WORKPLACE INDUSTRIAL RELATIONS IN BRITAIN

The DE/PSI/ESRC Survey

W. W. Daniel and Neil Millward

Gower

First published 1983 by Heinemann Educational Books
Reprinted 1984

Reprinted 1985 by
Gower Publishing Company Limited
Gower House
Croft Road
Aldershot
Hants GU11 3HR
England

British Library Cataloguing in Publication Data

Daniel, W. W.
    Workplace industrial relations in Britain : the
DE/PSI/SSRC survey.
    1. Industrial relations—Great Britain
    I. Title   II. Millward, Neil
    331'.0941   HD8391

ISBN 0 566 05152 4
        0 566 05153 2 Pbk

Typeset by Inforum Ltd, Portsmouth
Printed and bound in Great Britain by
Biddles Ltd, Guildford and King's Lynn

Preface

The survey on which this book is based was undertaken through collaboration between the Department of Employment (DE), the Policy Studies Institute (PSI) and the Economic and Social Research Council (ESRC). The DE and ESRC provided funds for the research and the PSI involvement in the enterprise was funded by a grant from the Leverhulme Trust. The research team worked under the guidance of a steering committee which included representatives of all three parties.

The initial development work for the survey, the questionnaire design and the direction of the data collection were largely carried out by Neil Millward with invaluable help from Patricia Wallace. He and Bill Daniel undertook the analysis and writing up of the survey which is reported in this book. In this they were helped by Martin Arnott and other colleagues in the Social Science Branch of DE and in PSI. Social and Community Planning Research (SCPR) administered the survey and made a major contribution to the design, and prepared the data for analysis in a way which went well beyond the call of duty. Colin Airey was principally responsible for the work at SCPR. Eileen Reid of PSI played a substantial part in the preparation of the text for this book. At all stages of the survey the members of the steering group, particularly Andrew Thomson, Chris Caswill and W.R. Hawes, assisted by William Brown, who acted as consultant to DE on the project, made an important contribution.

The average length of the interviews with managers was about one and a half hours. Many lasted two hours or more. Interviews with employee representatives lasted just under one hour on average. In some workplaces interviews were carried out with a manager and two or three employee representatives. Many of them took great pains to ensure that interviewers were given full and accurate answers to the many questions put to them. In short, our acknowledgement to the managers and employee representatives who answered our questions goes very far beyond a ritual expression of thanks.

It is hoped that this book will represent only the starting point in the analysis of the rich data embodied in the survey and that the survey will be the starting point in a series which will illuminate the developments in workplace industrial relations in Britain.

The analysis of the survey data, the interpretation of the findings and the organisation of the subject matter in this book are the responsibility of the authors. Any views expressed, implicitly or explicitly, are those of the authors and may not be taken to represent those of any of the sponsoring bodies.

Peter Brannen
Chairman, DE/PSI/ESRC Workplace Industrial Relations Survey Steering Committee.

Note: The Social Science Research Council (SSRC) recently changed its name to ECONOMIC AND SOCIAL RESEARCH COUNCIL (ESRC).

Contents

Notes on Tables and the Questions Asked in the Survey

General conventions adopted in tables

*   Fewer than 0.5 per cent.

—   Zero

§   Unweighted base is fewer than 20 and too low for percentages.   (A)

( ) Unweighted base is 20 or more but fewer than 50; percentages should be treated with caution.   (B)

Column and row percentages do not always add to 100 owing to the rounding of decimal points.   (C)

The proportions in subsidiary categories do not always add to the proportion in a composite category owing to the rounding of decimal points. For example, 71 per cent of senior manual shop stewards had their own offices or the use of an office, while 20 per cent had their own office and 52 per cent had the use of an office but no personal office.   (D)

Column and row percentages sometimes add to more than 100 because more than one answer was possible.   (E)

The proportions in subsidiary categories do not always add to the proportion in a composite category because more than one answer was possible. For example, the proportions of establishments where union representatives used the time off work provisions of the Employment Protection Act for different purposes added to substantially more than the proportion of establishments where the provisions had ever been used because, at some establishments, they had been used for a number of different purposes.   (F)

The base numbers for the individual categories in a variable do not add to the total base number because the necessary information was not provided in a number of cases.   (G)

The base numbers for the individual categories in a

variable do not add to the total base number because only
an illustrative range of categories was included. For
example, we occasionally use for analysis a variable which
combines elements of the nature of an establishment's
ownership and its industrial sector. It includes a column
for all private employers but provides information within
the private sector for only an illustrative selection of
industries such as manufacturing, construction and
miscellaneous services.

The weighted base numbers for the individual categories in a variable may not add to the total weighted base
number owing to the rounding of decimal points.   (H)

The different sources of information
As is the case with the text, where data are presented in tables without
the source of the information being identified it will have been provided
by the management respondent. Where the source is identified as the
manual or non-manual worker representative without any further
qualification, it will be the primary worker representative.

Unless otherwise specified, the information used for breakdown
variables, such as number employed at establishment, size of total
organisation, industrial sector, ownership and trade union membership
density, will be that provided by managers.

Arrangements for recording questions
Wherever information is first reported or referred to in the text, the
question in the interview schedule from which it is derived is recorded
in brackets at the end of the sentence. The verbatim questions are then
reported in Appendix A at the end of the book. Questions derived from
the management questionnaire have the prefix Q. Questions derived
from a worker representative schedule are prefixed WQ.

I Introduction

During the past 20 years industrial relations have been in the forefront of public and political debate in Britain. Reform of the industrial relations system has been part of every political party's manifesto. From time to time a contribution has been made to the debates by the publication of evidence, collected on a national basis and in a systematic manner, about the conduct of industrial relations in Britain at the places where people work. This evidence about industrial relations practices, gathered by the use of large-scale surveys, has required periodic updating as practices themselves have developed and the focus of public debate and policy making has changed. The first survey of workplaces, designed to gather information on a broad range of industrial relations practices, was sponsored by the Royal Commission on Trade Unions and Employers' Associations, the 'Donovan Commission', in 1966[1]. By 1972 the information gained from this survey was considered to be out of date in many respects and a new survey was carried out with a very different design[2]. That survey was repeated in 1973 with the aim of monitoring changes in the intervening fifteen months[3]. Those surveys did not, however, become established as an authoritative source of national information for the illumination and evaluation of industrial relations issues in the way that other surveys, carried out periodically, have become for certain other areas of social and economic life.

By 1979 the results of the 1973 survey were becoming less and less useful and the Department of Employment decided to sponsor a new survey of industrial relations practices which it was hoped would be the first of a regular series[4]. As development work proceeded, other organisations expressed interest in the enterprise and it became clear that if the full benefit for policy was to be derived from the study then there would be advantage in involving other parties. In addition to the survey's being used to provide information relevant to the policy concerns of a variety of users, advantage would be gained if the information were used to test more theoretical issues in the field of industrial relations, a process which, if it appeared to have less immediate policy relevance, could be expected to help policy analysis in the longer term. Accordingly, in order to create the best chance of gaining the full benefit from the survey, the Economic and Social Research Council (ESRC) and the Policy Studies Institute (PSI) joined with the Department in what became a unique collaborative enterprise. The survey became known as the DE/PSI/ESRC Workplace Industrial Relations Survey (1980).

The Department was the prime mover in the operation. Its main interest was to ensure that there was established a solid base for analysis of industrial relations practices and procedures as a background to policy making. The interest of the ESRC was to ensure that a rich, new data base about industrial relations was made available to the whole community of researchers and scholars in a form that was most useful to them. PSI was concerned that the information be used for medium term policy analysis and evaluation, from a perspective that was independent of the immediate requirements of government. Despite those differences of interest, each of the three parties recognised that it had much to gain both from its own involvement in the survey and from the involvement of the other two parties. Accordingly, accommodations were made and, at least in the judgement of those most closely involved, the collaboration represents a new and valuable arrangement for carrying out research relevant to public policy and scholarly enquiry. The accommodations are, however, reflected in this book. The authors have had two main aims in writing it. First, we aim to provide the general reader with a factual account of the results of the survey and an indication of the way in which those results are relevant to the policy concerns of government, employers and trade unions. Our second aim has been to provide the specialist reader with a preliminary analysis of the research results in a way that will enable and encourage the specialist to carry out more detailed analysis of the data in order to explore the main research and policy issues[5]. In these two ways we hope to stimulate, and ourselves later contribute to, a wide-ranging debate about the nature of industrial relations in Britain based upon the survey data.

The design of the survey

The design of the survey had three key features. First, we made the establishment our unit of analysis. Secondly, we carried out interviews with both management and worker representatives in establishments. Thirdly, the coverage was more comprehensive than that of any previous survey of its type.

As one of the main aims of the survey was to provide a basis for measuring change, the obvious starting point for the design might have appeared to have been the 1966 workplace industrial relations survey for the Donovan Commission. If we had adopted that design we would have been able immediately to produce clear results about changes since 1966. In fact, we judged that as so much scope for technical improvement had developed since that original and pioneering survey it was not desirable to take it as a model. The Donovan survey was, in reality, a collection of separate surveys of categories of people thought to fulfil important roles in industrial relations: works managers, supervisors, shop stewards and ordinary union members. It was not possible, therefore, to compare the answers to similar questions of managers and union representatives from the same place of work. Neither was it possible to add information from, say, a shop steward on a joint stewards' committee to information from, say, a manager, about the scope of bargaining at the same workplace. These limitations restricted severely the scope for analysis and made it impossible to build up a picture of industrial relations at the place of work. The 1972 and 1973 surveys represented an advance over the Donovan survey and did interview different parties from the same place of work. Unfortunately, in terms of their usefulness, *place of work* was defined in an idiosyncratic manner and the sampling frame was less good than those that have become available more recently. It was not possible to generalise the results of either the 1972 or 1973 surveys to any known or well-defined population of workplaces. Moreover, the results of the survey could not be used to estimate what proportion of all employees was covered by a particular practice or policy, such as what proportion of people worked at places where trade unions were recognised.

From the 1980 survey we wanted to be able to say both what proportion of workplaces operated a particular practice and what proportion of employees were covered by the practice. That distinction is so important in our analysis that it warrants a short digression in order to amplify it. A small proportion of workplaces employs a large proportion of the workforce. In our present survey, workplaces with 1,000 or more people represented only 2.5 per cent of establishments but accounted for 31 per cent of employees. Consequently, a practice that was very much more common in large workplaces might feature in a small proportion of workplaces but cover a larger proportion of the workforce. For instance, our findings suggested that one quarter of establishments operated a closed shop for some group of manual workers. But, as the closed shop was more common the larger the size of the establishment, the estimate from our findings is that 44 per cent of all manual workers worked in closed shops. Our sample was consciously designed to enable us to make both kinds of statement.

A key choice in that design was to make the establishment our primary unit for the collection of information. By *establishment* we mean an individual place of employment at a single address. Again, as the size of establishments and enterprises is one of the main sources of variation in policies and practice, and as there is often confusion between the two in popular debate and, indeed, in some scholarly writings, it is worth saying a word to emphasise the distinction. As already indicated, the establishment is a particular workplace defined in a geographical way. But most establishments are part of larger organisations. In our present survey, 80 per cent of all establishments were part of larger enterprises that operated more than one establishment. In relation to size, for instance, the issue of most interest and importance is whether the size of the establishment or the size of the total organisation is the major influence upon practices or characteristics. When we are referring to establishments we shall, in order to provide stylistic variation, talk in an interchangeable way about *workplaces, sites,* or *establishments* – or *plants*, when analysis is confined to manufacturing industry. When we are referring to the whole organisation of which the establishment is part we shall talk in a similarly interchangeable way about *enterprises* or *organisations* – or *businesses*, when analysis is confined to the private sector.

As our basic unit was the establishment, most of our questioning focused upon matters in relation to the establishment as a whole. As will be seen, however, we occasionally asked questions that focused upon just one sub-section of the establishment. Occasionally, too, we asked questions about the total organisation of which the establishment was part.

The second key feature of our design was that we talked to both management and worker representatives (often more than one) in the same establishment. Here we sought to ensure that worker respondents represented clearly defined sections of the workforce so that we might ask questions about those sections of both management and worker representatives, confident that they were thinking of the same group. As we generally spoke to a number of people in establishments it was possible for us to have some check on the reliability of our information. We were also able to collect information about a wider range of topics than is possible when there is only one respondent at the establishment, as is the common practice with industrial surveys.

The third and most important feature of our sample design that we want to highlight here was its comprehensiveness. We argue in our conclusions that this gave our results a distinctiveness and value far beyond that of the earlier surveys. The inclusion of the public sector had, especially, a major influence on our analysis and conclusions. All previous surveys of industrial relations had been restricted to particular industrial sectors, generally manufacturing and various parts of the private services sector. The analysis of the Donovan Commission has often been criticised as being based too exclusively on evidence about industrial relations practices in manufacturing industry, and, particularly, engineering[6]. The lack of an adequate sampling frame for the service sectors may have been part of the reason for the limited coverage of other surveys, but the availability of the census of employment removed this obstacle for the 1980 survey. There were, however, some limitations to the sectors covered. Primary industries (agriculture, forestry and fishing) were not covered by the census of employment and would have required special sampling procedures. As we were proposing to exclude establishments with fewer than 25 employees, for reasons given below, and small establishments predominate in primary industries, we judged that a special separate effort could not be justified.

The sample was limited to England, Scotland and Wales because of the different legislative and administrative frameworks applying to industrial relations in Northern Ireland and other territories of the United Kingdom. Establishments employing only members of the armed forces were also excluded. The other main exclusion from our achieved sample was not intended and arose from our failure to obtain access to establishments in the coalmining industry in time for interviews to take place. The survey may, therefore, be regarded as covering the manufacturing and service sectors of civil employment in Great Britain[7].

As our present survey was designed to cover a much greater variety of establishments than its predecessors, particularly in the service sectors with their mixture of public and private ownership, we needed a larger sample than earlier surveys, and a target of about two thousand was set. In the event, interviews were successfully carried out at 2,041 establishments[8].

With a target sample of two thousand establishments, we had to make a judgement about the size of establishments to be included. Previous surveys had all excluded small establishments, but they varied considerably in their assumptions about what size was too small to include in a survey of industrial relations. The Donovan Commission survey of managers had excluded establishments with fewer than 150 employees in manufacturing and those with fewer than 50 employees in construction. The 1972 and 1973 surveys generally excluded establishments with less than 250 employees, but dropped that figure to 100 in distribution[9]. The Warwick survey of manufacturing industry in 1977 excluded establishments with less than 50 full time employees[10]. There was clearly a wide range of variation in assumptions about the size of establishment for which questions about formal industrial relations became less relevant. The limitations of possible sampling frames and considerations arising from limited resources will certainly have also played a part in the choices made. We felt that there was evidence of formal industrial relations becoming more important for small establishments and judged that there would be advantages in including workplaces that were smaller than those previously covered. Accordingly, we included all establishments which had 25 or more employees, full time or part time. We judge that the inclusion of smaller workplaces added substantially to the value of the research. It enabled us to explore more fully variations in relation to size. Moreover, our findings confirmed that there was much happening in small workplaces concerning institutional labour relations. For example, of the private sector establishments with 25 to 49 employees, more than one half were found to have some union members, nearly one fifth had 80 per cent or more of their workforce unionised, two-fifths had a union recognised by management for collective bargaining, one third had a joint consultative or similar committee and three-quarters had a formal procedure for disciplinary cases.

The sample and overall response
The sample was drawn from the 1977 *Census of Employment,* the most comprehensive and up-to-date listing of employing units available at the time. A random sample of about 3,300 census units with a minimum of 25 employees was used. A substantial number of these turned out to be ineligible, either because they had closed down or had less than 25 employees. The overall response rate was 75 per cent, a considerable achievement by the survey contractor, Social and Community Planning Research (SCPR), for a survey which made such heavy demands on respondents. The overall response rate refers to the proportion of eligible addresses at which a complete management interview was obtained. Worker representatives were also interviewed in a substantial proportion of those establishments, as we describe in the next section.

The respondents
Our choice of respondents reflected the way in which we conceived of the industrial relations organisation of workplaces. But it is worth, first, describing the interviews we carried out, as that will provide a concrete basis on which to erect the ideas about organisation. Our aim was to interview both management and employee representatives, where employees were formally represented. At each establishment we interviewed, at a minimum, a management representative and, at a maximum, two management representatives and three employee representatives. Figure 1 provides a summary of the number of different types of respondent that we interviewed. Initially, interviewers were asked to identify and interview the senior manager at the establishment who dealt with industrial relations, or, in the case of non-industrial establishments, staff or employee relations. They were advised that, although in many large industrial establishments the words *industrial relations* would be included in the job title, often this responsibility would be merged with that of the personnel director or manager. Priority was to be given to obtaining an interview with the senior relevant person at an establishment. In some cases we expected that

Figure 1. Summary of number of respondents

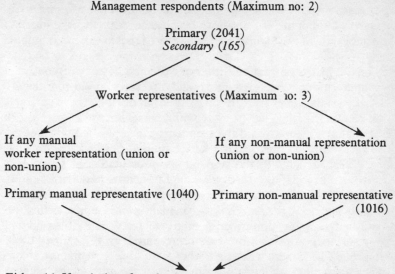

Management respondents (Maximum no: 2)

Primary (2041)
Secondary (165)

Worker representatives (Maximum no: 3)

If any manual
worker representation (union or
non-union)

If any non-manual representation
(union or non-union)

Primary manual representative (1040)   Primary non-manual representative
(1016)

Either (a) If majority of workers are manual and there was more than one
manual negotiating group

Secondary manual representative (216)

or   (b) If majority of workers are non-manual and more than one
non-manual negotiating group

Secondary non-manual representative (167)

the senior person, when interviewed, would be unable to answer all sections of the questionnaire, and would call on the help of, or refer the interviewer to, one or more of his colleagues. Respondents who provided the majority of the information have been styled *primary* respondents while we have called the others *secondary*. In the event, there was a secondary management respondent at 165 of the 2,041 establishments at which interviews were completed[11].

At some workplaces which belonged to larger organisations that had a number of establishments, interviewers were unable to obtain a complete interview with an appropriate manager at the sampled establishment and were referred to people at other levels of the organisation. The interview achieved was often *composite* in that some questions were answered by a representative at the establishment and some by a respondent in a different part of the organisation. In these instances, the establishment representative was always categorised as the *primary respondent* and the other respondent as the *secondary respondent*. In most of such cases the secondary respondent was an industrial relations or personnel manager or specialist at a head office or a regional or divisional office. In a proportion of cases (172 out of 2,041) the whole of the management interview was conducted outside the establishment at a different level of the organisation, because no suitable respondent at the establishment was available. A majority of these were in the public sector.

After we had identified and interviewed management respondents we sought, through them, to contact and interview worker representatives. In establishments with recognised trade unions for manual workers, an interview was sought with the senior shop steward (or similar lay representative) of the negotiating group which represented the largest number of manual workers[12]. Similarly, where non-manual unions were recognised, the senior lay representative of the largest non-manual negotiating group was sought for interview. In all cases, the negotiating groups and their senior representatives were identified by management and the permission of management obtained before the representatives were approached for interview[13]. Where either manual or non-manual workers were not represented by recognised trade unions but where there was some other form of representation, interviews were sought with the senior worker representative on the relevant committee. Whether they were union or non-union representatives, we described the representatives of largest groups as *primary worker representatives*.

In a number of cases where there were recognised trade unions our management respondents could identify no worker representative *at the establishment*. Such cases amounted to 192 for manual workers and 171 for non-manual groups. In these cases we did not try to identify and interview any alternative employee representative at another location. In establishments with worker representatives, interviews were obtained and completed in 84 per cent of cases for manual workers and in 85 per cent of cases for non-manual groups. Refusal by management to allow the interview was the single most common reason for non-response. The representative refused in only one per cent of cases. We judged that the heavy demands upon respondents in terms of absence from their normal work was one of the main reasons why managers did not always allow worker representatives to be approached.

Where there were recognised trade unions and more than one negotiating group we also set out to interview the senior worker representative of a second group. Where the majority of employees was manual our aim was to interview the senior representative of the second largest manual negotiating group. If the majority of employees was non-manual we sought the senior representative of the second largest non-manual group. Response rates for these *secondary worker representatives* were lower than for the primary: 72 per cent for manual representatives and 70 per cent for non-manual representatives. In a very few cases the interviewing of the worker representatives caused some difficulty, owing to absence in particular, and substitute respondents were interviewed.

In total, interviews were successfully carried out with 2,439 worker representatives and 2,205 managers, the bulk of them during the period May to August 1980. The results presented in this report derive from some 4,644 completed quesionnaires. Further details of the fieldwork and other methodological aspects of the survey are included in Appendix B to this report. A fuller account is available from the Economic and Social Research Council Data Archive for researchers wishing to carry out their own analyses of the data.

The structure of the interviews
As mentioned earlier, because interviews were carried out in establishments the bulk of our questioning focused upon what happened at establishment level. Of course, much that is very important for the practice of industrial relations occurs at other levels and in different contexts. Among large employers decisions are often taken at divisional, national and, sometimes, international levels and trade unions seek to influence decision making at all these points. Moreover, local meetings of trade union branches and employers' associations, their national conferences and regional and national joint negotiating bodies all represent important parts of the industrial relations system. In some cases good information is already available for those other parts of the system. In other cases they are more susceptible to study using methods different from the large-scale sample survey.

Although our present survey focused upon the establishment we were, of course, unable to cover everything of relevance to industrial relations that happened at the establishment. Moreover, it is often the case that policies, practices or procedures vary in relation to different groups of employees within establishments. Accordingly, it is worth saying a word about both the way we defined sub-units of the establishment and the way we selected particular units or events for study.

A key criterion for identifying particular parts of the establishment for special study was the recognition of groups for collective bargaining. Our aim was to distinguish groups of employees with common representational arrangements involving a trade union or group of unions recognised by management. In defining *recognition* we followed closely the main element of the legal definition in operation at the time[14], that is to say, recognition for collective bargaining. Groups of employees with common representational arrangements, in these terms, have often been referred to as *bargaining units* or *negotiating groups*. We assumed that in circumstances where groups were recognised for both manual and non-manual employees then the units were normally distinct. We further assumed that more than one bargaining unit could exist within each main occupational group. In relation to information on particular practices or events, we confined our inquiries to, at most, the two largest manual negotiating units and the two largest non-manual negotiating units.

As will already be clear, we distinguished between arrangements for representing manual and non-manual groups. Indeed, we tended to ask all our questions on representation and recognition separately for manual and non-manual categories. Occasionally we broke those main groupings down still further into broad occupational classes such as skilled, semi-skilled and unskilled manual workers. In addition, we also differentiated, in a few questions, between male and female, and between full time and part time employees.

On some topics an initial question established whether the particular practice or arrangement was common to all employees or whether different practices applied to different groups. Where practice varied, the detailed questions on that topic were normally asked of only the largest group. For instance, if an establishment had several different disputes procedures, most subsequent questions were asked of only the procedure covering the most employees. Similarly, where the question referred to recent events, such as industrial action, we asked detailed questions about only the most recent event. Clearly it was necessary for us to be selective in order for the survey to be manageable, but selection also carries the possibility of distortion and we make clear throughout the report where we have focused upon particular events and categories.

Analysis of the results

Generally the form of analysis that we have used as the basis for this report has been detailed tabular analysis. That is to say, we have analysed answers to particular questions in relation to a range of characteristics of establishments such as the number of people employed on site, the total number of people employed by the organisation, industrial sector, ownership, union density, composition of the workforce and so on. Where we found that there was one dominant influence upon answers, we explored associations with other characteristics while holding the dominant influence constant. This form of analysis provides the most effective means of meeting a number of aims, including the sorting out of the inter-relationships between characteristics in a fast and flexible way, quickly identifying the main influences upon the distribution of a particular characteristic and presenting results in a way that is readily understandable by a general readership. We hope that others will subject different parts of the survey to the more sophisticated forms of statistical analysis that are necessary and feasible for the full explanation of inter-relationships regarding particular defined areas.

Accuracy of the results
As with all sample surveys, there is always the possibility that the proportions, averages and other measures computed from the sample may not correspond to those of the population from which the sample was drawn. With a chosen confidence level of, say, 95 per cent, it is possible to give a rough estimate of the sampling error attached to measures of the sample characteristics. The sampling errors in this survey were greater than would have been the case if simple random sampling had been used because of the disproportionate sampling of larger establishments. Sampling error was, however, slightly reduced by using a stratified design. The net result was that sampling errors were roughly 25 per cent greater than those for a simple random sample of the same size. Taking this into consideration, the following table shows the approximate sampling error attached to a selection of proportions for the whole survey sample, assuming a 95 per cent confidence level.

	Percentage found by survey				
	5 or 95	10 or 90	20 or 80	30 or 70	50
Approximate sampling error (per cent)	1.3	1.6	2.3	2.5	2.8

To illustrate, the sampling error for a survey finding of 30 per cent is 2.5 per cent. In other words, we could be 95 per cent certain that where the survey results showed that 30 per cent of all establishments had a certain characteristic then the true proportion in the whole population of establishments was within the range 27.5 per cent to 32.5 per cent. Naturally, measures of characteristics of sub-samples are subject to greater sampling errors[15]. Appendix B contains examples of precise estimates of sampling error for major variables in the survey.

Units of analysis
As mentioned earlier, we designed the sample in such a way as to enable us to make two kinds of statement. First, a particular proportion of establishments operated a certain practice. Secondly, a specified proportion of workers was covered by that practice. We illustrated the importance of the distinction in relation to the closed shop. A third

requirement that we specified for the design was that we should be able to compare establishments of different sizes across the full range of establishment sizes. Previous surveys had shown the major importance of establishment size as a source of variation in a whole range of industrial relations practices. In practice, to generate enough larger establishments for satisfactory inter-size comparisons to be made, we had to sample larger units with greater frequency than smaller ones. For that purpose, the sample was stratified according to size of establishment at the time of the census and different sampling fractions applied accordingly. The figures in this report, unless otherwise stated, have been weighted to make them representative of all the establishments in the population.

Weighting
In broad terms, the weights applied for the analysis here were those necessary to restore the numbers in each size band to their proper proportions according to the census. Response rates were sufficiently uniform across industry sectors and size bands to make any additional weighting unjustified. For convenience the results have been weighted to a base of 2,000 establishments. Detailed supplementary work on the sample achieved, which was carried out in parallel with the preparation of this report, has suggested an alternative form of weighting which could be used for certain types of analysis[16]. We outline in Appendix B the details of the weighting used in this report and the suggested alternative.

The choice of respondents for the analysis
About two-fifths of all the questions asked in the survey were asked of both management and worker representatives. This presents us with a built-in check on the reliability of our information. But it also presented us with a dilemma as to whose accounts we should use as the basis for our analysis.

First, we should make clear that in most cases the picture revealed by the accounts of worker representatives was very similar to that revealed by management respondents. Indeed, the two accounts were generally so similar that they can reasonably be regarded as the same in sample survey terms. Such an outcome was especially gratifying in view of the lack of correspondence between different respondents' answers to the same factual questions which Parker reported from the 1973 survey[17]. It is especially remarkable, for instance, in relation to accounts of the most important level of bargaining over pay, and of whether there was bargaining over a range of issues, such as the introduction of new working methods, at the establishment level, the organisational level or not at all. In principle, there is very considerable scope for differences in answers to such apparently factual questions arising from differences in definition and perception. In practice, the answers were very similar.

Secondly, for the purposes of clarity, simplicity, consistency and economy we have normally confined ourselves to just one account when reporting the incidence of a particular practice or institution, the account being that of management. We adopted managers' accounts as the main basis for our figures chiefly because our management information was more complete. That is to say, we had management respondents from all our establishments while we had worker representative responses for only a sub-sample. Normally, before presenting management responses alone, we will have checked that they were generally consistent with corresponding worker representatives' responses. In other cases we have found it useful to show explicit comparisons between reports by different respondents to very similar questions. For instance, in Chapter VI we analyse separate accounts by management and union representatives of the amount of information given by management to worker representatives. We find that both accounts vary markedly in relation to ownership and that the pattern of variation arising from the parallel accounts is in accord. That congruence adds substantial weight to the credibility of the results.

Thirdly, and exceptionally, however, we found that in a few important instances there were differences between management and union accounts which led us to adopt a different approach to the analysis. For instance, management and union accounts of industrial action in the 12 months previous to the interview differed so much that we carried out a case by case analysis. That analysis revealed differences in the reporting of industrial action among manual and non-manual employees which were sufficient to warrant treating them differently. In that instance we decided, for a number of reasons set out in Chapter IX, to take the combined reports of the manager and the appropriate worker representative as our indicator of the occurrence of industrial action. Doing this had important implications for the reported levels of industrial action, for its relative frequency between manual and non-manual workers, and for the pattern of strike and non-strike action. It also has important implications for the assessment of results from single respondent surveys relating to such matters as strikes and other action. In our view, the results of our analysis of this area alone go a long way towards a justification for talking to more than one respondent in each establishment.

The contents of the book and some conventions used
Our survey had a number of different purposes, as opposed to being designed to illuminate one particular set of issues in great detail and with great clarity. Accordingly, many of the chapters in the book can be

read independently of the others, and there is some arbitrariness in the order in which the chapters appear. In Chapter II we examine the survey's results for a number of features of worker representation where trade unions are recognised. Analysis of the closed shop is discussed in detail in Chapter III. Chapter IV covers a number of features of workplace trade union organisation and its relationship to other units within the wider structure of trade unionism. Chapter V deals with various features of how management at establishment and higher organisational levels organise themselves for industrial relations matters. In Chapter VI non-union forms of representation are considered, as well as various practices in the field of consultation, participation and disclosure of information. In Chapter VII we focus upon collective and individual disputes procedures and practice. Chapter VIII examines various features of pay determination, both by collective bargaining and other methods, and associated practices concerned with wage and salary systems. Industrial action is dealt with in Chapter IX. Finally, in Chapter X we bring together some of the survey's evidence on what can be thought of as some of the outcomes of the industrial relations system at workplace level. The book finishes with a general summary, highlighting some of the implications of the results.

Where in the text or the tables we present information without explicity identifying its source, the data were derived from interviews with managers. Similarly, where information is attributed to manual or non-manual worker representatives without any further qualification, then the source was the appropriate *primary* worker representative. When reporting answers to questions we do not always quote the verbatim form of the question in the text. We do, however, note the question number, and the form of words used is listed in Appendix A, chapter by chapter. We adopted this arrangement because we had six different schedules, all of them of substantial length, and it was not practicable for us to reproduce them all in this report. Copies of the full schedules may be obtained from the ESRC Data Archive at the University of Essex or from the Policy Studies Institute.

The tables shown in the text were drafted to illustrate the main points made in the text. Accordingly, we did not adopt a standard or consistent format in our definitions of breakdown variables. Sometimes we did not include all categories. Categories were combined in ways that proved most appropriate to the subject matter being analysed and sometimes the combination varied. A separate volume of tables using standardised breakdowns is, however, published in parallel with this report and is also available from the Policy Studies Institute.

Notes
1. Government Social Survey, *Workplace Industrial Relations* (HMSO, London,

1968). Also referred to in the text as the Donovan Commission survey or the Donovan survey.

2. Stanley Parker, *Workplace Industrial Relations 1972* (OPCS, HMSO, London, 1974).

3. Stanley Parker, *Workplace Industrial Relations 1973* (OPCS, HMSO, L∘ndon, 1975).

4. It is almost certainly the case too that a boost was given to the idea of workplace surveys of industrial relations by the Political and Economic Planning (PEP) survey which resulted in the report, *Wage Determination in Industry* (W.W. Daniel, Political and Economic Planning No. 563, 1976). That report revealed a potential within sample surveys of establishments for exploring and analysing issues that went beyond the purposes for which the early workplace surveys had been used.

5. The data are available from the SSRC Data Archive to researchers with access to suitable electronic data processing facilities in such a form that none of the sampled establishments is identifiable. Application forms for the documentation and data tapes are obtainable from The Director, SSRC Data Archive, University of Essex, Wivenhoe Park, Colchester, Essex. The Archive's reference number is 1575.

6. H.A. Turner, 'The Royal Commission's Research Papers', *British Journal of Industrial Relations*, November 1968, and other papers in the same issue; H.A. Clegg, *The Changing System of Industrial Relations in Great Britain* (Basil Blackwell, Oxford, 1979), p. 46.

7. Orders III to XXVII of the 1968 Standard Industrial Classification.

8. One of these was subsequently judged to belong to the agriculture sector and has been excluded from the analysis.

9. The 'situations' within an establishment about which the questions were addressed were limited to those with 25 or more employees.

10. William Brown, Ed., *The Changing Contours of British Industrial Relations* (Basil Blackwell, Oxford, 1981).

11. In principle there might have been more than one secondary management respondent at an establishment; in practice this did not happen.

12. Manual and non-manual employees were defined, in terms similar to those used in the New Earnings Survey, in a document called the Basic Workforce Data Sheet, which was sent to management respondents before their interviews. Non-manual occupations were those of a managerial, professional or clerical nature; the remainder were to be counted as manual.

13. In methodological terms, identifying and contacting worker representatives through management may not be ideal. However, given the much greater difficulties of identifying shop stewards at a particular establishment through local union offices, we settled on this as the only practical method. Naturally, some stewards sought advice from their local or national officers about being interviewed and we were pleased that in the great majority of cases they subsequently agreed. Contacting non-union worker representatives could, in any case, be done only through management.

14. Recognition was defined in Section 11 of the Employment Protection Act, 1975, which was in operation at the time of our interviews. The provisions for intervention by ACAS in recognition disputes were repealed in the Employment Act, 1980, but the concept of recognition is still inherent in the legislation, for example, in relation to consultations about redundancies.

15. Tables of sampling errors for samples of different sizes are available in statistical textbooks and works on survey research. See, for example, Gerald Hoinville, Roger Jowell and others, *Survey Research Practice* (Heinemann Educational Books, London, 1978).

16. The weighting scheme used in this report restores establishments of different sizes to their correct proportions within the population of census units as recorded by the 1977 *Census of Employment*. Our statements are generalisable to the portion of the population that had 25 or more employees at the time of the census and also had 25

or more employees when the interview took place in 1980. We made no attempt to identify establishments created between 1977 and 1980 nor ones which had grown to more than 25 employees by 1980. The alternative weighting scheme detailed in Appendix B extends the population to which the sample can be generalised so that all establishments with 25 or more employees are included. However, this is possible only by assuming that establishments that grew to 25 or more employees during the three years were no different in relation to the survey variables from the ones that had 25 or more employees at both points in time.

17. Stanley Parker, *Workplace Industrial Relations 1973* (OPCS, HMSO, London, 1975). We attribute the greater correspondence in the present survey to four main factors. First, many of the questions were more strictly 'factual', the examples given by Parker involving a greater degree of judgement by respondents. Secondly, many of our questions were more specifically focused upon particular practices or groups of employees. Thirdly, we specified shorter recall periods and, fourthly, we selected respondents in a way more likely to ensure that they were knowledgeable about the practices or events in question. Further investigation of the correspondence between answers to the same questions is in progress and will be reported in due course.

II Trade Union Recognition and Associated Issues

The recognition of trade unions represents a key feature of institutional industrial relations. For the trade union movement, the achievement of recognition has symbolised strength and growth. For employers, the recognition of unions has involved the acceptance of a constraint upon management choice and action. Historically, recognition disputes have sometimes involved expressions of the most extreme form of industrial conflict. Conflict over recognition has persisted into recent years, although our present findings confirm that the more dramatic examples of recognition disputes are very much the exception to the most common ways in which recognition is brought about. The extent of trade union influence, as reflected in the extent and pattern of trade union recognition, is an important consideration for large parts of economic and social policy as well as employment and industrial relations strategies. In this chapter we plot the coverage, distribution and growth of trade union recognition as well as looking at a number of associated issues.

Traditionally trade union representation and recognition have been characteristic of manual rather than non-manual workers, although there has been substantial growth in white collar trade union recognition and membership during the past twenty years. Nevertheless, it remains the case that more manual than non-manual workers are trade union members and that trade unions are more widely recognised in relation to manual workers than they are to non-manual workers.

Moreover, it is also the case that manual and non-manual workers are almost invariably represented by different trade unions. Accordingly, it is both simpler and more consistent with the general practice of labour relations to analyse issues concerning levels of trade union recognition and membership separately for the blue collar and white collar groups. Initially, then, in this chapter, we summarise briefly the overall picture regarding levels of trade union membership and the extent of trade union recognition. Secondly, we present a more detailed analysis of the pattern for manual workers. Thirdly, we compare the picture for non-manual workers with that for manual grades. There are two further refinements to our information which rather complicate the exposition. First, in cases where managements negotiated with more than one bargaining group we asked a selected number of questions

Table II.1 Overall pattern regarding trade union recognition and membership

	All establishments	Nationalised industries	Public administration[1]	Private manufacturing	Private services
					Percentages
Any union recognised	67	100	94	68	42
					Column percentages
Both manual and non-manual unions recognised	38[2]	88	65	31	18
Manual union recognised but not non-manual	16	6	2	37	14
Manual recognised/no non-manual workers	*	1	1	—	*
Non-manual union recognised but not manual	7	*	15	*	6
Non-manual recognised/no manual workers	5	5	11	—	5
Neither manual nor non-manual unions recognised	33	—	6	32	58
					Percentages
Proportion of full-time employees who were union members (union density)[3]	62	97	89	68	55
Base: all establishments					
Unweighted	*2040*	*134*	*576*	*746*	*580*
Weighted	*2000*	*79*	*577*	*548*	*790*

[1] Public administration here includes all public employment other than nationalised industries but is predominantly central and local government
[2] See note C page xii

	All establishments	Nationalised industries	Other public corporations	Government	All private sector
					Percentages
Trade unions recognised for manual workers	58	98	(80)[1]	73	50
Trade unions recognised but all negotiations at higher level	1	2	—	4	*
Trade unions not recognised but represented	2	—	—	2	
					Column percentages
Level of trade union membership[2]					
None	28	—	(12)	10	37
1–49 per cent	24	2	(4)	50	17
50–89 per cent	16	13	(15)	20	15
90–94 per cent	4	11	(15)	1	5
95–99 per cent	7	26	(14)	5	6
100 per cent	21	48	(40)	14	20
Manual trade union members as a proportion of manual workers (union density)[3]	66	91	(97)	54	65
Base: all establishments that employed manual workers					
Unweighted	1899	130	32	482	1255
Weighted	1833	75	25	488	1245

* Fewer than 0.5 per cent

[1] See note B

[2] See note 1 at the end of the chapter

[3] Eight per cent of establishments had no information on the level of their trade union membership and a further six per cent were not able to provide detailed figures. The proportions having different levels of membership have been calculated on a base of all establishments that provided figures

about the second largest group, for both manual and non-manual categories. Secondly, we asked worker representatives as well as management respondents key questions about recognition. Our starting point and chief reference point in the chapter will be management's account of arrangements for the first negotiating group. We refer to refinements concerning second groups and the accounts of worker representatives where appropriate.

The overall pattern of trade union recognition and membership
Generally, our analysis showed that the three strongest influences upon the extent of trade union recognition were ownership[1], the size of establishments and the size of enterprises (Q24a, b; Q53a, b). A fourth and more complex source of variation was the workforce composition. Table II.1 shows the overall pattern of trade union recognition and membership in relation to the ownership of the establishment. Sixty-seven per cent of establishments recognised trade unions as representing some employees at the place of work. The sixty-seven per cent was made up of 38 per cent of establishments where both manual and non-manual trade unions were recognised; 16 per cent where manual unions were recognised but non-manual employees had no recognised unions to represent them and 12 per cent where non-manual unions were recognised but not manual unions.

In establishments where non-manual unions were recognised, but not manual unions, it was normally the case that there were no manual workers or that manual workers represented a very small proportion of the total workforce. Hence the frequency with which public service establishments appeared in that category. The striking feature of the public sector as a whole, however, was the frequency of some form of recognition. There were no nationalised industry establishments where trade unions were not recognised. In the public sector as a whole, only five per cent of management respondents reported that they did not recognise trade unions. Overall, the proportion of all employees who were trade union members broadly reflected the proportion of all establishments that recognised trade unions[2] (Q23c; Q52c).

The extent of union membership and recognition among manual workers
Table II.2 shows that when analysis was confined to establishments that employed manual workers and was focused exclusively upon the recognition of manual workers, there remained a marked difference between the public and private sectors. All nationalised industry establishments that employed manual workers recognised manual unions for negotiating pay and conditions. The same was true for only half the establishments in the private sector. Apart from establishments that

fully recognised manual trade unions, the table contains two other categories of interest. First, there were cases where manual unions were, in principle, fully recognised, but no negotiations with union representatives took place at the level of the establishment. Such cases accounted for one per cent of establishments and were most common among national or local government offices. Secondly, there were cases where managements were prepared to listen to representations from union officers on behalf of individual workers or groups of workers but did not formally recognise trade unions for purposes of collective bargaining. The sample survey method is far too crude a tool with which to explore all the refinements associated with a willingness to talk on a range of different topics that falls short of recognition. Within the limitations of our method, however, it appeared that establishments where managers spoke to trade union representatives as trade union representatives, but did not recognise them for purposes of collective bargaining over pay and conditions, accounted for about two per cent of the total. Such workplaces were heavily concentrated among the smallest establishments.

Variations in the level of trade union membership among manual workers broadly followed variations in the recognition of manual unions. There were, however, two notable exceptions to that general pattern. In local or national government, three-quarters of establishments recognised trade unions but only just over half of manual workers were members of trade unions. In the private sector, two-thirds of manual workers were trade union members but only half the

Table II.3 Manual union recognition[1] in relation to union density[2]

Percentages

	Manual trade union density (per cent)			
	1–24	25–49	50–89	90–100
All establishments	65	83	91	96
All private sector	47	70	93	95
Central/local government	82	94	89	89
Nationalised industry		(96)[3]		98

Base: establishments with any trade union members

[1] The percentages quoted represent the proportion of establishments where manual unions were recognised for negotiating pay and conditions, and bargaining took place at the establishment
[2] Union density is full-time union members as a proportion of all manual workers
[3] Generally, trade union membership in nationalised industries was so high that there was little scope for analysis in relation to union density. The proportion quoted is based on establishments with densities of 1–89 per cent and the base for the percentage is still fewer than 50. See note B

establishments recognised trade unions. That difference reflects the way in which union recognition appears to have been granted at substantially lower levels of union membership in the public sector compared with the private. Table II.3 shows the details. In private sector establishments where less than one quarter of manual workers were union members, 47 per cent of managements recognised unions, while in the large majority of public sector establishments with similar levels of manual union membership trade unions were recognised. There was also a marked contrast between public and private sector establishments where the level of union membership was between one quarter and one half.

In the private sector the other most striking feature of the distribution of trade union membership was the way in which it polarised at extremes. That is to say, over one third of establishments had no trade union members and nearly one third of establishments had 90 per cent or more of their manual workers in trade unions. The remaining one

Table II.4   Manual union recognition in relation to organisation and establishment size

Percentages

	All establish- ments	Number employed by organisation			
		25– 500	501– 2000	2001– 10,000	10,001 or more
Manual union recognised	58	38	66	69	71
Negotiations at higher level	1	*	1	*	2
Representation but no recognition	2	2	4	1	1
Base: all establishments employing some manual workers					
Unweighted	*1899*[1]	*395*	*251*	*358*	*695*
Weighted	*1399*	*599*	*212*	*280*	*491*

	Number employed at establishment					
	25–49	50–99	100–199	200–499	500–999	1000 or more
Manual union recognised	44	55	67	81	89	94
Negotiations at a higher level	1	1	2	*	5	1
Representation but no recognition	2	3	1	2	1	—
Unweighted	*323*	*347*	*363*	*355*	*246*	*265*
Weighted	*·704*	*486*	*317*	*194*	*82*	*51*

* Fewer than 0.5 per cent
[1] See note G

third were spread across the other 89 per cent. Another way of expressing the same distribution is that in one half of the cases where establishments had any trade union members, they had 90 per cent membership or higher. In one third of the cases where they had any membership they had 100 per cent membership. That pattern raises questions about the closed shop, which is considered in detail in Chapter III.

Apart from the nature of the ownership of establishments, the size of establishments especially and, to a lesser extent, the size of enterprises, were strongly associated with the extent of recognition. Table II.4 shows that there was a very strong and consistent tendency for manual unions to be more likely to be recognised the more people there were employed on site. In establishments that employed 1,000 people or more, 94 per cent recognised manual unions, while less than one half of establishments that employed 25 to 49 people recognised manual unions. Similarly, there was a tendency for establishments to be more likely to recognise manual unions the larger the total enterprise of which they were part. The main cut-off point here, however, was 500 employees in total. Where the total enterprise complement was 500 or fewer, a comparatively small number of establishments recognised manual unions. Where the complement rose to over 500, the proportion that recognised manual unions increased very substantially. Thereafter there continued to be an increase with each succeeding enterprise size band, but the rate of increase fell markedly. As we show later in our analysis, the pattern in relation to enterprise size was partly a consequence of a very marked difference between independent establishments and those that were parts of larger organisations. Independent establishments were very much less likely to recognise unions than were establishments that were part of larger enterprises, and independents were heavily concentrated in the overall enterprise size band where 500 people or fewer were employed.

As both size and ownership had very strong influences over the extent to which manual trade unions were recognised, it is of special interest to consider the interaction between the effects of size and ownership. Table II.5 shows variations for different ownership types in relation to establishment size. It is clear that, for nationalised industries, ownership was much more important than the size of establishments. The level of recognition was very high indeed in even the smallest establishments. That provided very little scope for there to be much increase in the level of union recognition as the size of establishment increased. In the private sector, by way of very marked contrast, there was an extremely strong relationship between the size of establishments and the level of recognition. Accordingly, the largest contrast between the public and private sectors occurred among the smallest establishments.

Table II.5   Manual union recognition in relation to ownership and establishment size

Percentages

Number employed at establishment	Nationalised industries/ public corporations	Central/ local government	All private sector
25–99	(93)[1]	66	40
100–499	92	82	66
500–999	(98)	87	89
1000 or more	(100)	93	93

Base: all establishments employing manual workers

[1] See note B

The analysis in Table II.5 was based upon the size of establishments as measured by the total number of employees employed on site. As, however, it was manual trade union recognition with which we were concerned, it was possible that the more critical measure of size would be the number of manual workers employed rather than the total number of employees. Of course, in general terms there is a strong positive association between the number of manual workers employed by an establishment and the total number of people employed, so the total number employed is a good proxy for the number of manual workers. At the same time, there are differences between sectors in the proportions of their workforce that are represented by manual workers. In particular, local and central government establishments tend to have a substantially lower proportion of manual employees than do other sectors. Accordingly, it was possible that the pattern revealed in Table II.5 might have partly reflected such differences. We therefore repeated the analysis using the number of manual workers as the measure of establishment size. The pattern revealed was very similar to that shown by Table II.5.

Unfortunately, it was not possible for us satisfactorily to repeat our analysis of the inter-relationship between size and ownership with regard to total organisation size. Nationalised industry establishments and government establishments were almost invariably part of very large enterprises. Accordingly, the only way in which we could extend our analysis of union recognition in relation to size and ownership was by confining the analysis to very large enterprises. The results showed that smaller private establishments that belonged to enterprises which employed 10,000 or more people were very substantially less likely to

Table II.6   **The recognition of manual unions in relation to establishment and enterprise size**

Percentages

Number employed at establishment	Number employed by organisation 25–500	501–10,000	10,001 or more
25–99	33	51	59
100–499	49	70	80
500–999	n.a.[1]	85	96
1000 or more	n.a.	91	94

Base: private sector establishments employing manual workers

[1] Cell size not applicable

recognise unions than counterparts in public administration or among the nationalised industries.

As the association between establishment size and union recognition was less marked in the public sector, it was more appropriate for us to confine our analysis of the inter-relationship between establishment size and enterprise size to the private sector (see Table II.6). In the private sector both the number of people employed on site and the number of people employed in total by the enterprise of which establishments were part exercised strong independent influences upon the extent of trade union recognition.

Table II.7   **Proportion of establishments that recognised manual unions in relation to independence**

Percentages

	Total	Number of manual workers employed 1–24	25–49	50–99	100–199	200 or more
All establishments	50	25	43	63	78	91
Independent establishments	31	16	24	50	(66)[1]	(67)
Establishments that were part of a group	58	28	55	68	81	92

Base: all private sector establishments employing manual workers

[1] See Note B

Table II.8 Manual union recognition in relation to selected industrial sectors

| | Manufacturing | | | | | | Construction | Professional/ Scientific | Services | |
	Vehicles	Mechanical engineering	Electrical engineering	Food/ Chemicals	Textiles/ Clothing	Miscellaneous manufacture			Finance	Miscellaneous
Number employed at establishment										
All establishments	72	70	68	61	58	77	62	61	27	30
25–99 employees	§[1]	57	§	(40)[2]	(43)	(55)	56	57	(30)	25
100–499 employees	§	86	(62)	(76)	(77)	86	(76)	66	(13)	(51)
500–999 employees	§	(95)	(97)	(77)	§	(98)	§	(73)	§	§
1000 employees or more	(96)	(100)	(95)	(81)	§	§	§	92	§	§
Number of manual workers										
1–24	§	§	§	§	§	§	(25)	56	(23)	(18)
25–99	§	59	§	(44)	(51)	72	67	63	§	29
100–499	(76)	94	(84)	86	(74)	92	90	81	§	(65)
500 or more	(96)	(100)	(100)	(94)	§	(94)	§	(96)	§	§

Base: establishments that employed manual workers

[1] See note A

[2] See note B

As we mentioned earlier in the chapter, a further characteristic of workplaces that complicated the analysis by establishment and enterprise size was whether they were independent or part of larger groups. Independent establishments were very substantially less likely to recognise manual unions regardless of the number of people employed by the establishment or the enterprise of which it was part (see Table II.7). As independent establishments were largely concentrated in the enterprise size band of 500 employees or fewer, the difference between the independents and others partly accounted for the tendency for there to be a larger contrast between enterprises in the smallest size band than between those in the larger size bands.

Variations in the extent of trade union recognition in relation to industrial sector partly reflected the characteristic size and ownership structure of different sectors (see Table II.8). At the same time, there remained sectoral differences that were independent of workforce size and ownership. For instance, the extent of recognition of manual unions in financial and personal services was generally very low, partly because establishments generally tended to be small in those sectors, and tended to employ relatively few manual workers. When establishments employing similar numbers of manual workers were compared, it remained the case that the level of recognition in those service industries was comparatively low, but it was clear that the number of manual workers employed was a more important influence on the extent of manual union recognition than was the industrial sector involved.

Table II.9 Manual union recognition in relation to proportion of women manual workers employed

Percentages

Number of manual workers employed	Total	Proportion of women among manual workers (percentage)				
		None–20	21–40	41–60	61–80	81–100
1–24	24	30	§[1]	10	32	14
25–99	50	62	(56)[2]	42	32	29
100–499	81	92	87	81	63	(61)

Base: private sector establishments employing 1–499 manual workers

[1] See note A
[2] See note B

A final substantial influence upon levels of trade union recognition was the proportion of women who were employed at the establishment. Again, that influence was more apparent when analysis was confined to the private sector (see Table II.9). The higher the proportion of women employed, the less likely was a manual union to be recognised.

Lack of recognition in establishments with relatively high union membership

We have looked at the extent and pattern of recognition of manual trade unions. Also of special interest is the other side of the coin or, more precisely, the extent to which unions were not recognised in circumstances where they had members and might expect to be recognised. In the private sector this was not uncommon. Nine per cent of private sector establishments reported that they had trade union members among manual workers but did not recognise unions. In one half of those cases 25 per cent or more of manual workers were members and in one quarter of cases membership was as high as 50 per cent or more. Workplaces where trade union membership was so high but where unions were not recognised are clearly of special interest, if only for their abnormality. They were most common among smaller establishments and especially smaller independent establishments. Table II.10 shows the distribution of establishments with any manual union membership but no recognition, in relation to establishment and organisation size. The workplaces with a relatively high level of membership but no recognition were almost exclusively small independent establishments or small establishments belonging to medium size or small organisations in the private sector.

The number of unions that were recognised at a workplace compared with the number with membership provided a second measure of the

Table II.10   **Proportion of establishments with manual union membership that did not recognise manual unions**

Percentages

Number employed at establishment	Number employed by total organisation		
	25–500	501–10,000	Over 10,000
25–99	12	11	5
100–499	12	8	5
500–999	n.a.[1]	3	1
1000 or more	n.a.	2	–
Base: establishments in private sector that employed manual workers			

[1] Cell size not applicable

Table II.11 Patterns of recognition and non-recognition of manual unions within establishments

Percentages

	All establishments	All private sector	Nationalised industries	Central/local government
Number of manual unions with members				
One	57	61[1]	45	49
Two	21	19	28	22
Three or more	22	18	26	28
Number of unions recognised				
One	53	58	48	46
Two	16	13	27	22
Three or more	19	15	25	25
Number of unions not recognised				
One	11	14	4	7
Two or more	5	7	1	4
Base: establishments having manual union members				
Unweighted	*1483*	*912*	*130*	*413*
Weighted	*1235*	*739*	*75*	*400*

[1] See note C

extent to which manual unions with members were not recognised (see Table II.11). The results showed more extensive non-recognition of trade unions with membership than did our previous analysis of establishments with manual union members but no recognition. Nine per cent of private sector establishments recognised no manual union despite having union members. Twenty-one per cent of private sector establishments did not recognise one or more unions that had members. The pattern of variation in that measure of non-recognition, however, was, like our first measure, closely related to the size of establishments and organisations.

The formality of recognition
To establish how far the recognition of manual unions was formally embodied in written agreements, we asked managers in establishments where manual unions were recognised whether they had any written agreements in which the largest negotiating group was recognised for negotiating pay and conditions (Q38a). We found that nearly

three-quarters (71 per cent) of establishments where manual unions were recognised reported that they had written agreements relating to their primary manual negotiating group and 15 per cent said they had more than one such agreement. In principle, we expected that arrangements would be more formal in larger organisations than in smaller ones and that they would be more formal in public enterprises than in private ones. In practice, we did find that there were differences of that kind but they were not at all as marked as would be expected. In particular, it was difficult to imagine that although they recognised unions, one fifth of the largest establishments belonging to the largest enterprises had no recognition agreement. Similarly, it was hard to believe that one quarter of all nationalised industry establishments were not covered by recognition agreements in relation to manual workers.

It is possible that the pattern revealed partly reflected differences related to the formality of agreements, which was what we set out to examine, but also, partly, differences in relation to the extent of centralisation. That is to say, it may well be that some of the largest establishments representing large enterprises and some of the public establishments that said they did not have written agreements were, in fact, covered by recognition agreements that had been signed by the parties at higher levels. When, however, we looked at the extent to which management representatives at establishments reported that they had written recognition agreements in relation to the most important bargaining levels over pay and other issues, we found no sign that in cases where negotiations were more centralised local managers were less likely to report that they had written recognition agreements. It did not appear that there was any easy explanation of the pattern we found.

The timing of recognition

In cases where people said they did have written recognition agreements with the largest negotiating group for manual workers we asked when the agreement was originally signed and how it was brought about (Q38b, c). The first of these two questions was designed to identify those types of establishment where the recognition of manual workers was growing. The second was intended to give some indication in a general way of the circumstances that gave rise to recognition. Of course, these questions depended on our earlier question about the existence of written agreements and we had reasons for feeling that answers to that had not reflected the full extent of written recognition agreements. In practice, it is unlikely that that will have detracted from the value of answers to the subsequent questions. Where people failed to report written recognition agreements because they operated at a level higher than that of the establishment then, normally, recognition

Table II.12 **How the recognition of manual trade unions was brought about**

Column percentages[1]

	All establishments	Number employed by organisation			
		25–500	501–2,000	2,001–10,000	10,001 or more
By discussion	73	(84)[2]	(88)	(63)	76
By extension	18	(7)	(7)	(36)	16
Industrial action involved	5	(6)	(—)	(—)	—
Ballot of workers involved	4	(7)	(4)	(—)	5
ACAS involved	1	(2)	(1)	(*)	*
Can't remember	5	(7)	(1)	(1)	9
Base: all signing recognition agreements in the previous five years					
Unweighted	*213*[3]	*33*	*27*	*43*	*88*
Weighted	*164*	*41*	*18*	*31*	*50*

[1] See note E
[2] See note B
[3] See note G

will have been well-established and routine rather than recent and dramatic.

There was, however, a further complication relating to the question on how recently the recognition agreement had been signed. Such a signing could represent initial recognition or the formalisation of recognition. Our instructions to interviewers made it clear that we included the signing of agreements where that represented the formalisation of recognition. We found that in a substantial minority of cases written recognition agreements had been recently signed. About one quarter of establishments had first signed agreements within the previous five years, and for about one in ten agreements had been signed within the previous 12 months. It was in the private sector where one fifth had signed agreements in the previous three years that there had been the most recent activity. It was the case, further, that recent activity was concentrated in smaller establishments belonging to smaller enterprises. Among establishments with 25 to 99 people that were owned by enterprises having 25 to 500 employees, 17 per cent had signed agreements in the previous year; 28 per cent in the previous three years; and 33 per cent in the previous five years (percentages here are cumulative).

Table II.12 shows managers' accounts of how recognition was brought about. The answers create a very different impression from that sometimes suggested by the more widely publicised recognition disputes of recent years. By far the most common answer was that recognition was brought about as a result of discussion and agreement. In only five per cent of cases was any industrial action or threat of industrial action involved, and in only one per cent of cases had the Advisory, Conciliation and Arbitration Service (ACAS) been called in to help. Four per cent of establishments that had signed recognition agreements in the previous five years had carried out some balloting of workers. Of course, 'discussion' may take many forms. It may be more or less heated and more or less prolonged. It also takes place within the framework of awareness of what can happen and does happen at other workplaces. Accordingly, the places where strikes or other industrial action occurred, where balloting was carried out or where ACAS was called in may well have been more important than they were common, as they may have created precedents, generated expectations and so on. It is also the case that references to ACAS and the use of ballots were more common in relation to the recognition of non-manual unions, as we show later.

Of special interest in Table II.12 is the number of cases where, by implication, the initiative for recognition came about from outside the establishment. These are the cases where recognition at the establishment came about through extension from other parts of the enterprise. In some of those cases, as has been observed elsewhere[3], the requirements of management organisation may be as strong an influence over the recognition of trade unions as any demands from the unions or particular groups of workers. As might be expected, there was some tendency for establishments where recognition had come about as a result of extension to be concentrated among the younger establishments but, surprisingly, there was no tendency for them to be more common where establishments had recently experienced a change of ownership. Recognition by extension was, of course, more common in establishments that were part of larger organisations and was especially frequent in local or central government offices.

Cases where union recognition had been introduced by extension tended to involve establishments that belonged to the largest enterprises. By contrast, industrial action was associated with recognition only in the smaller enterprises. Indeed, there were two main types of establishment where formal trade union recognition was likely to have been associated with industrial action or threat of such action. The first was the independent establishment in the private sector that employed fewer than 100 people (in such establishments industrial action was mentioned in 14 per cent of cases). The second was the relatively small establishment belonging to a small local authority (establishment size less than 100 employees and enterprise size less than 500 employees). Industrial action was mentioned in 15 per cent of such cases. It is clear that strikes or other forms of industrial action did play a substantial part in the achievement of recognition in small private sector firms and small local authorities.

Comparisons with second largest negotiating group and union representatives' accounts

Our accounts of the formalisation of recognition, its recency and how it was brought about have so far depended upon managers' accounts with reference to the largest negotiating group. As explained at the beginning of the chapter, we also had, first, some details concerning the second largest negotiating group (Q43a) and, secondly, the answers of union representatives to corresponding questions.

Where managers negotiated with more than one bargaining group for manual workers, their accounts showed that arrangements with the second group were similar to those for the first. The only differences were that they were very slightly less likely to have written agreements with the second group and slightly more likely to have only one such agreement. In cases where both management and union representatives were interviewed, there was a remarkable correspondence in their respective accounts of whether written agreements existed, how recently they had been signed and how they had been brought about. Accounts very rarely differed by more than one or two percentage points and very similar overall impressions were given.

The incidence of, and number of, lay trade union officers at workplaces

In about three-quarters of establishments where manual unions were recognised managers reported that the manual unions had stewards or union representatives (Q27a, b). In just over one half of the establishments they reported that there were senior stewards or convenors and in five per cent of cases they said that senior stewards or convenors spent all or nearly all their work time on trade union affairs concerning the establishment (see Table II.13; Q28a, b, c). The strongest influence upon whether establishments had stewards, convenors and full time convenors was the size of establishments. This was especially the case when analysis was based upon all establishments that employed manual workers, reflecting the tendency for larger establishments to be more likely to recognise manual unions. But it remained strongly the case when analysis was confined to those establishments that recognised trade unions. The difference between larger and smaller establishments was most marked in relation to the reported incidence of full time convenors. Full time convenors were rare in workplaces with fewer than 500 people, but nearly two-thirds of establishments with 2,000 or more employees had full time convenors for manual workers.

Table II.13   The incidence of manual representatives, convenors and full time convenors at workplaces

Percentages

	All establish-ments	Number of manual workers at establishment							
		1–9	10–24	25–49	50–99	100–199	200–499	500–999	100 or more
Any manual stewards or representatives	44	6	22	40	60	77	88	93	93
Any convenors/ senior stewards	31	5	17	28	39	47	67	75	90
Any full-time convenors	3	—	—	*	*	3	14	38	69
Base: establishments employing manual workers									
Unweighted	*1899*	*162*	*244*	*336*	*280*	*293*	*306*	*140*	*138*
Weighted	*1833*	*223*	*424*	*522*	*282*	*197*	*127*	*38*	*21*
Any manual stewards or representatives	74	20	45	72	85	93	96	94	95
Any convenors/ senior stewards	52	18	35	51	55	57	73	76	91
Any full-time convenors	5	—	—	1	*	4	16	38	70
Base: establishments recognising manual unions									
Unweighted	*1375*	*54*	*117*	*202*	*201*	*246*	*284*	*136*	*135*
Weighted	*1095*	*65*	*203*	*289*	*200*	*163*	*117*	*37*	*21*
Number of union members per manual steward	29	14	14	20	20	24	30	33	38
Number of stewards per convenor	4.3	1.3	1.5	2.0	3.1	4.6	5.4	7.7	7.2
Full-time con-venors as per cent of convenors	10	—	—	1	*	6	12	25	39

* Fewer than 0.5 per cent

A second way of looking at the incidence of lay representation at workplaces, however, was to express the number of stewards as a ratio in relation to the number of trade union members and to express the number of convenors as a ratio in relation to the number of stewards.

That analysis is shown at the foot of Table II.13 and reveals a very different picture in relation to establishment size than did the simple question of whether there were any stewards or convenors. While stewards and convenors were more common in larger establishments, the span of representation of stewards and convenors was smaller in the small establishments. In establishments with fewer than 200 employees, manual stewards generally represented about 20 trade union members. In establishments having 1,000 or more employees, the span of representation tended to be very much larger. Similarly, the ratio of convenors to stewards was higher in smaller establishments. It remained the case, however, that larger establishments had a higher incidence of full time convenors, even when they were expressed as a proportion of convenors, stewards or members. When establishments of similar size were compared there was no tendency for stewards, convenors or full time convenors to be more common in establishments that were associated with larger enterprises. There was a complex pattern relating to whether establishments were independent or not. Where unions were recognised and fewer than 100 manual workers were employed, then independent establishments were more likely to have both stewards and convenors. Where unions were recognised and 100 or more manual workers were employed, then independent establishments were less likely to have stewards and convenors. The difference was especially marked in relation to full time convenors.

The tendency for workplaces where a high proportion of women were employed to have less well-developed union organisation was again apparent. Even where unions were recognised, establishments that employed a higher proportion of women were less likely to have stewards, convenors and full time convenors.

While public sector establishments were more likely than private sector counterparts to recognise manual unions, union members tended, nevertheless, to be more fully represented in the private sector. The contrast was most marked when local or national government establishments were compared with private sector counterparts. The government workplaces, especially the smaller workplaces as measured by number of manual employees, were much less likely to have stewards and convenors. In the larger workplaces they were substantially less likely to have full time convenors. The differences here between public and private sectors may reflect the greater tendency for decisions to be taken at the establishment level in the private sector. Certainly, we found when we analysed the incidence of different kinds of representative in relation to the most important level for pay bargaining and also levels of bargaining over other issues, that stewards, convenors and full time convenors were much more common where plant bargaining prevailed.

Table II.14 The training of union representatives

	All establishments	Number employed at establishment						
		25–49	50–99	100–199	200–499	500–999	1000–1999	2000 or more
Whether any stewards trained in previous year	42	20	39	43	51	62	87	98
Proportion of stewards trained in previous year	*27*	*19*	*22*	*21*	*28*	*29*	*28*	*33*
Base: establishments with manual representatives and numbers given by managers								
Unweighed	*1085*	*86*	*137*	*194*	*248*	*198*	*116*	*106*
Weighed	*775*	*188*	*182*	*167*	*130*	*65*	*28*	*15*

The life time of full time convenors

Of some special interest was the existence of full time convenors. We have seen that they were the norm in establishments with more than 1,000 employees and we found, further, that many had been intro-duced in recent years. In nearly one quarter of cases where full time convenors operated they were first established within the previous five years (Q29c). It appeared, however, that the most rapid period of their recent growth had been the two years from 1975 to 1977. That was especially true for the smaller establishments that had full time con-venors. At establishments with fewer than 500 employees, over one quarter of the convenors owed their origins to that two year period. We have no direct evidence about why the number of full time convenors should have risen in the years 1975 to 1977, but the timing combined with previous research suggests that it may have been associated with the employment and industrial relations legislation of the mid-1970s[4].

The training of shop stewards

The desirability of improved and increased training for lay union representatives tends to be something about which there is wide agree-ment among industrial relations commentators and practitioners. There is less agreement about the purposes of such training[5]. The issues tend to focus upon who should control the content of courses. We had limited questioning about shop steward training in our present survey (Q30a, b, c, d; WQ32a, b, c, d). We asked both management and union representatives whether any manual stewards at the establishment had done courses during the previous year and, if so, how many. We also asked each party to evaluate training for shop stewards. In addition, to provide some evidence relevant to the debate about control over shop steward training, we asked about the location of training, who initiated it and whether management determined the content. Table II.14 shows that there had been some shop steward training of one day or longer during the previous year in 42 per cent of establishments. Such training was almost universal in the largest establishments, but it was much less common in smaller establishments that had stewards. Of course, there were many fewer stewards in smaller establishments than in larger ones. In establishments with 25 to 49 people, which had stewards, the average number was two, while in establishments of 2,000 people or more the comparative figure was 41. Accordingly, in order to establish a standardised measure of the incidence of shop steward training in relation to size, it is necessary to take into account the number of stewards at establishments of different sizes. The proportion of stewards who received training is shown in the second row in Table II.14. Overall, just over one quarter of all stewards had received training in the previous year. On the face of things that is a remarkably high figure, which might give the impression that all shop stewards in Britain would be trained over a four year period. It is, of course, by no means as simple as that. First, that estimate ignores the turnover in stewards. Our findings suggest that about one third of stewards change each year. Secondly, the only measure we have of the quality or quantity of training received by stewards is that it lasted one day or longer. At the same time the figures do suggest that there is a substantial amount of shop steward training being undertaken in one form or another.

Even when the number of stewards was taken into account, such training was clearly more common in large establishments (see Table II.14). In the largest establishments, one third of stewards had received training. In the smallest, the proportion dropped to one fifth. The variations in relation to type of employer were rather surprising. Manual shop stewards in the private sector were slightly more likely to have received training than counterparts in local or central government and very much more likely to have done so than stewards in the nationalised industries. It may be, again, that the greater tendency to decentralisation in the private sector contributed to that pattern. If that was the case, it was not reflected in variations relating to levels of decision making as revealed by our relevant questioning on levels of bargaining over pay and other issues.

According to management respondents, courses had been held at the initiative of trade unions in about three-quarters of the cases where they occurred and at the initiative of management in about one quarter of instances. At 17 per cent of workplaces where shop steward training had occurred, management determined the content of at least some shop steward training. It was in nationalised industries that management was most likely to initiate shop steward training and control content. As managers in one major part of the public sector were those most likely to exercise influence over shop steward training, it is interesting that managers in the other major part, local and central government, were least likely to do so.

Time off for shop steward training under the Employment Protection Act, 1975

The Employment Protection Act, 1975 made provision for trade unionists to have time off work for certain specified activities, including training. In our questioning of trade union respondents we explored the extent to which they had made use of that provision (WQ20a, b). Compared with the lack of impact made by many features of the Act[6], a relatively high use of the time-off provisions was reported by union representatives, especially manual stewards. Thirty-eight per cent of manual representatives reported that the provision had been used and

Table II.15   Use of time-off provisions in the Employment Protection Act

Percentages

	All establish- ments	Number employed at establishment				
		25–99	100– 199	200– 499	500– 999	1000 or more
Manual workers						
Provisions used	38[1]	25	45	54	53	55
Reason for use						
Steward training	24	10	30	41	40	50
Steward duties	22	14	29	30	34	38
Members' activities	8	5	12	12	10	13
Other reason or no reason given	2	1	2	6	3	3
Base: primary manual representative interviewed						
Unweighted	*955*	*206*	*174*	*209*	*166*	*200*
Weighted	*694*	*343*	*142*	*113*	*56*	*39*
Non-manual workers						
Provisions used	22	16	25	25	36	35
Reason for use						
Steward training	11	5	12	17	20	30
Steward duties	12	9	12	16	20	18
Members' activities	6	5	7	5	11	6
Other reason or no reason given	1	—	3	1	1	1
Base: primary non-manual representative interviewed						
Unweighted	*900*	*190*	*159*	*203*	*158*	*190*
Weighted	*639*	*301*	*140*	*107*	*54*	*37*

[1] See note F

about one quarter said that it had been used for shop steward training (see Table II.15). The strongest influence upon the use of the provision was the size of establishments, and one half of the largest workplaces had experienced use of the time-off provisions specifically for steward training. Even in cases where stewards existed, small independent establishments were least likely to have had requests for time off under the provisions. Only 19 per cent of manual unions in all independent establishments had used the provisions. That pattern is consistent with a whole range of findings showing that the employment legislation of the mid-1970s had least impact upon small firms and establishments[7].

Evaluations of shop steward training
In cases where stewards had received training, the very large majority

Table II.16   Management evaluation of manual representative/shop steward training

Column percentages

	All establish-ments	Private British	Private overseas	Nationalised industries	Central/ local government
A great deal	32	31	33	42	26
A fair extent	52	51	57	53	58
Not very much	13	15	8	4	15
Not at all	3	3	2	1	1
Mean score[1]	+1.0	+0.9	+1.1	+1.3	+0.9
Base: establishments where manual stewards were trained					
Unweighted	*570*	*333*	*63*	*51*	*111*
Weighted	*296*	*176*	*24*	*22*	*66*

[1] The mean score has been calculated by giving scores of +2 to 'a great deal'; +1 to 'a fair extent' −1 to 'not very much'; −2 to 'not at all'; and 0 to 'can't say' or not answered. As there was a differential rate of non-response the percentage distributions have been recalculated using those who gave a rating as the base

of managers felt that the training was valuable. Eighty-four per cent judged that training did help stewards in their work as representatives. About one third of managers said that it helped them a great deal. Only three per cent felt that shop steward training was of no value (see Table II.16). Management respondents in nationalised industries and private firms with overseas ownership were most positive. More had reservations in central or local government offices and privately owned British firms. Within the private sector, manufacturing establishments generally, and particularly those involved in mechanical or electrical engineering, were most likely to have reservations about steward training.

There was a strong association between managers' evaluations of shop steward training and the degree of industrial peace they had experienced. Where workplaces had experienced relatively long strikes, about one quarter of managers felt that shop steward training was of little or no help. In places where there had been no industrial action the corresponding proportion was ten per cent. The pattern does suggest that managers tended to expect to derive benefits from shop steward training in the form of absence of industrial action. On the other hand, it was also clear that managers tended to be more in favour of shop steward training the higher was the level of trade union organisation at workplaces. For instance, training was judged to be more useful where there was a closed shop and where a higher proportion of manual workers were union members.

Table II.17 **Comparison of management and manual steward evaluations of manual steward training**

Column percentages

	Management representative	Union representative
A great deal of help	31	82
A fair extent	55	15
Not very much	12	2
Not at all	2	1
Mean score[1]	+1.0	+1.8
Base: establishments where manual representatives were interviewed		
Unweighted	*373*	*373*
Weighted	*178*	*178*

[1] See note to Table II.16

However favourable managers were to shop steward training overall, the shop stewards themselves were even more enthusiastic (WQ32d). Table II.17 shows the comparison in cases where both managers and shop stewards gave evaluations. It is clear that the large majority of stewards gave the highest rating to training and nearly all felt it was useful. At the same time, it is, of course, a very familiar survey finding that people give a high retrospective rating to training and educational courses that they have undertaken[8], although it is also true that such findings normally refer to courses that people have been on themselves, whereas here we are also dealing with ratings of courses for others.

Both parties were so favourable towards shop steward training that there was little scope to explore inter-relationships between management and union evaluations. That is to say, it would have been interesting to explore whether or not union representatives rated training more highly in circumstances where management regarded it less favourably. In practice there was little scope for such analysis, but any tendency there was suggested congruence between management and union judgements. Where managers rated training more highly, so did union representatives.

From union representatives we collected a little more information on the details of shop steward training. Those details are shown in Table II.18. Generally, it will be seen that training was mainly undertaken in working hours, was most frequently provided at a trade union location, although educational establishments made substantial provision for shop steward training, and that union representatives' accounts of who initiated courses and who determined content were broadly in line with

Table II.18   Details of manual steward training according to worker representatives

Percentages

	All establish-ments	Private sector	Nationalised industries	Central/ local government
Time of training				
In work hours	93	95	(81)[1]	89
Location				
Trade union location	62[2]	60	(72)	67
Educational establishment	41	42	(28)	40
Workplace	7	5	(2)	16
Initiative				
Management	20	23	(9)	13
Union	91	89	(92)	97
Content				
Management decided content of some courses	14	15	(15)	10
Base: manual union respondents reported manual steward training				
Unweighted	*373*	*270*	*32*	*64*
Weighted	*178* •	*131*	*12*	*32*

[1] See note B
[2] See note E

those of managers. Beyond that general picture, two further points are worthy of note. First, nationalised industries once again compared unfavourably with other sectors in their provision for shop steward training. That pattern is surprising, given the general tendency for trade union organisation to be well-developed in nationalised industries. Secondly, educational establishments featured more prominently among locations for providing courses than they did among the sources of training for personnel managers, as we shall see in Chapter V. At the same time, educational establishments still provided help for less than one half of the establishments whose shop stewards experienced training. The educational system generally did not appear to play a major part in vocational training in the field of industrial relations.

Office and secretarial facilities for senior stewards
Generally, it appeared that substantial majorities of senior stewards for manual workers had access to some office services. Ninety-five per cent had access to a telephone (Table II.19). Nearly three-quarters had

Table II.19   Facilities for senior stewards

	Manual representatives	Non-manual representatives
	Percentage	
Any office facilities[1]	71	74
Own office	20	18
Use of office	52	56
[Provided in previous five years]	[36]	[33]
Any access to telephone	95	94
Own telephone	23	30
Use of telephone	72	64
[Provided in previous five years]	[45]	[38]
Other office help[1]	73	84
Secretarial assistance	29	35
Use of photo-copier[2]	41	44
Use of typewriter	31	39
[Provided in previous five years]	[33]	[31]
Agreement over facilities		
Provided by formal agreement with management	22	23
Rating of facilities		
Facilities very good (percentages)	29	30
Base: establishments where representatives in column headings were interviewed and unions were recognised		
Unweighted	*972*	*922*
Weighted	*707*	*655*

[1] See note D
[2] Other office help was secretarial assistance, access to photo-copier or access to a typewriter. The proportion listed as having access to a photo-copier was made up of people who did not have secretarial assistance but did have photo-copying facilities. The same principle applied to use of a typewriter

secretarial assistance or access to a photo-copier or a typewriter. Seventy-one per cent had at least the use of an office. It appeared that there had been a marked tendency for facilities of all types to be introduced in the previous five years. The proportions with different facilities dropped considerably when we focused upon the proportion of senior stewards who had their own offices (20 per cent), their own telephone (23 per cent) and secretarial assistance (29 per cent). In very large establishments, those with 2,000 or more employees, however, four-fifths of senior stewards had their own offices and nearly all had their own telephones and some secretarial assistance. Frequently, facilities were provided for within formal, written agreements with

Table II.20   Facilities for senior stewards in relation to size

Percentages

| | All establish- | Number employed at establishment | | | | |
		25–99	100–199	200–499	500–999	1000 or more
A. Manual workers						
Own office	20	8	16	32	44	61
Own telephone	23	17	14	26	46	62
Secretarial help	29	26	23	34	39	54
Base: manual worker representatives where unions were recognised						
Unweighted	*972*	*209*	*176*	*214*	*171*	*202*
Weighted	*707*	*350*	*144*	*117*	*56*	*40*
B. Non-manual workers						
Own office	18	10	21	21	34	41
Own telephone	30	25	28	29	44	59
Secretarial help	35	29	35	39	53	43
Base: non-manual worker representatives where unions were recognised						
Unweighted	*922*	*194*	*161*	*210*	*161*	*206*
Weighted	*655*	*308*	*142*	*112*	*55*	*38*

management, and that was especially the case in our largest establishments, where nearly one half of the workplaces had written agreements that specified facilities for senior stewards. Generally, however, worker representatives did not rate very highly the facilities provided for senior stewards. Twenty-nine per cent said they were 'very good', but one fifth gave an unfavourable rating and that proportion was high for answers to questions of this type.

By far the strongest source of variation in the provision of facilities was the size of establishments (see Table II.20). That was especially true so far as a personal office was concerned. The provision of secretarial help showed the weakest association with establishment size and the strongest association with other characteristics of workplaces. With regard to ownership, there was little marked variation in relation to the characteristics that are frequently the basis for differences in our later analysis, such as the comparison between public and private employers and the contrast between independent establishments and those that were parts of groups. The most striking variation in the provision of facilities for senior manual stewards lay between establishments that were owned by overseas companies and those that were domestically owned. Overseas employers were very substantially more likely to provide facilities for senior stewards. So far as the trade union characteristics of workplaces were concerned, secretarial services, especially, tended to be more frequently provided where union density was high and where there was more local bargaining. In each case the association was independent of establishment size.

The provision of facilities for non-manual senior stewards was very similar to that for manual counterparts. Non-manual stewards were slightly more likely to have their own telephone and secretarial services (see Table II.19). Associations between facilities and establishment size were not so strong for non-manual employees (see Table II.20). Similarly, the contrast between overseas and domestic companies was not so great. In terms of ownership, the striking contrast for non-manual stewards was between the public and the private sectors. For establishments employing fewer than 500 people, facilities for senior non-manual stewards were substantially better in the private sector. For larger establishments they were substantially better in public employment.

Table II.21 **Number of manual trade unions at establishment and pattern of bargaining in multi-union workplaces**

Column percentages

Number of manual trade unions	All establishments	Number employed at establishment				
		25–99	100–499	500–999	1000–1999	2000 or more
One	56[1]	71	46	27	13	4
Two	20	17	25	16	15	14
Three-five	23	10	27	48	55	41
Six and more	2	—	2	7	14	38
No information	*	*	—	*	2	1
Base: establishments recognising manual unions						
Unweighted	*1375*	*347*	*551*	*226*	*131*	*120*
Weighted	*1095*	*590*	*379*	*77*	*32*	*17*

Pattern of bargaining in multi-union workplaces

Column percentages

Joint negotiations	35	40	31	40	31	36
Separate negotiations	60	56	64	54	68	62
Base: more than one manual union recognised						
Unweighted	*749*	*88*	*282*	*158*	*111*	*110*
Weighted	*424*	*141*	*186*	*55*	*27*	*15*

Multi-unionism

A recurrent criticism of the British industrial relations system is that the number of different trade unions with which any particular management has to deal makes the business of management very much more difficult. The suggestion is that the form of trade union representation within establishments exacerbates the problems of organisational rigidities and inflexibility. Multi-unionism, it is argued, makes difficult the effective use of manpower, promotes difficulties over job demarcation, has an in-built tendency to generate leap-frogging pay claims and imposes substantial demands upon management time when consultation, discussion and negotiation has to be duplicated over a number of different bodies and conflicting demands have to be reconciled[9].

Certainly our findings confirmed that multi-unionism was very widespread in Britain (Q23a). In establishments that recognised manual trade unions, one quarter had three or more manual trade unions with members at the workplace. Nearly one half had more than one manual union. The strongest influence upon the number of unions at establishments was the number of people employed. At establishments with a complement of 2,000 or more people, over three-quarters had three or more manual unions and 38 per cent had six or more. At the same time, while the number of recognised unions was large, the number of bargaining groups was fewer (Q25c). Table II.21 shows the number of recognised unions at establishments of different sizes and Table II.22 analyses the number of manual bargaining groups in relation to the number of recognised trade unions.

Table II.22   Number of manual bargaining units in relation to number of recognised unions

Column percentages

Number of bargaining units	All establishments	Number of recognised unions				
		One	Two	Three	Four	Five or more
One	76	100	42	30	39	33
Two	15	—	58	24	25	18
Three	6	—	—	46	9	16
Four or more	3	—	—	—	27	33
Base: all establishments recognising manual unions						
Unweighted	*1375*	*620*	*241*	*183*	*146*	*182*
Weighted	*1095*	*662*	*199*	*111*	*60*	*58*

It is clear that, while nearly one half of establishments that recognised trade unions had more than one manual union, three-quarters dealt with only one bargaining unit. The contrast between number of unions and number of bargaining units was most marked for 'arger

Table II.23 **Management and union preferences regarding negotiating through one bargaining unit or multiple units**

	Manual workers		Non-manual workers	
	Management	Union	Management	Union
All establishments with more than one union			Column percentages	
Prefer joint (one unit)	62	58	40	50
Prefer separate (more than one unit)	25	38	38	39
No preference	4	2	8	7
Not stated	9	2	14	4

Base: more than one union and both management and union representative interviewed

Unweighted	*505*	*505*	*538*	*538*
Weighted	*164*	*164*	*354*	*354*
			Column percentages	
One bargaining unit				
Prefer joint	78[1]	79	64	70
Prefer separate	6	15	*	11
No preference	1	2	5	12
Not stated	16	4	30	8

Base: more than one union; management and union representatives interviewed; joint negotiation practiced

Unweighted	*186*	*186*	*112*	*112*
Weighted	*104*	*104*	*88*	*88*
			Column percentages	
Two or more units				
Prefer joint	52	44	33	43
Prefer separate	38	52	51	48
No preference	7	2	8	6
Not stated	3	1	8	3

Base: more than one union; management and union representatives interviewed; separate negotiations practiced

Unweighted	*319*	*319*	*426*	*426*
Weighted	*160*	*160*	*266*	*266*

* Fewer than 0.5 per cent
[1] See note C

establishments. While over three-quarters had three or more unions, 43 per cent dealt with only one bargaining group and a further 31 per cent with only two.

Certainly there was on the part of both management and union representatives a preference for negotiating jointly in one bargaining unit rather than having separate units for different groups of manual workers (Q45a, c; WQ17a, c). In Table II.23 we show a comparison of management and union preferences in circumstances where both management and union representatives were interviewed. As far as manual workers were concerned, there was a slight tendency for management representatives to be more in favour than union counterparts of joint negotiations, but as far as non-manual grades were concerned, there was a slight tendency for union representatives to favour one bargaining unit more strongly than did management representatives.

The relationship between the preferences of management and union representatives, however, is perhaps better shown by Table II.24. Where there was more than one union recognised but only one bargaining unit, management and union representatives agreed in the large majority of cases that that was the better arrangement. In a minority of cases, management preferred the existing arrangement, but the union representative would have preferred separate bargaining. There was a similar pattern for both manual and non-manual grades. Where separate bargaining was practised, views were very much more diverse. In

Table II.24   The inter-relationship between management and union preferences regarding joint or separate negotiating units

Column percentages

| | One bargaining unit | | Two or more units | |
	Manual	Non-manual	Manual	Non-manual
Both prefer joint	76	82	33[1]	23
Management prefers joint/union separate	17	18	24	17
Union prefers joint/ management separate	5	*	14	25
Both prefer separate	2	*	28	35

Base: both management and union representatives expressed a preference regarding joint or separate bargaining

Unweighted	186	112	319	426
Weighted	104	88	160	266

* Fewer than 0.5 per cent
[1] See note C

Table II.25 Reasons for preferring one bargaining unit

Column percentages[1]

	Manual workers		Non-manual workers	
	Management	Union	Management	Union
Easier/quicker/avoids duplicated activity	51	27	43	15
Avoids friction/bad feeling between groups	33	19	12	15
Avoids leapfrogging/ continuous bargaining	20	6	10	7
Issues are similar for all groups	10	16	25	23
Avoids divide and rule/ strengthens union group	1	29	4	30
Promotes unity/ cooperation	5	9	8	10
Always worked well	5	3	6	8
Different views help better outcome	4	13	7	14
Other answers	3	8	4	4
Not stated	2	1	7	7
Base: all relevant management and union representatives				
Unweighted	*435*	*318*	*333*	*266*
Weighted	*230*	*168*	*227*	*182*

[1] See note E

only a minority of cases did both parties agree that the existing arrangementment was preferable. As far as manual workers were concerned, there was agreement in one third of cases that a change to one bargaining unit would be preferable and that proportion was higher than the 28 per cent of cases where both parties wanted to retain separate units. The pattern for manual workers appeared to offer substantial scope to move away from multi-union bargaining. As far as non-manual unions were concerned, there was also a substantial minority (nearly one quarter) where the answers of both parties indicated a preference for a change, but the balance of preference was more in favour of the *status quo*.

Tables II.25 and II.26 summarise the reasons management and union representatives gave for their preferences regarding joint or separate bargaining (Q45b, c; WQ17b, c). As far as managers were concerned, the chief advantages of dealing with one bargaining unit were, first, that a set of negotiations could be completed all together

Table II.26   Reasons for preferring more than one bargaining unit

Column percentages[1]

	Manual workers		Non-manual workers	
	Management	Union	Management	Union
Issues/problems vary	69	60	67	71
Easier to settle with one at a time	10	3	4	3
Required by higher level arrangements	9	10	16	10
Always worked well	5	4	2	4
Only practicable method	2	3	3	2
Union representatives have different views/ disagree	2	18	5	8
Means that views of different groups are heard	1	17	*	9
Not stated	15	5	11	4
Base: all relevant management and union representatives				
Unweighted	*189*	*296*	*194*	*250*
Weighted	*96*	*192*	*103*	*145*

[1] See note E

rather than being wastefully duplicated over two or more units; secondly, negotiating through one body reduced friction and rivalry between different groups and, thirdly, it avoided a continuous round of bargaining with the leap-frogging inherent in that process. It was striking that union representatives expressed many of the same reasons as managers for their preference. In addition, however, union representatives favoured one joint body, first, because they thought that all the unions combining together strengthened their position and made it more difficult for management to play off one group against another and, secondly, because they thought that the combination of a range of different views on issues led to better outcomes.

Reasons for preferring separate negotiations were dominated by one view among both management and union representatives. This was the view that as different groups had different problems, circumstances and requirements and generated different issues, then it was appropriate to deal with them separately. Beyond that there was the view that it was easier to settle with one group at a time rather than struggling with all together. In some instances it was reported that higher level institutions or arrangements required separate bargaining at workplace level.

Table II.27 Union recognition and densities: non-manual and manual groups compared

Percentages

	All private sector	Private manu-facturing	Private services	All public sector	Nation-alised industries	Public admini-stration
Non-manual unions						
Union recognised						
(per cent)	30	32	29	90	94	89
Union density[1]	31	39	21	61	90	57
Base: all establishments that employed non-manual workers						
Unweighted	*1328*	*746*	*578*	*706*	*133*	*573*
Weighted	*1339*	*548*	*785*	*650*	*78*	*571*
Manual unions						
Union recognised						
(per cent)	50	68	35	76	98	73
Union density	65	75	39	67	91	58
Base: all establishments that employed manual workers						
Unweighted	*1255*	*736*	*515*	*644*	*130*	*514*
Weighted	*1245*	*542*	*697*	*588*	*75*	*513*

[1] Union density is the proportion in per cent of the relevant group of employees who were union members. See note 2 at the end of the chapter

The comparative pattern for non-manual unions

All the questions that we have reported upon in this chapter we asked also about non-manual unions. Occasionally we have referred to the findings for non-manual groups as we have gone along, but chiefly we have focused upon manual unions. In this section we summarise the comparative position concerning trade union recognition for the two main classes of employee as revealed by our questioning. Generally, and in terms of the bulk of the matter that we could explore through our method, the pattern of response with regard to non-manual unions was remarkably similar to that for manual unions. There were, however, two major differences. It remained the case that unions were less widely recognised for non-manual workers than for manual workers and union membership was lower among non-manual workers. Secondly, there were important differences in the pattern of variation in non-manual union membership and recognition compared with the pattern for manual unions. First, the most marked difference was one of degree rather than one of kind and was related to ownership. We stressed that ownership was a major source of variation with regard to manual unions, but there were even greater differences in levels of non-manual recognition according to whether employers were public or private and whether establishments were independent enterprises or parts of large organisations. Table II.27 summarises the main details. Differences between the public and the private sectors were dramatic. The large majority of all public sector establishments recognised non-manual unions (90 per cent). In nationalised industries the very large majority of non-manual employees were union members. In other parts of the public sector the majority of non-manual workers were union members. Indeed there was very little difference in the public sector between manual and non-manual workers as far as recognition and densities were concerned. In the private sector, by contrast, the position was very different. Levels of non-manual recognition and membership were substantially lower than for manual employees and dramatically lower than for the public sector. In the public sector as a whole 90 per cent of establishments recognised non-manual unions and 61 per cent of non-manual employees were union members. In the private sector 30 per cent of establishments recognised non-manual unions and 31 per cent of non-manual workers were members. In independent establishments the proportion where non-manual unions were recognised fell to 16 per cent. The recognition of manual unions was twice as common in the same establishments.

Secondly, as with the recognition of manual unions we found that there was a very strong and consistent tendency for a non-manual union to be more frequently recognised the greater the number of people employed at the establishment. In both instances that trend was largely the result of the pattern in the private sector. When analysis was confined to the private sector it appeared that the relationship between recognition and establishment size was even stronger for non-manual groups than it was for manual groups. As far as manual workers were concerned, however, it was apparent that the total size of the establishment was principally a proxy for the number of manual workers employed on site. That is to say, when we analysed the recognition of manual unions in relation to establishment size within different manual worker size bands, it was apparent that the number of manual workers employed was a more important source of variation than the total number of people employed. Indeed, that is just what might be expected intuitively. So far as non-manual workers were concerned, however, the picture was very different. In private employment, the total number of people employed on site was a much more important source of variation than the number of non-manual workers (see Table II.28). The difference between manual and non-manual workers in this respect was very striking and it suggests that, in the private sector generally, the recognition of non-manual unions was in some sense subsidiary to the recognition of manual unions. The pattern for non-

Table II.28 **Recognition of non-manual unions in relation to number of non-manual employees and total number employed at establishment**

Percentages

| Number of non-manual employees at establishment | Total number employed at establishment | | | |
	Under 100	100–499	500–999	1,000 or more
1–24	20	43	§[1]	§
25–99	33	48	(63)[2]	§
100–499	n.a.[3]	46	73	90
500 or more	n.a.	n.a.	(57)	89

Base: private sector establishments employing non-manual workers

[1] See note A
[2] See note B
[3] Cell size is not applicable

manual recognition also has important implications for ideas about influences upon the growth of white collar unionism which we take up in the concluding section to this chapter.

Thirdly, as with manual recognition there was a strong tendency in the private sector for non-manual union recognition to be more common the larger was the size of the total enterprise of which the establishment was part, independently of the size of the establishment. Similarly, when establishments of similar size were compared, there was a very strong tendency for independent establishments to be less likely to recognise non-manual unions than were establishments that were parts of groups. For instance, at private sector establishments employing fewer than 10 non-manual workers, only two per cent of independent establishments recognised non-manual unions, compared with 36 per cent of counterparts that were part of larger organisations. Similarly, for the same establishment size category, 50 per cent of establishments belonging to enterprises employing over 10,000 people in total recognised non-manual unions compared with only eight per cent of counterparts where the total enterprise size was 500 employees or fewer. Even when private sector establishments employing 100 to 199 non-manual workers were compared, independent establishments were half as likely to recognise non-manual unions as establishments that belonged to groups, and establishments where the total enterprise size was 500 or less were half as likely to recognise non-manual unions as counterparts where the enterprise employed 10,000 or more. It was clear in the private sector that, independently of establishment size, the total size of the enterprise and whether or not establishments belonged to larger organisations were very strongly associated with non-manual union recognition. Indeed, it appeared that they were more strongly related to non-manual recognition than they were to manual union recognition. Again, the pattern has implications for ideas about the growth of white collar unionism which we discuss in our concluding section.

Apart from the differences in the extent of recognition, union densities and patterns of recognition there were very few marked contrasts between the largest non-manual unions and the largest manual unions reflected in answers to other questions relevant to recognition that we have discussed in this chapter. Written recognition agreements were reported to a very similar extent. Non-manual recognition agreements were concluded with similar recency to agreements with manual unions. There were, however, interesting differences between the manual and non-manual in the ways that recognition had been brought about. There were no cases of recent white collar recognition that had been associated with industrial action. By contrast, the use of ballots and references to ACAS were sightly more common in cases of non-manual recognition.

It was the case, too, that lay trade union officers at the place of work were slightly less common among non-manual unions. The difference was most marked in relation to full time convenors and that difference was most apparent in large establishments. For instance, two-thirds of establishments with a complement of 2,000 or more people had full time manual convenors while one quarter of the same establishments had full time non-manual convenors. At the same time, one quarter is still an unexpectedly high figure for non-manual unions.

Multi-unionism was even more common among non-manual workers than among manual workers and dealing with more than one bargaining unit was also slightly more common. We examined management and union preferences regarding joint or separate bargaining for non-manual workers in an earlier section where we showed that both managers and worker representatives were more inclined to favour separate bargaining for different groups of non-manual workers than for different groups of manual employees.

Training for non-manual lay union representatives was slightly less common overall. That was the case whether the measure adopted was the proportion of establishments where there was any steward training or the proportion of stewards who received any training. At establishments which had both manual and non-manual representatives, 29 per cent of the manual stewards received training in the previous year but only 17 per cent of non-manual counterparts. The gap between the frequency of manual and non-manual training was most marked in smaller establishments and enterprises. For instance, in those estab-

Table II.29 Comparison of worker representatives' evaluations and accounts of shop steward training

	Manual representatives	Non-manual representatives
	Column percentages	
Evaluations of training		
A great deal of help	78	71
A fair extent	18	26
Not very much	1	—
Not at all	1	—
Can't say	2	3
Mean score	1.7[1]	1.7
	Percentages	
Details of shop steward training		
Undertaken in working hours	91	90
Location		
Place of work	10[2]	9
Trade union location	59	60
Educational establishment	38	28
Other	8	15
Some training undertaken at management initiative	25	15
Management has some influence over content	20	11
Base: both manual and non-manual workers' representatives interviewed and gave details of shop steward training		
Unweighted	*204*	*204*
Weighted	*76*	*76*

[1] See notes to Table II.16
[2] See note F

lishments representing organisations that employed 500 people or fewer, 29 per cent of manual stewards received training, but only seven per cent of non-manual representatives did so.

Managers were slightly more approving of training for non-manual representatives than for manual stewards. By contrast, slightly fewer non-manual representatives themselves gave the highest assessment of the value of training for stewards (see Table II.29). With regard to the other details about training that we collected, the chief difference in practices as between manual and non-manual training was the role of management. Management was substantially more likely to initiate training for manual stewards and to have some influence over the content of training for such stewards.

Growth in trade union membership and recognition

Our findings on levels of trade union membership and recognition confirm that there was substantial trade union growth during the 1970s. Analyses of trade union growth have normally been carried out with union density as the key measure. In this chapter we have generally focused upon trade union recognition as the critical measure of the coverage of trade unions, although we have occasionally included trade union density in our tables showing the extent of recognition. In fact, there was generally in our findings a very strong positive association between union densities and levels of recognition. There were interesting and important deviations from that association, such as the tendency for establishments in public administration to recognise unions with substantially lower levels of membership density than were associated with recognition in private sector establishments. Generally, however, if we had used union density as our principal measure of union coverage we would have found much the same pattern of variation as we found through focusing upon recognition. Accordingly, in view of the extent to which density has been used in studies of growth it is legitimate to switch the focus in this concluding section from recognition to density.

We calculated from our survey that in 1980 the overall union density was 62 per cent. (Our overall figure was calculated by expressing all full time employees who were union members as a proportion of all full time employees. See note 2 at the end of the chapter.) It was not possible for us to compare that figure with the official statistics published by the Department of Employment and based upon returns from individual trade unions[10]. The Department's figures have well-established limitations and overstate actual membership[11]. In addition, of course, we excluded from our analysis establishments that employed fewer than 25 people, where union membership is much lower. When we compared our overall figure of 62 per cent with that for full time employees employed in comparable establishments from a national sample survey of individuals carried out shortly after our survey[12], the survey of individuals revealed a union density of 65 per cent for full time employees. It was clear that the two figures were consistent. We had no way, however, of comparing our figures with those that existed in previous periods, owing to the lack of comparable surveys carried out 10 or 20 years previously. Nevertheless, whatever their weaknesses as a measure of the actual union density at any time, the official figures provide a sound basis for identifying changes over time. They provide clear evidence of union growth through the 1970s.

That raises the question of what our survey can contribute to an explanation of that growth. We found that the chief sources of variation in union recognition and density were ownership, the size of establishments, the size of enterprises and workforce composition. By implication, our findings would suggest that if the public sector were extended, or the size of workplaces increased, or the size of enterprises enlarged or the male proportion of the workforce increased, while all other considerations remained equal, then there would be union growth. Conversely, if the private sector became relatively larger, if small establishments became more common, if the size of corporations were reduced and a higher proportion of women worked, then trade union membership would decline. In his classic study of growth in white collar unionism, Bain concluded that the disposition of employers to recognise unions, government encouragement of recognition, and employment concentration were the main conditions necessary for the growth of trade union membership[13]. If, in our survey, ownership is taken as a proxy for the disposition of employers to recognise unions associated with government encouragement, and establishment size is taken as a measure of employment concentration, then his conditions accorded with two of the characteristics that we found to be most strongly associated with union recognition and density. Our analysis, however, suggests the following further refinements. First, we found that, in the private sector, the size of enterprises was very strongly associated with union recognition and density, independently of the size of establishments. That was especially true for non-manual groups. While, in general, establishment and enterprise size are positively associated with one another, they are distinct dimensions of size and the total number of people employed by an enterprise may not be taken to be a measure of employment concentration. In many very large enterprises employees may be numerous but diffuse. Our findings suggested that enterprise size was an additional and distinct influence upon trade union recognition and density which was especially strong for non-manual employees.

Secondly, so far as manual employees were concerned it was clear from our analysis that when, in the private sector, establishment size emerged as so strongly associated with recognition and density it was as a proxy for the number of manual workers employed on site. The characteristic of workplaces strongly associated with unionism was the manual complement rather than the total size of the workforce. For manual grades, then, the concentration of manual employment was the key source of variation. The pattern for non-manual grades was, however, different. In the private sector, the total number of people employed on site was substantially more strongly associated with non-manual union recognition and density than the number of non-manual employees. The impression created was that in the private sector the recognition of non-manual unions was partly a spin-off from other characteristics of workplaces rather than associated directly with the concentration of *non-manual* employment.

Thirdly, in our analysis it was apparent that, as far as ownership was concerned, there was, in addition to the major distinction between public and private employers, a further distinction to be made between independent establishments and those belonging to multi-establishment companies. All other things being equal, independent establishments were much less likely to recognise unions and densities were lower. The contrast was especially marked for non-manual workers.

Fourthly, we found that in the private sector the recognition of manual unions and union density were strongly related to the proportion of women employed, independently of the other main sources of variation. So far as non-manual groups were concerned, the picture was slightly different. Non-manual union density in the private sector was consistently related to the proportion of women non-manual workers, but the pattern of recognition of non-manual unions was less strongly related to the proportion of women employed. That pattern provided a further illustration of the way that the recognition of non-manual unions in the private sector appeared to be less dependent upon the characteristics of the non-manual workforce. More generally, the association between the proportion of women employed and union densities and recognition was also relevant to ideas about trade union growth. Overall our analysis was consistent with the view that union recognition and density were mainly the result of government and management policies and practices, especially in relation to the implications of managing large numbers of people, rather than the inclinations and wishes of individual workers[14]. The variation in relation to the workforce composition, however, did provide an exception to the general pattern. That type of variation implied that the characteristic attitudes of different groups of employees towards trade unionism might also play a part in trade union recognition and density, at least in the private sector.

Notes

1. By *ownership* we refer chiefly to whether establishments were parts of the public or the private sectors, but we also use the term to cover whether establishments were independent or part of larger organisations as, in the private sector, there were substantial differences according to whether establishments were relatively small firms or were parts of a corporation.

2. We did not ask managers how many part time workers were members of trade unions. Accordingly, union density among all employees, manual and non-manual combined, was measured by expressing all full time employees who were union members as a proportion of all full time employees. Where we distinguish between manual and non-manual union density, then the measure is full time workers who were union members as a proportion of all workers.

3. See, for instance, the account of the United Biscuit case in W.W. Daniel and Neil McIntosh, *The Right to Manage?* (Macdonald, London, 1972), and the 'Resistance' case in Neil Millward and John McQueeney, *Company Take-overs, Management*

Organisation and Industrial Relations (Department of Employment, London, 1981).

4. We have already referred to the evidence of the Warwick survey (William Brown, Ed., *The Changing Contours of British Industrial Relations* (Basil Blackwell, Oxford 1981)) that the legislation of the mid-1970s contributed to the growth of personnel specialists on the management side. In addition, George Sayers Bain, in *The Growth of White-collar Unionism* (Oxford University Press, 1970), has shown the importance of legislation and government encouragement for the development of unionisation.

5. T. Schuller and S. Henderson, 'Worker Representatives and the Articulation of Training Needs,' *Industrial Relations Journal*, Vol. 11, No. 2, 1980; J. Lover, 'Shop Steward Training: Conflicting Objectives and Needs', *Industrial Relations Journal*, Vol. 7, No. 1, 1976; W.E.J. McCarthy, *The Role of Shop Stewards in British Industrial Relations*, Research Paper No. 1, Royal Commission on Trade Unions and Employers' Associations.

6. W.W. Daniel and Elizabeth Stilgoe, *The Impact of Employment Protection Laws* (Policy Studies Institute No. 577, London, 1978); W.W. Daniel, *Maternity Rights: the experience of employers* (Policy Studies Institute No. 596, London, 1981).

7. See note 6.

8. See W.W. Daniel and Harriet Pugh, *Sandwich Courses in Higher Education* (Political and Economic Planning No. 557, London, 1975).

9. See, for example, Sir Charles Carter and John Pinder, *Policies for a Constrained Economy* (Heinemann Educational Books, London, 1982).

10. 'Membership of trade unions in 1980', Department of Employment *Gazette*, February 1982.

11. George Sayers Bain and R. Price, *Profiles of Union Growth* (Basil Blackwell, Oxford, 1980).

12. The figure is derived from the comparison survey of the general population carried out by OPCS as part of the 1981 Policy Studies Institute survey of the position of ethnic minorities in Britain.

13. George Sayers Bain, *The Growth of White-collar Unionism* (Oxford University Press, 1970).

14. See, for instance, the analysis of white collar unionisation in K. Prandy, A. Stewart and R.M. Blackburn, *White Collar Work* (Macmillan, London, 1983).

III The Closed Shop

The institution of the closed shop is one of the most controversial aspects of industrial relations in Britain, involving basic philosophical issues and having important implications for the relative power of trade unions and employers. We approached the institution of the closed shop as a distinctive form of the relationship between management and trade unions, aiming to complement other research already in progress[1] by providing systematic survey evidence on the extent of the closed shop and some of its important characteristics. In line with the emphasis in our survey on factual questions about workplace practices, we did not explore the many philosophical and practical issues which surround the closed shop[2]; nor did we try to investigate its effects on individuals, employing organisations, the trade unions or the economy as a whole. What we have done is to analyse the closed shop as an aspect of organisation which varies in relation to distinct and identifiable characteristics of workplaces. We look at the distribution of the institution in British industry, its coverage, the extent to which it has grown in recent years and the pattern of variation as between different sectors of employment.

The extent of the closed shop

Table III.1 summarises our findings on the extent of the closed shop (Q31a, b, c; Q32a, b, c; Q62a, b, c; Q63a, b, c). The proportion of all employees at our establishments who were covered by a closed shop (27 per cent) came close to the proportion of all establishments that operated any form of closed shop (25 per cent). There was, however, a substantially different pattern for manual workers than there was for non-manual workers. Accordingly, the respective patterns are shown separately followed by the picture for all employees. It was reported by 25 per cent of establishments which employed manual workers that at least some manual workers normally had 'to be members of a trade union in order to have or keep their jobs'. In cases where a closed shop operated for any manual workers it generally embraced all manual workers. That was true in 90 per cent of establishments that had any form of closed shop for manual workers.

The more people who were employed at an establishment the more likely the establishment was to operate a closed shop. In consequence, the proportion of establishments that operated a closed shop for manual workers very substantially understated the proportion of manual

Table III.1 The extent of the closed shop

	Total	25–500	501–2000	2001–10000	10001 or more
		Number employed by organisation			
Manual workers					Percentages
Any manual workers in a closed shop	25	14	26	31	38
All manual workers in CS	23	12	25	29	34
Proportion of manual workers in CS	44	15	41	52	54
Base: all establishments employing manual workers					
Unweighted	*1899*[1]	*395*	*251*	*358*	*695*
Weighted	*1833*	*599*	*212*	*280*	*491*
Non-manual workers					Percentages
Any non-manual workers in a closed shop	10	3	8	9	19
All non-manual workers in CS	7	2	5	6	12
Proportion of non-manual workers in CS	9	4	6	6	12
Base: all establishments employing non-manual workers					
Unweighted	*2034*	*415*	*265*	*390*	*755*
Weighted	*1989*	*630*	*230*	*314*	*556*
All employees					Percentages
Any employees in a closed shop	25	30	37	48	56
All employees in CS	6	13	10	13	7
Proportion of employees in CS	27	24	31	33	36
Base: all establishments					
Unweighted	*2040*	*417*	*265*	*391*	*756*
Weighted	*2000*	*635*	*230*	*315*	*558*

[1] See note G

workers who were covered by the closed shop. In fact, nearly half (44 per cent) of all the manual workers employed by our establishments normally had to be trade union members in order to keep their jobs.

The closed shop was substantially less common among non-manual workers. In 10 per cent of establishments that employed non-manual grades there was a requirement for some non-manual workers to be trade union members. Compared with the pattern for manual workers, it was less frequently the case that such non-manual closed shops were comprehensive. That was especially true at larger establishments. As a result, the proportion of non-manual employees represented by our establishments who were covered by a closed shop (nine per cent) was close to the proportion of establishments that operated a closed shop.

Other possible measures of the extent of the closed shop
The information that we have presented so far on the extent of the closed shop has relied upon management accounts of whether any workers had to be members of trade unions in order to keep their jobs and, if so, how many. In view of the controversial nature of the closed shop, it was possible that management accounts would differ substantially from other measures that we had of the extent to which trade union membership was a condition of employment. In addition to managers' accounts we had, first, the answers of worker representatives to parallel questions (WQ34a, b, c, f; WQ35a, b, c). Secondly, from our analysis of union density, discussed in the previous chapter, we had a measure of how far all or nearly all workers in different categories were, in practice, trade union members, independently of what anyone said about whether that was a condition of employment.

Table III.2 shows a comparison of the answers of management representatives to our principal questions on the closed shop with those of their trade union counterparts. The patterns for manual workers and for non-manual workers are shown separately. In each instance the figures are based on cases where interviews were achieved with both management and union representatives. That is to say, the comparison is based upon strictly comparable establishments and if both respondents were fully informed and interpreted the questions in the same way then their answers should have been identical. The answers were not identical but they were very similar indeed. So far as manual workers were concerned, answers to the question of whether any workers had to be union members were very close. Union representatives were slightly more likely to say that they did not know whether it was the case that some workers were required to be union members and slightly less likely to say that some but not all manual workers needed to be union members. The pattern is consistent with the possibility that there was a closed shop among some group other than that represented by the particular manual union officer.

Similarly, management and union accounts of whether closed shops required workers to be trade union members before they could be

Table III.2 Comparison of the responses of management and union representatives to questioning on the closed shop

	Manual workers		Non-manual workers	
	Management representative	Worker representative	Management representative	Worker representative

			Column percentages	
Existence of closed shop				
All workers in a closed shop	43[1]	44	13	15
Some workers in CS	4	2	7	4
No workers in CS	52	48	80	74
No information	*	5	*	7
				Percentages
Pre-entry/post-entry				
Any workers in a pre-entry closed shop	21	18[2]	15	14
All pre-entry	14	13	12	13
Some pre-entry	7	4	2	1
No information	1	4	8	24
Exemptions[3]				
Some exemption	51	40	60	57
Issues over closed shop arrangements				
Some issue	3	4	3	4

Base[3]: cases in which both management and worker representatives were interviewed

Unweighted	*972*	*972*	*922*	*922*
Weighted	*707*	*707*	*655*	*655*

[1] See note C
[2] See note D
[3] For the proportion of establishments where there were exemptions and where some issue was reported the base becomes those establishments where there was a closed shop and where both management and worker representatives were interviewed

employed (pre-entry) or required recruits to join unions after becoming employed (post-entry) revealed proportions of a very similar order. With the exception of the existence of exemptions in the case of manual workers there was also a high level of congruence between managers' and trade union accounts of the extent to which there were agreed exemptions to the closed shop and the extent to which the arrangements had given rise to issues in the recent past (Q35a, b; Q37a; WQ39a, b; WQ41). These results are discussed in more detail in a later section.

Apart from the accounts of manager and worker representatives, a third measure that was of interest in assessing the extent and implications of the closed shop was the proportion of employees who were, in practice, members of trade unions. It was possible, owing to the controversial implications of the closed shop, that managers and trade unionists would be reluctant to report that people were required to be trade union members in order to keep their jobs. We might find that workplaces at which everyone or nearly everyone was a trade union member were substantially more common than those at which managers or trade unions reported that a closed shop existed. In practice, it seemed that that was not the case. We have seen that in 23 per cent of establishments that employed manual workers management respondents said that all manual workers were required to be trade union members. In 25 per cent of establishments employing manual workers, trade union membership was a condition of employment for *some or all* manual workers. Ignoring those establishments which did not have information or numbers on manual trade union membership, we found that 21 per cent of managers gave a figure for manual trade union membership that was 100 per cent of their manual labour force; 28 per cent gave a figure that was 95 per cent or more; and 32 per cent gave a figure that was 90 per cent or more. Accordingly, reports concerning the closed shop were consistent with figures on levels of trade union membership. At the same time, it was clear that substantially more establishments had very high levels of manual trade union membership than reported that they had a comprehensive manual closed shop. The respective reports were about one third having 90 per cent or more trade union membership, compared with one quarter reporting a closed shop for some manual workers.

Changes in the extent of the closed shop
Whichever measure is taken of the coverage of the closed shop, our findings show that the institution has grown substantially over the past twenty years. McCarthy estimated that in 1962 three and three-quarters million people were closed shop members[3]. That number represented 16 per cent of all employees, employed and unemployed, at the time. We found that 27 per cent of all employees covered by our establishments were in a closed shop. We explore evidence on the extent of change and relate our findings on the closed shop to other recent research more fully in our conclusions in Chapter XI.

Sources of variation in the distribution of the closed shop
As will have been apparent from our account of the overall distribution of the closed shop, the institution was much more common among manual workers and, indeed, was relatively rare among non-manual

Table III.3 **The coverage[1] of the closed shop among manual workers in relation to ownership and size of the establishment**

Percentages

Number employed at establishment	Public sector		Private sector	
	Nationalised industries/ public corporations[2]	Central or local government	Part of group	Independent establishment
All establishments with manual workers	72	22	49	21
25–99	(83)[3]	23	33	12
100–499	88	33	45	20
500–999	(80)	8	50	§[4]
1000+	(55)	16	59	(45)

Base: establishments with manual workers

[1] Coverage was measured by the proportion of manual workers who were in a closed shop.
[2] In this instance publicly owned establishments other than nationalised industries and central or local government establishments were grouped with nationalised industries because they had more in common on this question with those industries than with government employment
[3] See note B
[4] See note A

workers. In view of that, we shall concentrate our analysis of variations in the distribution of the closed shop upon the pattern for manual workers and refer to the comparative picture for non-manual workers where that is appropriate.

There were four major sources of variation in the incidence of the closed shop and they interacted in complex ways. These were ownership, the size of the establishment, the size of the organisation of which the workplace was part and the composition of the workforce. It will be apparent that these principal sources of variation were the same as those that distinguished between establishments that recognised trade unions and those that did not. Indeed, the overall picture showed that the closed shop tended to be a pole on the continuum of union density rather than part of a dichotomy which varied independently of density and recognition.

First, there were very marked differences in the extent of the closed shop as between different types of employer in terms of ownership. Trade union membership was a condition of employment for nearly three-quarters of the manual workers employed by nationalised industries or public corporations. In contrast, that was the case for only about one fifth of manual workers employed by independent establishments in the private sector and by national or local government employers (see

Table III.3). More instructive than the differences in overall levels of closed shop membership, however, were the differences in the association between establishment size and the closed shop for the different types of employer. In general terms, there was a strong tendency for the closed shop to be more common in larger establishments. By contrast, there was among nationalised industries or public corporations no tendency for the closed shop to be more common in larger establishments. Among central or local government employers, too, there was no sign of any association between levels of closed shop membership and size of establishment. The incidence of the closed shop was relatively low in public administration, especially in larger establishments. In contrast to the pattern for both major types of employer in the public sector, there was, in the private sector, a strong and consistent tendency for more manual workers to be required to be trade union members the larger the size of the establishment. That was true whether the establishment was an independent business or whether it was part of a larger business. Within each establishment size band the closed shop was also more common in establishments that were part of a group than it was in independent establishments. That difference, of course, was consistent with the tendency, discussed later in this section, for trade union membership to be more often a condition of employment in larger organisations.

The way in which establishment size was a strong and consistent source of variation in the incidence of the closed shop in the private sector but was not at all associated with the closed shop in the public sector is as important as it is striking. If the distribution of the closed shop is plotted within the private sector alone then it appears that the size of establishments and organisations explains most of the differences. It is only when the public sector is included in the analysis that it becomes immediately clear that other influences are also strong. The pattern for nationalised industries showed how important was ownership as a source of variation and suggested that the overall view of trade unions taken by the governing body of an enterprise has a major influence upon institutions like the closed shop. In view of the way in which size appears to be such a dominant source of variation when the private sector is analysed on its own, it is especially instructive that it should be overwhelmed by ownership when sectors are compared.

Apart from any general view of trade unions that might be held by the governing bodies of nationalised industries and might encourage institutions like the closed shop, it was also the case that nationalised industries were invariably very large enterprises and there was a general tendency for the closed shop to be more common in establishments belonging to larger enterprises. It was clear, however, that the overall size of nationalised industries did not on its own account for the

Table III.4 The closed shop and establishment size

		Number employed at establishment						
	Total	25–49	50–99	100–199	200–499	500–999	1000–1999	2000 or more
Manual workers								Percentages
Any manual workers in a closed shop	25	17	25	24	41	42	52	49
All manual workers in CS	23	16	22	22	36	37	40	42
Proportion of manual workers in CS	44	19	31	30	48	47	61	55
Base: all establishments employing manual workers								
Unweighted	*1899*	*323*	*347*	*363*	*355*	*246*	*142*	*123*
Weighted	*1833*	*704*	*486*	*317*	*194*	*82*	*34*	*17*
Non-manual workers								Percentages
Any non-manual workers in a closed shop	10	7	9	11	18	19	25	19
All non-manual workers in CS	7	6	7	7	6	9	8	5
Proportion of non-manual workers in CS	9	8	7	6	11	9	12	9
Base: all establishments employing non-manual workers								
Unweighted	*2034*	*364*	*379*	*397*	*378*	*249*	*143*	*124*
Weighted	*1989*	*778*	*527*	*344*	*206*	*83*	*34*	*17*
All employees								Percentages
Any employees in a closed shop	25	18	24	25	42	43	54	52
All employees in CS	6	6	7	7	6	8	7	4
Proportion of employees in CS	27	14	19	18	31	28	38	33
Base: all establishments								
Unweighted	*2040*	*367*	*380*	*399*	*378*	*249*	*143*	*124*
Weighted	*2000*	*785*	*528*	*347*	*206*	*83*	*34*	*17*

Table III.5   Coverage[1] of closed shop for manual workers in relation to size of establishment and size of total organisation   Percentages

Number employed by establishment	Number employed by organisation		
	25–500	501–10000	10001 or more
25–99	13	39	42
100–499	16	47	51
500–999	n.a.[2]	36	58
1000 or more	n.a.	62	56
Base: all employing manual workers			

[1] See note to Table III.3
[2] Cell size is not applicable

difference between these and private employers. When analysis was confined to very large enterprises, it remained the case that nationalised industries more frequently operated closed shops than counterparts in the private sector.

In the private sector, as we have stressed, the size of establishments and organisations were the main sources of variation in the incidence of the closed shop and the pattern warrants further illustration and discussion. Table III.1 showed that the number of manual workers in a closed shop increased steadily the larger was the total number of people employed by the total organisation. Fifteen per cent of manual workers in enterprises employing 25 to 500 people were required to be trade union members. By contrast, the same was true for over half the manual workers employed by enterprises with a total workforce complement of 2,001 or more. Similarly, Table III.4 shows that there was a marked tendency for more manual workers to be required to be trade union members the larger was the size of the establishment. Indeed, it was difficult to say which measure of size was the more important source of variation, although Table III.5 suggests that, perhaps, surprisingly, overall enterprise size was more important than establishment size. Certainly for establishments employing fewer than 1,000 people there was, among establishments employing a similar number of people, a very strong and consistent tendency for a higher proportion of manual workers to be required to be trade union members the larger was the size of the overall enterprise. When enterprise size was held constant there was a tendency for a higher proportion of manual workers to be in closed shops the larger was the size of the establishment, but that tendency was not especially strong and consistent. As was the case with trade union recognition, the variation in relation to enterprise size was partly a reflection of differences between independent establishments

Table III.6 Existence[1] of any closed shop for manual workers in relation to number of manual workers and total number of employees at the establishment

Percentages

Total number employed at establishment	Number of manual workers at establishment			
	1–24	25–99	100–499	500 or more
Fewer than 100	8	21	n.a.[2]	n.a.
100–499	—	15	41	n.a.
500–999	§[3]	§	56	59
1000 or more	§	§	§	70

Percentages

	Number of manual workers at establishment							
	1–9	10–24	25–49	50–99	100–199	200–499	500–999	1000 or more
Any manual workers in a closed shop	6	9	19	23	36	53	62	73
Base: private sector establishments employing manual workers								
Unweighted	*85*	*122*	*216*	*192*	*208*	*198*	*106*	*105*
Weighted	*131*	*237*	*376*	*210*	*142*	*80*	*30*	*17*

[1] In each half of the table the extent of the closed shop was measured by the proportion of establishments where any manual workers were in a closed shop
[2] Cell size is not applicable
[3] See note A

and those that were part of larger organisations. Independent establishments in each size band were less likely to have closed shops than counterparts that belonged to larger organisations and independent establishments were concentrated in the lowest enterprise size band.

Also reflecting the pattern with regard to union recognition, there was some tendency for the number of people employed at the establishment to be a proxy for the number of manual workers employed so far as the closed shop for manual workers was concerned (see Table III.6). That is to say, it appeared that the number of manual workers employed was a more important source of variation than the number of people employed, although it also seemed that in larger workplaces the overall size of the establishment was an independent source of variation.

There were substantial differences between different industrial sectors in the extent to which union membership was a condition of employment for manual workers, but those differences partly reflected

Table III.7 **Extent[1] of closed shop among manual workers in relation to proportion of female manual workers**

Percentages

Number of manual workers	Proportion of manual workers who were women		
	Over 70 per cent	30–70 per cent	30 per cent or fewer
25–99	7	16	26
100–499	(24)[2]	37	52
500 or more	§[3]	66	68

Base: private sector establishments with manual workers

[1] Extent of the closed shop measured as in Table III.6
[2] See note B
[3] See note A

variations in relation to size and ownership. For instance, 81 per cent of manual workers employed in transport and communications were members of closed shops, but that was largely because that sector was dominated by nationalised industries. Just over half the manual workers employed in manufacturing industry had to be trade union members in order to keep their jobs. The same was true of only 18 per cent of manual workers employed in miscellaneous services. That contrast, however, was largely a consequence of the fact that such service establishments were characteristically small, while manufacturing establishments were characteristically large. Within manufacturing industry, vehicle manufacture, and food, drink, tobacco and chemicals had relatively high levels of closed shop membership, while electrical engineering and textiles or clothing had relatively low levels. Those differences were moderated when the effect of variations in establishment size were taken into account, but they did tend to persist across the size bands.

A final major source of variation in the incidence of the closed shop among manual workers was the proportion of the manual workforce who were women. As Table III.7 shows, there was a strong and consistent tendency, within establishment size bands, for the closed shop to be less common the higher the proportion of the manual workforce who were women.

Pre-entry or post-entry
A major distinction in forms of the closed shop is made between those where recruits are required to be members of the trade unions before they are taken on and those where recruits may join after selection or appointment. These forms are known, respectively, as the pre-entry and post-entry closed shop. Our findings showed that by far the most

common form was the post-entry version. Eight per cent of all manual workers employed by our establishments were in a pre-entry closed shop, compared with 44 per cent of all manual workers who were in some form of closed shop. That meant that 18 per cent of manual workers who were required to be trade union members needed to have an appropriate trade union card before they were eligible to apply for their jobs. The proportion of non-manual workers who worked in the pre-entry closed shop was negligible in survey terms. It represented one half of one per cent of all non-manual workers employed by our establishments.

Table III.8 summarises the details of the pre-entry closed shop among manual workers. It is clear that, as was the case with the closed shop generally, nationalised industries or public corporations were the types of employer most likely to operate pre-entry closed shops. Our findings on the distribution of any form of closed shop in the private sector showed that there was a strong and consistent tendency for the proportion of workers covered to increase the larger was the size of establishments and of organisations. That pattern was not reflected in the distribution of the pre-entry closed shop. Indeed, where a closed shop of any kind did operate in a small establishment or enterprise, it

Table III.8 Details of pre-entry closed shop among manual workers

Percentages

	All establish-ments	Public sector		Private sector	
		Nationalised industries/ public corporations	Central/ local government	Part of group	Indepen-dent establish-ment
Any manual workers in a pre-entry closed shop	5	10	3	5	5
All manual workers in pre-entry CS	3	7	3	3	3
Proportion of closed shop workers in pre-entry CS	18	24	12	17	24
Proportion of all manual workers in pre-entry CS	8	16	3	8	5
Base: all establishments employing manual workers					
Unweighted	*1899*	*162*	*482*	*1441*	*287*
Weighted	*1833*	*100*	*488*	*1316*	*382*

Table III.9   Time allowed to join post-entry closed shops for manual workers

Cumulative percentages

	All establishments	Private sector	Nationalised industries	Central/local government
		Type of employer		
Right away/within 1 week	24	29	18	11
Within 2 weeks	34	38	22	28
Within 1 month	66	69	60	58
Within 3 months	86	88	80	82
Over 3 months	91	91	94	89
Not stated	9	9	7	12
Base: establishments with a post-entry closed shop				
Unweighted	*471*	*307*	*86*	*64*
Weighted	*357*	*215*	*55*	*72*

tended to be slightly more likely for the form to be pre-entry than was the case for larger workplaces. The implication of the pattern is that while the post-entry closed shop was associated with the organisational characteristics of workplaces, the pre-entry closed shop was related more to characteristics external to the establishment such as the control of entry into occupations in the wider labour market. That is to say, it is likely that where a small firm operated a closed shop it was often because it employed people in particular occupations where the pre-entry closed shop was more common. Certainly the membership of pre-entry closed shops was relatively high in small units when expressed *as a proportion of closed shop members*. For instance, among independent establishments employing 25 to 99 people, 43 per cent of the closed shop members were members of the pre-entry form, whereas only 18 per cent of all closed shop members belonged to the pre-entry form.

Further evidence of influence upon the pre-entry closed shop was provided by the way in which the incidence of the pre-entry form varied more in relation to types of occupation within organisations than in relation to types of organisation. That is to say, where the coverage of pre-entry closed shops among manual workers was not universal, it tended to be concentrated very much upon skilled manual occupations (Q31d, e; Q32d, e).

Table III.10 Comparison of management and union responses to questioning on the length of time allowed to join a post-entry closed shop

Cumulative percentages

	Manual workers		Non-manual workers	
	Management representative	Worker representative	Management representative	Worker representative
Within one week	26	32	33	32
Within two weeks	34	45	38	41
Within one month	68	76	63	69
Within three months	86	96	77	95
Over three months	93	97	81	97
Other answer	7	3	19	3

Base: establishments where both management and union representatives answered questions on time allowed to join a post-entry closed shop

Unweighted	*315*	*315*	*121*	*121*
Weighted	*220*	*220*	*79*	*79*

Time to join the post-entry closed shop

Where establishments operated a post-entry closed shop, we examined how long people were given to join a union after they became employed (Q31j; Q32h; Q62j; Q63h; WQ34j; WQ35k). For manual workers the most common period was one month. One quarter were required to join immediately or within their first week of employment while, expressing the percentages cumulatively, one third were required to join within two weeks and two-thirds within a month (see Table III.9). There were clearly wide variations in the time before people were required to join, but the variations were not distributed in any systematic way. There was a slight tendency for people to be required to join sooner in larger establishments, but it was only after the two week period that that tendency became apparent.

Of course, these figures are based upon the accounts given by management representatives. When we compared them with the answers of union representatives, in establishments where both management and union respondents gave time periods, we found the picture shown in Table III.10. It is clear that manual union representatives tended to expect manual workers to join earlier than did management representatives. As a result of this divergence of view, there appeared to be scope for potential disputes over this aspect of closed shop agreements but, as we shall see in a later section, such problems were rarely mentioned by employer and worker representatives in our interviews. Apart from that difference, answers of management and union representatives appeared remarkably congruent. It was also apparent that the periods of grace enjoyed by non-manual workers were of the same order as those applying to manual workers.

The check-off

The check-off, or the deduction of union dues at source by management on behalf of the trade union, has long been associated with the closed shop. It is argued that once a closed shop is established there are strong pressures for measures to be taken to prevent lapses in trade union membership and the check-off provides one such measure.

In fact, we found that the check-off was very widespread among our establishments, and much more widespread than the closed shop (Q37b; Q68b; WQ42a). Nearly one half of all establishments that employed manual workers had a system for deducting the trade union dues of manual workers from their pay. That proportion represented three-quarters of workplaces that recognised unions for manual workers. As far as non-manual workers were concerned, a slightly lower proportion of all establishments operated the check-off, reflecting the lower level of recognition of white collar unions, but in cases where white collar unions were recognised, a slightly higher proportion

Table III.11   Extent of check-off among manual workers

Percentage

	All establish- ment	Public sector		Private sector	
		Nationalised industries/ public corporations	Central/ local government	Part of group	Indepen dent establish ment
Proportion of establishments operating check-off as per cent of all employing manual workers	45	94	59	54	17
Base: all employing manual workers					
Unweighted	*1899*	*162*	*482*	*1441*	*287*
Weighted	*1833*	*100*	*488*	*1316*	*382*
Proportion operating check-off as per cent of all recognising unions	75	99	77	79	51

of establishments deducted trade union dues than did so for manual workers.

Table III.11 shows that, for manual workers, the check-off was almost universal in nationalised industries and public corporations. National or local government and larger businesses in the public sector operated the check-off in the large majority of cases where they recognised manual trade unions. In contrast, in the private sector, one half of independent establishments that recognised unions deducted union dues. When we isolated private sector establishments it was apparent that the check-off was one of those rare institutions covered in our inquiry which varied more strongly in relation to organisational size than to establishment size. There was a strong tendency for the check-off to be more common the larger the size of the total organisation of which an establishment was part. There was little sign that the incidence of the check-off varied in relation to the number of people employed at the establishment.

Overall, the general impression created by our findings was that any link between the check-off and the closed shop was largely tenuous. That is to say, it was clear that recognising a closed shop and operating the check-off both tended to be parts of more elaborate or formalised industrial relations practices. At the same time, it certainly did not appear to be the case that the closed shop created such a need for the check-off that it occurred very much more frequently under the circumstances of the closed shop than under others. There was a tendency for establishments to be more likely to operate a check-off for manual workers the larger the proportion of manual workers who were trade union members. But that association was clearly a continuous trend

Table III.12 Some details of closed shop arrangements for manual workers in relation to check-off

Percentages

	Check-off operated	No check-off
Written closed shop agreement	76	46
Concluded within past five years	36	9
Some exemptions specified	56	13
Disputes procedure	53	22
Issue arisen over closed shop arrangements	5	6

Base: private sector establishments with a closed shop for manual workers

Unweighted	481	61
Weighted	294	61

Table III.13   Details of closed shops for manual workers

Percentage

	All establish-ments	Public sector		Private sector	
		Nationalised industries/ public corporations	Central/ local government	Part of group	Indepen-dent establish-ment
Number of closed-shop arrangements					
Single arrangement	86	92	86	88	78
Agreement					
Some agreement	87	97	88	88	73
Written	74	92	85	77	47
Oral	13	5	3	11	26
Lifetime					
Within previous five years	36	32	55	38	14
Exemptions					
Some exemptions	50	70	59	53	28
Procedure					
Any cs procedure	51	75	63	55	25
Special procedure	25	48	41	26	8
Issues over closed shop					
No issue	89	92	91	90	85
Issue arisen	4	1	1	3	7
Base: all establishments with a closed shop for manual workers					
Unweighted	*645*	*127*	*81*	*543*	*56*
Weighted	*460*	*80*	*88*	*385*	*53*

rather than a dichotomous contrast between workplaces that had a closed shop and those that did not. Indeed, there was only a very slight difference between workplaces with a closed shop for manual workers and those with a high level of trade union membership but no closed shop. It certainly seemed that the circumstances and considerations that led managements to deduct trade union dues at source extended very much further than those associated with the desire to avoid problems over the closed shop.

As it was so common for those workplaces that did have a closed shop to operate the check-off, there was little scope for useful analysis of the way in which the deduction of dues by management interacted with the form of the closed shop and managements' experience of the closed shop. Table III.12 shows the contrasts that were possible and confirms that the check-off did tend to be part of more elaborate closed shop arrangements. It was strongly associated with written closed shop agreements, the specification of exemptions, formal disputes procedures and agreements that had been concluded more recently.

Details of closed shop arrangements

Table III.13 summarises some of the details of closed shop arrangements covering manual workers in circumstances where these existed. In the large majority of cases where manual workers were required to be members of trade unions there was a single closed shop arrangement in operation (Q33a; Q64a) and that arrangement was agreed by management with the trade unions (Q34a; Q65a). Generally closed shop agreements took a written form. Just over one third of agreements had been introduced within the previous five years (Q34b; Q65b). Here, however, it was not always clear whether that meant that the present form of the closed shop arrangement had been introduced within the previous five years or whether a closed shop arrangement had been introduced for the first time in that period. In about one half of cases the closed shop arrangement made agreed provision for some manual workers to be exempted from the requirement to be members of a trade union (Q35a; Q66). In a similar proportion of cases there was an agreed procedure for dealing with disputes over the requirement to be a trade union member (Q36a, b; Q67).

When the variations in these details, shown in Table III.13, were compared with differences in the coverage of the closed shop, shown in Table III.3, then a clear pattern emerged. Where closed shops were most widespread, the arrangements covering them were most formal and well-developed. For instance, nationalised industries or public corporations were most likely to have closed shop arrangements. They were also most likely to have written agreements governing the closed shop, to have agreed exemptions and have agreed procedures for dealing with disputes. By contrast, independent establishments in the private sector were least likely to have closed shop arrangements. In cases where they did, they were also least likely to have written agreements governing their arrangements, or agreed exemptions or agreed procedures for dealing with disputes.

It also tended to be the case that where establishments had closed shops covering both manual and non-manual workers, non-manual closed shops were slightly more likely to involve written agreements, specified exemptions and agreed procedures for resolving disputes (see Table III.14).

Table III.14   Comparison of details of non-manual and manual closed shops

Percentages

	Establishments with non-manual closed shops		Establishments with both manual and non-manual closed shops	
			Non-manual	Manual
Form of arrangement				
Single arrangement	83		81	89
Agreement				
Some agreement	89		90	89
Written		85	87	85
Oral		4	3	4
Lifetime				
Within previous five years	43		43	36
Exemptions				
Some exemptions	58		66	62
Procedure				
Any CS procedure	59		67	63
Special procedure		28	31	34
Issues over closed shop				
No issue	82		85	91
Issue arisen	4		3	2
Base: as specified in column headings				
Weighted	*293*		*246*	*246*
Unweighted	*204*		*164*	*164*

Exemptions from the closed shop

We have seen that about one half of manual workers covered by closed shop arrangements were subject to agreements that specified some grounds for exemption. Table III.15 shows managers' accounts of the type of exemption, where one or more were specified. The most commonly specified was religious belief, which was specified in just under one third of manual closed shop cases. Conscience and non-membership of a union prior to the closed shop arrangement were specified in 10 per cent and 13 per cent of cases respectively. The pattern of variation in the extent of agreed exemptions was very striking. We saw earlier that the variations according to type of employer strongly suggested that those employers who were most likely to have closed shop arrangements were also more likely to have more elaborate arrangements which included specified exemptions. Table

Table III.15 Nature of closed shop exemptions in relation to type of employer (manual workers)

Percentages

	All establish- ments	Public sector		Private sector	
		Nationalised industries	Central/ local government	Part of group	Independent establish- ment
Some exemption	49[1]	79	61	54	28
Nature of exemption					
Religious belief	30	53	48	35	19
Conscience	10	14	13	11	19
Employees who were not union members before closed shop was introduced	13	38	8	13	4
Part time/ temporary	6	2	9	6	5
Apprentice/long service/key worker	6	7	5	6	4
Other reason	5	3	8	7	2

Base: all establishments with a closed shop for manual workers

Unweighted	*645*	*127*	*81*	*543*	*56*
Weighted	*460*	*80*	*88*	*385*	*53*

See note F

III.15 confirms that pattern. Nationalised industries, where closed shops were most common, were also most likely to include the most frequent grounds for exemption, which were religious belief or conscience and non-membership of a union prior to the introduction of a closed shop arrangement[4].

A more complex and interesting pattern was, however, revealed in the private sector when we examined the distribution of exemptions in relation to enterprise and establishment size (see Table III.16). The results showed conflicting trends. There was a very marked tendency for exemptions to be *more* common the larger the size of the *enterprise*. At the same time, exemptions were *less* common the larger the size of the *establishment*. A possible explanation of those apparently conflicting trends would be as follows. Larger enterprises tended to have more elaborate labour relations managements and to have better developed

Table III.16   Exemptions from closed shop in relation to size of establishment and size of organisation

Percentages

Number employed at establishment	Number employed by organisation		
	25– 500	501– 10,000	10,000 or more
25–99	(22)[1]	(51)	(72)
100–499	(39)	47	57
500–999	n.a.[2]	(20)	56
1000 or more	n.a.	(37)	43

Base: private sector establishments with a closed shop for manual workers

[1] See note B
[2] Cell size is not applicable

closed shop arrangements, including the specification of exemptions. At the establishment level, however, the impact of more elaborate labour relations management in larger workplaces was countered by greater anonymity. That is to say, exemptions were more acceptable in smaller workplaces where all workers were known to each other and the grounds for exemption could be tested against personal acquaintanceship. The consequence of the two distinct forces influencing the specification of exemptions in the private sector was that exemptions were most common in the smallest workplaces belonging to the largest enterprises.

Issues arising from closed shop arrangements
Following our question on whether there was an agreed procedure for closed shop disputes, we asked both managers and worker representatives if the closed shop arrangements had given rise to any issues at their establishment in the previous three years (Q37a; Q68a; WQ41). As we have already indicated, such issues arose infrequently according to both sets of respondents. As Table III.13 showed, four per cent of managers in establishments with a manual closed shop reported that any issue had arisen in the previous three years. That proportion represented one per cent of all establishments that employed manual workers and was not sufficiently high to provide much scope for analysing sources of variation in the type of issue. There was some indication, however, that smaller enterprises in the private sector, in that minority of cases where they did operate closed shops, were slightly more likely to report issues. Where managements did report some issues, these chiefly arose from requiring that new recruits should join the union (two per cent) and from disputes over which union

people should join (one per cent). The proportion of establishments with a closed shop for manual workers where the union had created difficulties by withdrawing membership from an employee was too low to measure (less than half of one per cent).

Notes
1. The Department of Employment commissioned John Gennard and his colleagues to carry out an analysis of the closed shop. We refer to the papers so far arising from that study in our discussion of the closed shop in our conclusions. The full report will be published later this year.
2. Charles Hanson, Sheila Jackson and Douglas Miller, *The Closed Shop*, (Gower, Aldershot, 1982).
3. W.E.J. McCarthy, *The Closed Shop in Britain*, (Basil Blackwell, Oxford, 1964).
4. Gennard and his colleagues carried out an analysis of the contents of union membership agreements which we discuss further in our conclusions. See J. Gennard, S. Dunn and M. Wright, 'The Extent of Closed Shop Arrangements in British Industry', Department of Employment *Gazette*, January, 1980.

IV Trade Union Organisation

In previous chapters we have occasionally made links with the wider system of industrial relations outside the workplace. In this chapter we discuss trade union organisation in relation to that wider system, beginning with the local units of the trade union to which worker representatives belonged.

Trade union branches – their size and composition

We use the term 'branch' for local units to which worker representatives belonged, although some unions have a different term. It is important to remember that the data refer to the branch *to which our respondents belonged*: worker representative respondents were not selected to provide information on a statistically representative sample of trade union branches. It is clear that the larger unions were over-represented in our sample, since union representatives were the senior lay representatives of the largest and second largest bargaining units at sampled establishments. Moreover, large trade union branches were more likely to be reported on than small ones. For these reasons the results are presented briefly. Further analysis could attempt to compensate for the selection biases and use the results as a guide to trade union branches in general, but we have not attempted this.

The main characteristics of union branches we examined were their size, the composition of their membership and their general attendance levels (WQ6a, d, e). Additional questions concerned how the branch fitted into the pattern of communication between worker representative respondents and their members (WQ6f, g). Respondents found the question on branch size particularly difficult to answer. Overall, nearly one quarter could provide no estimate. Tables IV.1 and IV.2 summarise the results on branch size and composition for the branches to which manual and non-manual representatives belonged, where estimates could be given.

Typically, primary manual respondents belonged to a branch of four hundred or so members. Their branches ranged in size from less than fifty to several thousands with about one half in the range between 200 and 2,000 members. Non-manual respondents reported belonging to rather smaller branches – typically with 300 or so members, about one half of which were within the range from 100 to 900 members. Individual trade unions varied considerably in terms of their typical

Table IV.1 Size and composition of union branches (manual workers)

	All primary manual representatives	Union of primary representatives				All secondary manual representatives
		TGWU	GMWU	AUEW	NUPE	
Number of branch members[1]						
Average	861	580	979	989	812	1400
Median[2]	438	293	483	750	443	550
						Column percentages
Branch composition						
Own workplace only	21	34	17	4	17	11
Own workplace plus others of same employer	24	19	32	1	56	5
Multi-employer	53	47	50	95	27	82
Not answered	2	*	1	*	*	2
Base: manual worker representatives belonging to recognised trade unions						
Unweighted	*972[3]*	*234*	*124*	*132*	*126*	*211*
Weighted	*707*	*174*	*90*	*81*	*98*	*103*

[1] Base excludes 22 per cent of establishments overall where branch numbers were not reported
[2] Median linearly interpolated from grouped data
[3] See note H

branch size, but this is very much a matter of the composition of the branch, to which we now turn our attention.

Branch composition can be described in terms of three main types: 'workplace based' branches, where all branch members of the trade union in question are employed at the same establishment; 'single employer' branches, where membership is drawn from more than one establishment of the same employer; and 'multi-employer' branches. The last two categories are sometimes referred to as 'geographically based' branches[1]. The three categories are shown in Tables IV.1 and IV.2, and their occurrence shows considerable variation. Of the four trade unions most frequently mentioned by manual respondents, the Amalgamated Union of Engineering Workers (AUEW) stands out as almost invariably having multi-employer branches. The National Union of of Public Employees (NUPE) branches were reported as predominantly single employer, obviously reflecting its public sector concentration, while the remaining two large general unions – the Transport and General Workers' Union (TGWU) and the General and Municipal Workers Union (GMWU) – had a mixture of all three types,

Table IV.2   Size and composition of union branches (non-manual workers)

	All primary non-manual representatives	Union of primary representatives						All secondary non-manual represen-tatives
		ASTMS	NALGO	APEX	ACTSS/ TGWU	TASS/ AUEW		
Number of branch members[1]								
Average	681	716	1253	(273)[3]	(244)	(471)		716
Median[2]	320	657	494	(116)	(88)	(521)		255
						Column percentage		
Branch composition								
Own workplace only	18	7	12	39	34	20		15
Own workplace plus others of same employer	47	21	68	13	32	11		60
Multi-employer	27	67	15	45	27	67		25
Not answered	8	5	5	2	8	2		—
Base: non-manual worker representatives belonging to recognised trade unions								
Unweighted	*922*[4]	*128*	*164*	*52*	*62*	*57*		*167*
Weighted	*655*	*52*	*121*	*19*	*42*	*30*		*106*

[1] Base excludes 27 per cent of establishments overall where branch numbers were not reported
[2] Median linearly interpolated from grouped data
[3] See note B
[4] See note H

with multi-employer branches being most frequent. Of these four unions reported by manual representatives, workplace based branches were most common in the TGWU, which more frequently than any other union had the most members in establishments where it had membership.

Non-manual union branches (Table IV.2) were more commonly single employer than were manual union branches, partly a reflection of their tendency to occur more frequently in the public sector, where non-manual employees are more numerous. Thus the typical National and Local Government Officers' Association (NALGO) branch was single employer. The Association of Clerical, Technical and Supervisory Staff (ACTSS, the white collar section of TGWU) and the Association of Professional, Executive, Clerical and Computer Staff (APEX) had the most workplace based branches while the Technical and Supervisory Section (TASS) of the AUEW largely had multi-employer branches.

Overall, there seemed to be a clear association between branch size and composition: workplace based branches were reported as being considerably smaller than geographically based branches. This is

Table IV.3   Frequency of meeting and attendance at manual union branch

Medians

	All branches	Work-place	Type of branch	
			Single Employer	Multi-Employer
Number of branch members				
Median[1]	438	110	450	880
Number of members generally attending				
Median	30	23	35	32
Number of branch meetings in previous year				
Median	10	5	10	14
Number of occasions respondent attended meeting				
Median	5	5	7	5
Base: establishments where manual worker representatives belonged to recognised trade union and where branch membership given				
Unweighted[2]	*760*	*250*	*196*	*314*
Weighted	*497*	*146*	*135*	*216*

[1] All medians linearly interpolated from grouped data
[2] Non-response varied between questions. Base given is for question with highest non-response and therefore is a minimum

apparent from the nine individual unions reported in Tables IV.1 and IV.2, but also when these two characteristics are directly related. The median size of workplace based branches was 110 members for manual unions, compared with 438 members for all types of branch. For non-manual unions the comparable figures were 54 and 320.

Frequency of branch meetings and attendance
As well as being generally smaller, workplace branches were reported as having different patterns of attendance. Table IV.3 shows how branch size, frequency of meetings and attendance varied for the three types of branch to which primary manual worker representatives belonged. Workplace branches typically met less than once every two months whereas multi-employer branches met more often than every month. Naturally our respondents, being selected as the senior shop steward or convenor at their establishment[2], reported attending almost every branch meeting where it was workplace based. In geographically based branches they typically attended a smaller proportion of meetings, although in absolute terms this came to as many.

Asked about general attendance at branch meetings of their union, respondents at workplace branches could almost invariably give estimates, since they normally attended themselves. Estimates of general attendance at geographically based branches were much less forthcoming – in the most extreme case of multi-employer branches, 25 per cent of primary manual respondents were unable to give estimates. The estimates given, however, were generally based on first-hand knowledge and show a noteworthy pattern. In essence, workplace branches were typically attended by a much higher proportion of members than geographically based branches – about one fifth, compared with about one twentieth for primary manual respondents' branches; about one third, compared with about one twentieth for non-manual respondents' branches. Multi-employer branches generally had lower attendances than single employer branches. Indeed, the pattern of attendance at branch meetings appears to have an obvious link with the ease of communication between officers and members and the ease of travel. Meetings of workplace branches, the majority of which were held at the workplace, presented the fewest problems in these respects and had highest attendance. The association between the frequency of meetings and the generally lower levels of attendance (shown in Table IV.3, but also apparent for non-manual branches) may also have significance.

A further suggestion from Table IV.3 is that shop stewards attend branch meetings much more frequently than the typical branch member, especially in geographically based branches. A similar difference was observed in 1966 by the Donovan Survey[3]. Unfortunately, because of the different sampling bases and definitions of respondents, it is not possible to say whether this difference has widened or narrowed in the period between 1966 and 1980.

Workplace representatives – methods of appointment

Worker representatives were asked questions about how they and other lay representatives in their union were appointed at their particular place of work (WQ1a, b, c, d, e, f, g; WQ3a, b, c, d, e, f). As with results relating to union branches, these results cannot be treated as strictly representative of all unions, because our respondents were normally members of the largest union in multi-union negotiating groups. However, the largest manual and non-manual negotiating groups consisted of a single trade union in most cases (82 per cent for manual workers, 78 per cent for non-manual workers), so that the effects on the overall picture of ignoring minority unions are likely to be small.

As we reported in Chapter II, in about three-quarters of establishments in which management recognised manual trade unions for collective bargaining there was at least one shop steward or union representative at the establishment. For non-manual unions the proportion was roughly two-thirds. It was in establishments where man-

Table IV.4   Details about the appointment of union representatives

	Manual unions			Non-manual unions		
	Senior represen- tative	Ordinary represen- tatives	Sole represen- tative	Senior represen- tative	Ordinary represen- tatives	Sole represen- tative
					Column percentages[1]	
Method of appointment						
Show of hands	67	71	71	57	60	49
Postal ballot	3	3	2	11	9	7
Non-postal ballot	23	21	13	23	25	22
Other	3	5	7	4	7	10
No election	1	*	5	2	*	7
No information	3	—	2	3	—	5
					Percentages	
Whether any election in previous year						
Election held	56	65	38	68	68	51
Whether representatives have, technically, to stand for re-election					Percentages	
Yes	76	75	53	75	76	65
Whether representatives have, in practice, to stand for re-election					Percentages	
Yes	73	75	51	74	73	50
					Column percentages[1]	
Frequency of elections						
Every year	58	60	61	73	76	76
Every second year	35	37	28	21	18	13
Other arrangement	4	4	6	4	4	5
Number of candidates[2] – whether two or more					Column percentages[1]	
Always	16	20	14	13	12	13
Mostly or sometimes	15	21	4	16	20	7
Rarely	12	14	8	13	12	12
Never	50	42	69	55	54	64
No information	7	3	5	3	2	4
Base: respondents belonging to recognised unions						
Unweighted	*791*	*791*	*181*	*712*	*712*	*210*
Weighted	*485*	*485*	*222*	*417*	*417*	*238*

* See note C
[2] Base changes to instances where elections held in previous year

agement recognised unions for collective bargaining that interviews with worker representatives were sought, and normally obtained, and therefore in these establishments that questions about shop steward appointments were relevant. We sought in our questions to distinguish the methods of appointment of senior stewards and ordinary (non-senior) stewards. However, in many cases the distinction did not hold, since there was only a single shop steward at the establishment for the trade union in question. These we term 'sole stewards'. Table IV.4 shows how senior stewards, ordinary stewards and sole stewards were appointed in the case of the union to which primary manual and non-manual respondents belonged.

For all types of representative, the most common method of election was by a show of hands at a meeting. Ballots of one kind or another were reported as being used in about one quarter of cases for manual stewards, and in just over one third of cases for non-manual stewards.

Since the proportion of stewards appointed by ballot, and particularly ordinary stewards, who were more numerous in large establishments, is rather higher in large establishments than in small ones, it is probable that the proportion of stewards appointed by ballot is greater than the proportions (based on establishments) shown in Table IV.4. In other words, probably more than one quarter of manual stewards and more than one third of non-manual stewards are appointed by ballots. Further analysis might be able to produce more precise estimates. But the above results are broadly in line with the 1966 Donovan survey of shop stewards[4] which reported that 'a show of hands was more than twice as frequent as a ballot'. If there was a trend between 1966 and 1980, it is likely that it was a modest one in the direction of balloting, no doubt partly due to the rise in membership of non-manual trade unions, whose use of ballots is greater.

Another important feature of the pattern of results is that the use of ballots for electing workplace representatives, although the minority practice, occurred in almost all the major trade unions. There were eleven manual unions and twelve non-manual unions for which we have sufficient results for separate tabulation[5], and all included at least one case where an election by ballot was reported.

The *type* of ballot used for appointing workplace representatives also varied between manual and non-manual groups. Postal ballots were rarely mentioned for manual steward elections (three per cent of cases), but were more common for non-manual union representatives (about 10 per cent of cases). Interestingly, this difference in the type of ballot used cannot be explained by differences in the geographical dispersion of stewards' constituencies, because the question referred to establishment level representatives. Moreover, the difference persists if only unions with workplace based branches are considered. The varying traditions and more recent growth of white collar trade unions may lie behind the difference.

Beside their method of appointment, worker representatives were also asked whether, once appointed, they were required to submit to periodic re-election. Two questions were asked, one relating to the technical requirements of their union (as perceived by respondents and perhaps stated in rule books, standing orders and so on), and the other relating to the normal practice. The first of these questions proved the more difficult to answer, some six per cent of respondents being unable to say whether stewards were technically required to stand for re-election. However, comparison of the two sets of answers, where both were given, showed that, for all three types of steward and for both manual and non-manual cases, periodic re-election was more commonly practised than was technically necessary. About three-quarters of senior and ordinary stewards had, in practice, to stand for periodic re-election, although for sole stewards the proportion was nearer one half. This compares with an estimate of 56 per cent for all stewards covered by the Donovan Commission survey in 1966 and suggests little, if any, change in practice in the intervening period.

Where respondents reported that, in practice, stewards or representatives in their union were required to stand for re-election, they were asked how often re-election took place and whether there had been elections within the last year. Annual re-elections were reported most frequently. Bi-annual elections were, broadly speaking, half as common as annual elections for manual representatives and one third as common for non-manual representatives. About one per cent reported that re-elections were less frequent than every two years and a further one per cent reported that there was no fixed interval for re-elections for ordinary stewards. For senior stewards the longer interval was reported in about three per cent of cases for manual workers and in four per cent for non-manual workers.

The existence of elections does not, of course, imply that elections were always contested and, indeed, the majority of stewards in the Donovan Commission survey reported that they had never been opposed when standing for re-election: nearly one half of them said that they had been persuaded to take on the job of shop steward when no-one else wanted it. Much the same situation appears to have existed in 1980. In about one half of establishments there was never more than a single candidate for shop steward elections, and in a further one in eight establishments other candidates were reported as rare. In about one in seven establishments there were always two or more candidates, and inclusion of cases where there were 'mostly' multiple candidates brought the proportion to about one fifth. These proportions varied, however, for the different types of steward. Sole stewards, normally the

Table IV.5   Electoral constituencies[1] of senior stewards (manual unions)

Column percentage

	All establishments	Number of manual stewards at establishment						
		2	3	4–5	6–10	11–20	21 –40	41 or mor
Union members	76	88	78	74	70	56	32	27
Stewards of own union	17	6	14	15	21	32	54	50
All manual stewards including those of other unions	4	3	—	2	5	9	12	20
No information	3	3	8	9	4	3	2	3
Base: establishments with senior manual stewards								
Unweighted	*805[2]*	*90*	*82*	*97*	*176*	*124*	*83*	*57*
Weighted	*501*	*93*	*68*	*71*	*92*	*45*	*19*	*7*

[1] Constituencies are those people who elected senior stewards
[2] See note G

only one for their union in their establishment, were more likely never to be opposed in elections. Senior and ordinary stewards in non-manual unions had very similar patterns of electoral opposition, but in manual trade unions there was a greater tendency for ordinary stewards to be opposed by other candidates. Part of this pattern of variation is explicable in terms of the size of the workforce: sole representatives tended to exist where there were fewer members to represent, and senior stewards where there were sufficient members to require several ordinary stewards, normally in larger establishments.

The constituency for electing senior stewards or convenors varied with the size of the shop steward body. Where there were few stewards, union members themselves tended to elect the senior shop steward; but where there were many shop stewards it became more common for shop stewards to elect the senior steward rather than for ordinary union members to do so (Table IV.5). This finding provides a ready explanation for the finding of Brown, Ebsworth and Terry[6], who showed that, for a sample of GMWU stewards at least, election by fellow stewards was more common in larger workforces. Their observation that election of senior stewards by fellow stewards was more common in engineering than elsewhere also seems to be worth modifying: on the basis of our data this appears to be an artifact of the greater size of workforces in engineering and when workforce size – or, more precisely, the size of the steward body – was controlled for, engineering seemed no different from any other sector. The fact that a similar pattern is apparent for non-manual senior shop stewards, despite their greater prevalence outside private manufacturing, reinforces the suggestion that the relationship arises from organisational factors rather than factors peculiar to any particular sector of industry or the trade unions in it.

Other positions in their union held by stewards

An indication of the involvement of shop stewards in the wider affairs of their union was sought from all trade union respondents. They were asked if any stewards in their union at their workplace had held in the last year any other positions in the union besides that of shop steward (WQ5a). This was followed by a request for the details of the positions held (WQ5b). Primary manual representatives reported the holding of another union position by themselves or other stewards in 34 per cent of cases. Secondary manual respondents reported it in 26 per cent of cases. For non-manual representatives the corresponding figures were 42 per cent and 32 per cent.

The types of other position held by stewards showed a similar pattern for the four types of respondent. The most frequently mentioned was membership of a branch committee, including being a branch officer such as secretary or chairman. These accounted for about two-thirds of cases and were mentioned by about one quarter of all steward respondents. Membership of district committees was mentioned about one half as often as membership of branch committees. The next most frequently mentioned position was that of delegate to a national conference. About one third of respondents mentioning any union position reported such a delegate from their establishment, equivalent to about one in eight of all establishments. Representatives on the top governing body of the union were mentioned by two per cent of primary manual respondents, six per cent of primary non-manual respondents and eight per cent of secondary non-manual respondents. This greater reported membership of the top governing bodies of their unions by non-manual representatives appeared to be a reflection of the generally smaller size of non-manual unions[7]; but it is noteworthy that for other positions there was little difference in the pattern between manual and non-manual unions. In addition, these results show a significant contrast with the report of the Donovan survey. On the basis of a similar question it was reported that 23 per cent of shop stewards held another office in their union and that branch committee membership accounted for most cases. However, membership of national and other bodies above branch or district level were apparently so infrequent that they were not mentioned at all in the report[8]. Mention of them in significant numbers in 1980, and particularly by non-manual respondents, may be another indicator of the relative increase in white-collar unionism over the period – or perhaps of the rather partial picture of shop steward activity given by the Donovan survey's sample from six of the largest trade unions, all of them predominantly manual. The holding of other union positions is naturally reported more often by respondents at larger establishments because larger establishments generally have more shop stewards – although less stewards *per member*, as we saw in Chapter II.

What is perhaps of more significance is whether shop stewards from larger establishments have a greater likelihood of being members of higher level bodies of their union. This could be tested in establishments of different sizes by relating the information on union positions to the data on the number of stewards at the establishment, confining the analysis to cases with a single recognised trade union. We have not yet carried out such an analysis, but it could provide a useful complement to the more direct study of trade union governing bodies.

Contact with local full time officers

The amount of contact between workplace based trade union representatives and the full time officers of their union was a matter explored in the Donovan survey and subsequently by Brown, Ebsworth and Terry[9] in their survey of GMWU stewards. The Donovan survey was of shop stewards in general and did not seek to distinguish senior from ordinary stewards; the survey by Brown and his colleagues did make that distinction. Our informants were senior (or sole) stewards and we asked them about only their own contact with full time officers, considering that their knowledge of other stewards' contacts with officials would be less reliable (WQ18a). Additional questions asked about the frequency of their contact with full time officers and management together and, secondly, with national officials or their union head office (WQ18b; WQ19a). Table IV.6 summarises the results of the first two of these questions for manual and non-manual primary worker representative respondents, in relation to workforce size.

Typically, senior manual stewards had contacted their local full time officials two or three times over the previous year. For non-manual senior stewards the typical (median) figure was twice per year. Both sets of results showed a strong association with the number of employees (manual or non-manual) at the establishment. Analysis in relation to union membership density did not indicate any association with frequency of contact, so it is probable that the most relevant indicator of size would be the number of union members. Further analysis showed that frequency of contact was similar across the public and private sectors and in both manufacturing and service industries. We did not observe any association with the main level of pay bargaining for the

Table IV.6 Number of meetings in previous year between senior[1] stewards and full time officials of their union

| | All establish-ments | Number of employees at establishment[3] | | | | | | | Unweighted base | Weighted base |
		1–24	25–49	50–99	100–199	200–499	500–999	1000 or more		
Number of meetings with local full-time official										
Manual steward	2.5	1	2	2	3	4	5	7	955	694
Non-manual steward	2	—	1	1	2	3	4	10	900	639
Number of meetings with local official and management										
Manual steward	1	—	1	1	2	2	3	3	955	694
Non-manual steward	—	—	—	—	—	1.5	2	7	900	639

Medians

Base: worker representatives in establishments with recognised trade unions

[1] In cases where there was only one steward that steward was included in the senior steward category

[2] Medians linearly interpolated where ties occurred

[3] Where information on manual stewards is provided the number of employees is the number of manual workers. Where the information is about non-manual stewards, the number is the number of non-manual workers

group of workers represented by our respondent[10]. The implication of this, together with the strong association with workforce size, is that contact between senior stewards and full time officers is not confined to the main periodic pay negotiations but is more often in connection with a variety of problems affecting individuals or particular sections of the workforce. As we shall see in Chapter VII, union officials were quite commonly brought in by management to help settle grievances and disputes when the initial stages of formal procedures had failed to resolve a problem. It is likely that contact between senior stewards and full time officers was often a precursor to these more formal interventions.

Meetings involving senior stewards, full time officials and management were considerably less frequent than bilateral meetings on the trade union side. Typically, senior manual stewards reported one of these trilateral meetings in the past year; non-manual respondents typically reported none. Again the correlation with establishment size was strong for both sets of respondents (Table IV.6). There were no apparent sectoral differences, nor was there any clear association with the level of pay bargaining. There was, however, a tendency for more frequent meetings to be reported by manual senior stewards when trade union density was high (80 per cent or more), a tendency that persisted when workforce size was controlled in the analysis.

It might be expected that meetings between full time officials, senior shop stewards and management, being relatively rare occurrences, would take place when serious problems at the establishment were at issue. We asked no direct questions about what was discussed and when, but we tested the suggestion indirectly in two ways, first in relation to the occurrence of industrial action and, secondly, in relation to respondents' assessments of the general industrial relations climate at their establishment[11]. Both the occurrence of industrial action and poor assessments of the industrial relations climate were associated with the frequency of contact between senior stewards and full time officials. However, all three variables were positively related to size. When workforce size was controlled in the analysis, there was still a slight tendency for more frequent meetings to occur in establishments with experience of industrial action and in those with a poor assessment of the industrial relations climate. There was also a fairly strong association between the occurrence of industrial action and the frequency of meetings between senior shop stewards, full time union officials and management. When examined in relation to workforce size, however, this turned out to be confined to small and medium size workforces (less than 500 manual or non-manual employees). In establishments above this size it was common for there to be a full time senior steward or convenor; in these establishments fewer meetings with local union officials and management took place.

Table IV.7 Proportion of senior shop stewards[1] who contacted their national official or union head office in the previous year

Percentages

| | All establishments | Number employed at establishment[1] | | | | | | Unweighted base | Weighted base |
		1–24	25–49	50–99	100–199	200–499	500–999	1000 or more		
Manual steward	41	43	29	40	43	56	57	62	955	694
Non-manual stewards	45	31	45	46	49	59	60	63	900	639

Base: worker representatives in establishments with recognised unions

[1] See notes 1 and 3 to Table IV.6

Contact with national union officers

Senior stewards reported having contacted their national official or union head office over the past year in just under one half of establishments (Table IV.7). Again, the occurrence of such contact was associated with larger establishments, although for manual senior stewards both the largest and the smallest establishments appeared to have more contact than those of intermediate size. In both the manual and non-manual cases senior stewards more often reported contact with national officials than did sole stewards. Head office contact by manual senior or sole stewards was not associated with the most important level of pay bargaining but, for non-manuals, it occurred more often where bargaining was at the level of the whole organisation (55 per cent) than where it was at the establishment level (38 per cent). This difference persisted when only private sector establishments were considered. In addition, contact by non-manual stewards occurred more often in smaller establishments which had experienced industrial action, but less often in larger establishments that had experienced such action. For manual respondents there was no association with industrial action.

Intra-union shop steward meetings

Shop stewards may meet each other in a variety of settings, and we asked respondents about a number of these, sometimes distinguishing between meetings and more formalised committees. In the first instance we considered meetings of stewards other than branch meetings involving only stewards of the same union (WQ29a, b, c, d). Nearly one half of all primary respondents reported such meetings. Excluding establishments where there was only a single steward of the union in question, the proportion reporting such meetings was 60 per cent in the case of manual stewards and 56 per cent for non-manual stewards. In larger workforces, which generally had more stewards, meetings were more often reported than in smaller workforces. Where there was a full time shop steward or convenor at the establishment (usually but not always of the union to which our primary respondent belonged) the proportion reporting intra-union stewards' meetings rose to 73 per cent for manual unions and 79 per cent for non-manual unions. It was also higher, for both manual and non-manual stewards, where the most important level of pay bargaining was the establishment or a group of establishments within the same organisation ('divisional', in the terms used in Chapter VIII).

The characteristics associated with the occurrence of intra-union stewards' meetings were also associated with their frequency. Typically these meetings took place about once per month for manual stewards and a little less often for non-manual stewards. Where there was a full time manual steward, two-thirds of respondents reporting meetings said that they happened once per month or more often. A clear majority of all respondents reported that their meetings were always held during working hours. A majority also reported that minutes of the meetings were regularly taken. These two characteristics were also associated with workforce size, the presence of full time stewards, and pay bargaining at establishment level.

Joint shop stewards' committees and meetings
In establishments where manual (or non-manual) workers were represented by two or more trade unions, we asked primary respondents if there was a committee that included representatives from their own union and the other unions present (WQ27a). Such 'multi-union' establishments, as we saw in Chapter II, were a minority of those with any trade union membership and it was in a minority of these that a joint shop stewards' committee was reported by our primary worker representatives (32 per cent in the case of manual respondents, 17 per cent in the case of non-manual respondents). Typically, the committees had representatives from three unions (WQ27e). Several establishment characteristics were associated with the presence of such committees, the clearest being workforce size and the number of unions recognised by management for collective bargaining (Table IV.8). Establishments with two or more manual trade unions present were more than twice as likely to have a joint stewards' committee if they had more than 500 manual workers than if they had less than 100 such workers, and twice as likely if they had five recognised unions than if they had only two. Committees were also more common where there was a full time shop steward or convenor. A striking comparison was between multi-union establishments where all the manual (or non-manual) unions negotiated with management as a single group and those where they negotiated separately or in several groups. Joint shop stewards' committees were considerably more common in the former (Table IV.8). There was also a slight tendency for the presence of a joint stewards' committee to be associated with pay bargaining at the level of the establishment. The combination of these two circumstances – establishment level pay bargaining and a single negotiating group – might have been expected most often to give rise to the existence of joint stewards' committees. In fact, roughly one half of such establishments had a manual stewards' committee; one half did not. (In the case of non-manual stewards this combination of circumstances was too rare to justify separate analysis.) Thus periodic joint negotiations over pay at establishment level appears to be an insufficiently compelling circumstance for the creation of a joint shop stewards' committee; nor is the absence of such bargaining a condition for non-existence. This suggests that pay is only one of the

Table IV.8   Proportion of establishments where worker representative reported a joint committee of stewards [1]

	Manual representatives	Non-manual representatives
		Percentages
All establishments	32	17
		Percentages
Number employed at establishment		
25–99	24	9
100–499	36	26
500 or more	57	50
		Percentages
Number of recognised unions		
Two	24	13
Three	39	21
Four	45	15
Five or more	53	28
		Percentages
Number of negotiating groups		
One	38	22
Two	25	10
Three	24	20
Four or more	39	28
		Percentages
Full-time union representative		
Full-time steward at establishment	57	(57) [2]
No full-time steward	29	16
		Percentages
Most important level of pay bargaining		
National, industry or region	30	16
Organisation, divisional (single employer)	36	19
Establishment	37	23
Base: worker representatives in establishments with two or more recognised unions		
Unweighted	*602*	*605*
Weighted	*332*	*400*

[1] A joint committee of stewards was one with stewards drawn from two or more unions
[2] See note B

issues with which such committees may deal and, although we collected no direct information on the matters discussed, some further light could be shed on the committees by analysing their existence in relation to, for instance, the scope of bargaining at the establishment.

We also asked how frequently joint committees met and about the

Table IV.9 Characteristics of joint shop stewards' committees

	Manual representatives	Non-manual representatives
		Column percentages[1]
Frequency of meetings		
Once a month or more often	49	35
Less than once a month but at least every 3 months	29	48
Less than once every 3 months	12	9
Other answers	6	5
No information	2	*
Time of meetings		Column percentages
Always in working hours	81	76
Sometimes in working hours	8	12
Never in working hours	8	7
No information	2	5
Formality of committee		Column percentages[2]
Committee has a written constitution	49	61
Committee has standing orders	42	36
Committee has a minute book	74	72
Committee has any of the three items listed[3]	79	81
Base: establishments where worker representative reported presence of a joint shop stewards' committee		
Unweighted	*256*	*159*
Weighted	*108*	*69*

[1] See note C
[2] See note E
[3] That is to say, a written constitution, standing orders or a minute book

times of their meeting and their formality (WQ27b, c, d). These features of the committees were associated with very much the same set of characteristics as was the existence of the committees; particularly they were associated with larger workforces and greater numbers of recognised unions. For present purposes we simply note the overall picture, as shown in Table IV.9. Roughly one half of manual and one third of non-manual committees met at least once a month. In roughly three-quarters of cases the meetings were reported as always being held in working hours, indicating a high degree of acceptance by management. The committees appeared to be run on formal lines in most cases: four-fifths had either a written constitution, standing orders or a minute book. Written constitutions were reported for one half of the manual committees, and a little more frequently than that for non-manual committees.

Joint meetings of shop stewards from two or more trade unions in the same establishment are not always as formalised as the existence of a committee implies. With this in mind we asked a further set of questions about joint shop stewards' meetings, irrespective of the existence of a joint stewards' committee (WQ28a, b, c, d). In the manual case, about one fifth of respondents where there were two or more unions present reported such meetings. Two-thirds of these were where there was a committee. In consequence, the proportion of relevant establishments having either a joint stewards' committee or joint stewards' meetings was 38 per cent, compared with 32 per cent which had a joint committee. The analogous proportions for non-manual workers were 26 per cent and 17 per cent, rather more non-manual meetings being reported where there was no committee.

Joint stewards' meetings, apart from those of a joint stewards' committee, were less frequent than those of the joint stewards' committee. In terms of their constitutional documents and minutes they were also less formal. They were, however, just as likely to take place during work hours as were joint stewards' committee meetings.

Single employer meetings of shop stewards
In workplaces that are part of multi-establishment organisations, shop stewards from one establishment may meet with those from other establishments of the same employer to discuss common issues, quite apart from any meetings organised by their union branch. They may meet sufficiently regularly and formally to constitute a 'committee'. Such committees have a long history in the engineering industry where they are often known as 'combine committees' but they have received little study elsewhere in manufacturing or in the services sector[12]. Our questions sought to establish the existence of such meetings, irrespective of whether they were regarded as meetings of a committee, and we shall refer to them as 'combine meetings'. We also asked about their frequency, how long they had been taking place, the reasons for starting them and about management's support for them (WQ30a, b, c, d, e, f, g, h).

Overall, manual respondents reported the existence of such meetings in 43 per cent of establishments that were part of larger organisations (Table IV.10). For non-manual workers the proportion was very similar (42 per cent). Meetings were more often reported in the public sector, particularly in the nationalised industries, than in the private sector. In the private sector combine meetings were more frequently reported by stewards in workplaces belonging to larger enterprises. In

Table IV.10   Characteristics of shop steward combine meetings

	Combine meetings confined to one organisation[1]		Combine meetings covering more than one organisation	
	Manual represen- tatives	Non-manual represen- tatives	Manual represen- tatives	Non-manual represen- tatives
				Percentages
Whether meetings held[2]				
Yes – meetings held	43	42	13	11
				Medians
Frequency of meetings				
Months	2 months	3 months	2 months	2 months
				Percentages
Attendance at meetings				
Respondent attended meetings	97	90	80	78
			Column percentages	
Lifetime of meetings				
Up to three years	21	13	5	21
Three to five years	18	17	19	25
Five to ten years	29	30	22	12
Ten years or more	31	39	54	42
Difficulties over organising			Column percentages	
meetings				
Difficulties experienced	11	10	1	7
No difficulties	79	79	66	76
Answer unclear or no information	10	11	33	16
Financial help from				Percentages
management				
Help received	36	32	7	8
Base: establishments where worker representatives reported meetings of combine meetings				
Unweighted	*388*	*397*	*152*	*112*
Weighted	*255*	*242*	*86*	*73*

[1] Combine meetings confined to one organisation were meetings of stewards drawn from different establishments belonging to the same employer
[2] Base, for this row, is establishments that were part of multi-establishment enterprises and that recognised unions
[3] See note C

the public sector the reverse was the case – the largest organisations were less likely to have combine meetings.

Worker representatives reported the existence of combine meetings more often where there was high trade union membership density, a comprehensive closed shop and a full time senior steward or representative at the establishment. The most marked difference, however, was between establishments with different pay bargaining arrangements. Manual stewards reported combine meetings in 58 per cent of cases where they assessed the most important level of pay bargaining to be above the establishment but single employer, compared with 28 per cent where the establishment was the most important level. For non-manual representatives the comparable figures were 51 per cent and 19 per cent.

The relevance of the level of pay bargaining was also evident when we examined how often combine meetings were held. (Respondents reported that they attended the meetings themselves in over 90 per cent of cases, so the results on this and subsequent questions are clearly based on personal knowledge.) Meetings were held most frequently where pay bargaining was for all establishments in an organisation and least frequently where pay bargaining was at establishment level. Typically the frequency was at least every three months but not as often as once per month.

About one third of respondents reported that the combine meetings attended by stewards of their establishment had been going on for over ten years. The typical figure was seven years for manual respondents and eight years for non-manual respondents. There was little variation in these figures in relation to levels of pay bargaining or the other characteristics that were associated with the occurrence of combine meetings. There was, however, considerable variation across industrial sectors. The sector where the longest established combine meetings were reported was transport and communications. The sector with the most recently established combine meetings was health services. These differences were apparent for manual and non-manual representatives. Within manufacturing, the engineering sector did not stand out as having longer established combine meetings than other sectors and individual industries have too few cases for more detailed analysis.

Just over one half of respondents, both manual and non-manual, reported that the main reason for starting the combine meetings that they attended was to exchange ideas and information with stewards or representatives from other establishments. About one tenth said that it was union policy to have such meetings and a further one tenth mentioned some aspect of negotiations with management. Another tenth said the meetings had been started to deal with specific problems, while a similar proportion mentioned trade union unity or strength. The last two mentioned reasons were given more often by manual than non-manual respondents. Otherwise the patterns of response to this question were similar. There were no obvious patterns of variation in these responses in relation to other characteristics of the combine meetings or of the establishment of our respondents.

Finally, we asked whether or not respondents had had any difficulties in organising combine meetings and whether or not they had received assistance in attending them from management. About one in ten of respondents reported difficulties in organising combine meetings. There were no differences in the proportions between the private sector and the public sector as a whole, but in the nationalised industries non-manual respondents reported difficulties more frequently. There was a general tendency for difficulties to be reported where trade union density at the establishment was high (80 per cent or more). Another noteworthy variation was in relation to the level of pay bargaining. For manual respondents, difficulties were reported most often when the most important level of pay bargaining was at the establishment. For non-manual workers, difficulties were more common for all types of single employer bargaining. There were also differences in relation to how long established were meetings. For example, meetings that had been started up in the five years prior to the survey were three times more likely than longer established meetings to have encountered difficulties, according to manual respondents.

Length of time established, however, had no observable effect on whether the meetings received financial support from management. But this characteristic of combine meetings did show considerable variation between sectors in the case of manual stewards. Whereas about one third overall reported financial assistance, this proportion was nearly one half in the private sector and less than one quarter in the public sector. Non-manual respondents reported financial assistance with combine meetings much less frequently (less than 10 per cent of cases) and there was no difference between public and private sectors. Manual respondents more often reported financial assistance where manual trade union membership was high and also where pay bargaining was at the level of the whole organisation. Both sets of respondents reported it more frequently in industrial and commercial establishments (the private sector plus public sector trading organisations) where managers had assessed the financial performance of the establishment as above the average for their industry.

Multi-employer meetings of shop stewards
The final type of shop steward meeting that we asked about in the survey was a meeting involving shop stewards or representatives from several different employing organisations (WQ31a, b, c, d, e, f, g, h). Meetings of this kind were much less common than single employer combine meetings and were reported by roughly one in eight of our respondents (Table IV.10). They were least common in the nation-

alised industries, where industry specific trade unions are most prevalent. Generally, our respondents were less likely to attend them than they were to attend single employer combine meetings and this factor, together with the relatively small numbers involved, has suggested a more limited analysis of their characteristics. As Table IV.10 shows, compared with single employer combine meetings, multi-employer combine meetings were of more recent establishment for non-manual stewards, but of longer standing for manual stewards. They met with similar frequency – about once every two months. Respondents, especially manual respondents, less often reported experiencing difficulties in organising multi-employer meetings than single employer meetings, but also reported no difficulties less often, a result that suggests that they were more often independent of both management and official union support. Indeed, support from management in the form of travel, accommodation and administrative assistance was uncommon, being reported in roughly one case in twelve. The reasons given for starting the meetings, where they could be given, were similar to those given for single employer combine meetings. Again, the predominant type of reason was one emphasising the exchange of ideas and information between representatives in different establishments.

Notes

1. W.E.J. McCarthy and S.R. Parker, *Shop Stewards and Workshop Relations*, Research Paper No. 10, Royal Commission on Trade Unions and Employers' Associations (HMSO, London, 1968).
2. All the survey evidence in this chapter was obtained from worker representatives belonging to recognised trade unions. For ease of expression we will refer to them as 'shop stewards' or 'stewards' whether they were manual or non-manual representatives.
3. Government Social Survey, *Workplace Industrial Relations* (HMSO, London, 1968).
4. Government Social Survey, *op. cit.*
5. The minimum in this instance was ten observations.
6. W. Brown, R. Ebsworth and M. Terry, 'Factors Shaping Shop Steward Organisation in Britain', *British Journal of Industrial Relations*, July 1978, pp. 139–59.
7. In non-manual unions too small for separate tabulation, membership of the governing body was much more frequently reported: by 13 per cent, compared with six per cent overall.
8. Government Social Survey, *op. cit.*
9. Brown, Ebsworth and Terry, *op. cit.*
10. By contrast, Brown, Ebsworth and Terry (*op. cit.*) reported more frequent contact in manufacturing than in the public service, a weak association with establishment size and a strong association with national level wage bargaining.
11. The precise questions used to obtain these measures are given in Chapters IX and X respectively. The assessments of the general state of industrial relations referred to here were those of the appropriate worker representative respondents.
12. H.A. Clegg, *The Changing System of Industrial Relations in Great Britain* (Basil Blackwell, Oxford, 1979).

V Management Organisation for Industrial Relations

A recurrent complaint about British business and administration is that the industrial relations and personnel functions within management have not been adequately developed. Critics have, first, suggested that people with an interest in, and understanding of, those management functions have not been adequately represented on the governing bodies of enterprises[1]. Secondly, they have argued that the people involved in personnel work have carried less weight in management teams than, say, engineers or accountants because they have tended to have a less 'professional' training[2]. We sought, in our survey, to sketch the factual background relevant to those views. We analysed the extent to which our workplaces employed personnel or industrial relations managers and examined the qualifications, training and experience of people engaged in personnel work[3]. We also explored the extent to which personnel or industrial relations specialists were represented on boards or governing bodies and looked at the way in which managers drew upon external help, advice and consultancy in the personnel field. There was, however, one main limitation to our information in this area. The impressions created by previous workplace surveys about industrial relations led us to expect that we would be chiefly talking to personnel managers in the broadest sense of the function[4]. We designed our questioning on the roles and activities of respondents with the idea that answers would enable us to carry out an analysis of personnel management in its organisational context. If we established information on the background, qualifications and position in the managerial hierarchy of our respondents, then we would be determining the position of personnel management generally. In fact, although, generally, we spoke to the senior person at the establishment with responsibility for personnel matters, we found that fewer than one half of our primary[5] management respondents spent the major part of their time on personnel work, and that only about one quarter were employed as personnel managers. Accordingly, those respondents provided a more limited and patchy basis for exploring the position of personnel administration than we expected. At the same time, the nature of our respondents also provided the first substantive finding concerning personnel management: personnel work is chiefly carried out by people who are not formally employed as personnel specialists. Many of those who spend a major part of their time upon personnel

Table V.1   Respondents' management function in relation to establishment size

	All establishments	Number employed at establishment						
		25–49	50–99	100–199	200–499	500–999	1000–1999	2000 or more
								Percentages
Major part of time spent on personnel/industrial relations matters	42	24	37	51	74	87	94	95
								Column percentages
Function in job title								
Personnel/industrial relations	24¹	7	17	30	55	74	87	93
Personnel	20	6	14	27	52	65	72	62
Industrial/employee relations	3	2	3	3	3	10	14	30
General management	44	55	47	41	20	18	12	4
Works management	5	2	8	8	6	*	–	1
Branch management	18	26	17	12	11	3	1	3
Finance	5	5	7	5	6	2	–	–
Technical	2	2	2	4	1	1	–	–
Sales	1	2	1	–	1	–	–	–
Not stated	1	*	1	1	–	1	*	–
Base: all establishments								
Unweighted	2040	367	380	399	378	249	143	124
Weighted	2000	785	528	347	206	83	34	17

*Fewer than 0.5 per cent
(See page D)

work are general managers or administrators. The number of workplaces in Britain which do not have personnel managers has tended to be substantially understated by the tendency for previous research to exclude smaller workplaces from its analysis.

The management function of respondents

Table V.1 summarises the management functions reflected by the titles of our respondents (Q11a). Most were engaged in general, branch or works administration. That was certainly the case for establishments employing fewer than 200 people. Size, as measured by the number of people employed on site, was the strongest single source of variation in the extent to which establishments were represented by people whose title identified them as being principally engaged upon personnel work[6]. The relationship was very strong and consistent. Nearly all our largest establishments were represented by a personnel or industrial relations manager: hardly any of our smallest establishments were, as might well be expected and, indeed, appropriate.

The size of establishments was much more important than was the total size of organisations of which establishments were part. When we compared establishments of similar size, there was no general tendency for establishments to be more likely to be represented by personnel people the larger was the size of the total organisation of which they were part (see Table V.2). It is true that the smallest enterprises were least likely to be represented by personnel managers, but it was also the case that organisations of intermediate total size were most likely to have personnel specialists at their establishments.

Beyond the influence of establishment size, there were tendencies for personnel managers to be more common among overseas owned companies in the private sector and among nationalised industries in the public sector. In terms of industrial sector, manufacturing industry in general, and especially electrical engineering (57 per cent) and vehicle manufacture (49 per cent), was particularly likely to have personnel respondents. Outside manufacturing, financial services (37 per cent) and public administration (35 per cent) were the sectors where personnel managers were most common. These differences, however, were partly a consequence of variations in the size of the characteristic establishment in sectors. For instance, the high figure for manufacturing industry generally was a result of the tendency for establishments to be larger in that sector. Indeed, when workplaces employing 25 to 99 people were isolated, then manufacturing industry (eight per cent) was among the sectors least likely to be represented by a personnel manager. By contrast, although distribution was relatively unlikely to be represented by a personnel specialist overall, it was relatively likely to be so when analysis was confined to establishments of similar size. At

Table V.2   **Respondents in personnel functions in relation to establishment and organisation size**

Percentages

Number employed by total organisation	Number employed at establishment			
	25–99	100–499	500–999	1000 or more
25–500	5	26	n.a.[1]	n.a.
501–10,000	23	52	84	81
10,001 or more	14	39	68	93
Base: all establishments				

[1] Cell size not applicable

the same time, the construction industry and personal services were relatively unlikely to be represented by personnel managers, both overall and when establishments of similar size were compared.

We explored the extent to which the existence of specialist personnel management was associated with the extent of worker organisation at workplaces. That is to say, we looked at the extent to which there was any relationship between whether workplaces had personnel managers and the level of trade union membership and activity. We found, overall, that there was a strong association between our measures of specialisation in personnel management and our measures of trade union organisation and activity. That association, however, was largely a consequence of the fact that both management and trade union sophistication were very strongly associated with establishment size. Nevertheless, when we confined analysis to establishments of similar size, we did find some evidence that personnel managers were more common where trade unions were recognised and a high proportion of workers were members of unions. It was, of course, more appropriate to explore that relationship in smaller workplaces, as nearly all the larger establishments were represented by managers who had personnel titles and spent most of their time on personnel work. In smaller establishments (those having 25 to 99 people and those having 100 to 499 people) management respondents were more likely both to spend the major part of their time on personnel matters and to be nominally personnel specialists in cases where trade unions were recognised and where more than one half of the workforce were trade union members. For instance, in workplaces employing 25 to 99 people where there were no manual trade union members, only one quarter of management respondents spent most of their time on personnel work and only seven per cent had personnel titles. By contrast, in cases where over one half of manual workers were trade union members, 38 per cent

Table V.3   Respondents' functions

Column percentages

| | All establishments | Whether major part of time spent on personnel/industrial | |
		Yes	No
Personnel/industrial relations	24[1]	52	3
Personnel	20	45	3
Industrial relations	3	7	*
General management	44	26	58
Works management	5	4	6
Branch management	38	13	21
Finance	5	2	7
Technical	2	2	2
Sales	1	1	2
No information	1	*	1
Base: all establishments			
Unweighted	*2040*	*1202*	*838*
Weighted	*2000*	*835*	*1165*

*Fewer than 0.5 per cent
[1] See note D

of respondents spent the bulk of their time on personnel matters, and 16 per cent had personnel job titles.

While only one quarter of our respondents had titles which located them in the personnel function in the widest sense, a higher proportion spent a major part of their time on personnel matters (see Table V.1; Q13). Even so, the proportion remained less than one half. Moreover, even in cases where respondents spent the bulk of their time on personnel matters, nearly one half were not personnel specialists in terms of their title (see Table V.3). The pattern reinforced the initial impression that, in a substantial proportion of establishments, much personnel work was done by general managers and administrators rather than by specialists. That was especially marked in workplaces which employed fewer than 500 people. The variations in the proportion of establishments represented by people who spent a major part of their time on personnel matters without the establishment having a personnel manager closely followed variations in the proportion who had personnel titles. Table V.1 showed how both proportions increased steadily in relation to establishment size. At the same time there was, among small establishments, a substantial gap between establishments

Table V.4   Activities and responsibilities of respondents

Percentages

	All establish- ments	Whether major part of time on personnel issues		Whether personnel specialists	
		Yes	No	Personnel/ IR job title	Other job title
Disciplinary cases	92	94	90	96	93
Recruitment	89	90	90	88	91
Training	80	82	79	74	90
Settling/nego- tiating terms of employment	64	75	57	82	68
Job evaluation/ grading	60	70	53	73	67
Industrial relations procedures	59	76	48	84	66
Responsibility for systems of pay	48	45	50	42	49
Base: all establishments					
Unweighted	*2040*	*1202*	*821*	*828*[1]	*374*
Weighted	*2000*	*835*	*1146*	*430*	*405*

[1] For the comparison between people who had personnel job titles and those who had other titles the base is people who spent a major part of their time on personnel matters

represented by personnel specialists and those represented by people who spent a lot of their time on personnel matters but did not have a personnel job title. That gap narrowed steadily the larger was the size of establishments.

The roles and responsibilities of respondents

We asked respondents whether each of a range of different work responsibilities and activities formed part of their job (see Table V.4; Q13). The answers, frankly, were not very instructive. That appeared to be a result of two influences. First, the same description of an activity could have quite different meanings in different types of establishment and, secondly, there was a range of possible forms of involvement in the same activity. For instance, over 90 per cent of respondents said that determining, or negotiating, terms of employment formed part of their job. There was very little variation according to whether or not people spent a major part of their time on personnel matters, or whether or not they had personnel job titles. It is likely that people felt able to agree that that responsibility formed part of their job no matter whether they spent all their time developing and refining terms and conditi< ns of employment and nego:iating these with trade union representatives, or whether they had full discretion about whom to appoint to a particular job and at what rate of pay, or whether they occasionally found themselves in a position to give an opinion on such matters.

A more interesting pattern should have appeared when we isolated people who both spent the bulk of their time on personnel issues and carried the term *personnel* in their titles. In principle, the isolation of such people should have enabled us to compare like with like. In practice, it appeared, again, that the form of the question enabled people with a very wide range of type and level of involvement in an activity to say that it formed part of their responsibilities and, consequently, answers did not produce illuminating differences.

Indeed, we were not able to identify any pattern of variation that was illuminating other than where we analysed responsibilities by the measures of the centralisation of collective bargaining that were built into the schedule (see Chapter VIII). Variations emerged when we isolated workplaces where pay increases were subject to collective bargaining and those where they were not, and when we identified the most important level of bargaining. Similarly, there were differences when we analysed responsibilities in relation to whether or not different aspects of employment, such as the introduction of major change or the number of people recruited, were subject to collective bargaining, and, if so, at what level. The principal finding was that, where there was a pattern of the centralisation of collective bargaining over pay increases and other aspects of employment at company level, then our management respondents were much less likely to say that they were engaged in determining or negotiating terms and conditions of employment, or in setting up industrial relations procedures or that they had responsibility for payments systems. The striking feature of this pattern was the extent to which the centralisation of collective bargaining at the company level produced a result that differed markedly from all other arrangements, whether that was national level bargaining, plant bargaining, no bargaining or no recognition of trade unions. It appeared that when a range of decisions was resolved through collective bargaining at company level, then that pattern was associated with a greater tendency for a whole range of decisions to be centralised than was the case when other levels of collective bargaining were important or there was no collective bargaining. The pattern will give a special interest to our analysis in Chapter VIII of the most important levels of bargaining over pay and over some other issues.

Table V.5   The education and qualifications of respondents who spent a major part of their time on personnel work

	All spending major part of time on personnel/industrial relations	Whether personnel specialist	
		Personnel/ IR job title	Other job title
		Column percentages[1]	
Formal qualifications for			
personnel work	34	50	18
No formal qualifications	61	44	80
No information	4	6	2
		Percentages	
Nature of qualifications[1]			
Member of professional			
association only	20	30	8
Degree/diploma in business/			
social science	8	10	6
Degree/diploma in personnel/			
industrial relations	3	6	1
Professional qualification	2	2	2
No information	2	2	2
Base: respondents who spent a major part of their time on personnel work			
Unweighted	*1202*	*828*	*374*
Weighted	*835*	*430*	*405*

[1] See notes C and D

The education, qualifications, experience and training of personnel managers

In order to provide further measures of the degree of professionalism among personnel managers, we asked those respondents who said that they spent a major part of their time on personnel work whether they had two or more years experience in personnel work and whether they had undergone formal training in personnel matters during the previous two years (Q16). In cases where they had staff to help them, we asked similar questions in relation to their most recent recruit (Q16). The purpose of the questioning focused upon the recruit was to gauge whether the new generation of people coming into personnel work was being prepared for the work differently from the previous one. Again, the fact that so many of our respondents were not formally employed within the personnel function and had not taken on a recruit who was formally concerned with personnel work meant, for the sample as a

Table V.6   The occupational experience of respondents who spent a major
part of their time on personnel work

	All spending major part of time on personnel/industrial relations	Whether personnel specialist	
		Personnel/ IR job title	Other title
	Column percentages		
Two or more years experience of personnel work	86[1]	89	84
No experience or fewer than two years experience	9	4	13
No information	5	7	3
	Percentages		
Locus of experience			
At same establishment	41	42	39
Same employer different establishment	20	15	25
Different employer	25	31	19
No information	*	1	*
Base: respondents who spent a major part of their time on personnel work			
Unweighted	*1202*	*828*	*374*
Weighted	*835*	*430*	*405*

*Fewer than 0.5 per cent
[1] See note D

whole, that the questions did not fully achieve the purposes for which
they were designed. At the same time, the replies are of interest and it is
worth, initially, looking at them in turn and in relation to whether
respondents were personnel specialists.

One third of those respondents who said that they spent a major part
of their time on personnel work said that they had a formal qualification
relevant to personnel work (see Table V.5). People had the opportunity
to mention more than one qualification, but in most cases they mentioned only one and that consisted of membership of an occupational
organisation (such as membership of the Institute of Personnel Management which, of course, includes an examination requirement). In
eight per cent of cases people had degrees or diplomas in one of the
social sciences or a business related subject, and in three per cent
of cases they had degrees or diplomas in personnel management or
industrial relations. Even when analysis was confined to people who
both spent a major part of their time on personnel work and had job
titles relevant to the function, only one half had any formal qualifica-

tion. It also remained the case that, for nearly two-thirds of those with some qualification, the qualification consisted of membership of an occupational organisation.

The general impression created by our findings was that education and training for personnel work consisted largely of on-the-job training and training that was specific to the organisation in which people worked. Eighty-six per cent of those respondents who said they spent a major part of their time on personnel work also said that they had had two or more years of experience of that kind of work. That proportion varied little in relation to whether or not people had personnel job titles (see Table V.6). It has to be assumed that people who were not personnel specialists were generally saying that they had had two or more years of experience carrying the range of personnel responsibilities within a general management or administrative job, or what-

Table V.7 The occupational training of respondents who spent a major part of their time on personnel work

	All spending major part of time on personnel/industrial relations	Whether personnel specialist	
		Personnel/ IR job title	Other job title
		Column percentages	
Course of one day or more on personnel in previous two years	61	71	50
No courses on personnel in previous two years	34	22	47
No information	5	7	3
		Percentages	
Type of course			
Internal (own organisation)	26	24	28
Professional association	14	21	8
Commercial/consultancy	13	19	8
Educational institute	9	12	6
Industrial training board	1	1	1
Employers' association	1	1	1
Other	3	4	2
No information on type of course	*	*	1
Base: respondents who spent a major part of their time on personnel work			
Unweighted	*1202*	*828*	*374*
Weighted	*835*	*430*	*405*

*Fewer than 0.5 per cent

ever, that they were currently doing. Normally, people's experience had been gained at their present establishment, and in nearly two-thirds of cases it had been gained with the same employer.

Sixty-one per cent of people who spent the bulk of their time on personnel issues did say that they had received training of one day or more in the previous two years. The most common type of such training was an internal course provided by the respondent's own organisation (see Table V.7). Then followed courses provided by occupational associations, consultants or commercial training organisations. The education sector provided few of the training opportunities undertaken by practising managers.

Variations in the extent to which respondents had formal qualifications and had recently undertaken any training closely followed differences in the extent to which establishments employed personnel

Table V.8 **The formal personnel qualifications, training and experience of respondents in relation to establishment size**

	All establish-ments	Number employed at establishment				
		25–99	100–199	200–499	500–999	1000 or more
						Percentages
Major time on personnel/ industrial relations						
(a) Some formal qualification	34	25	33	47	51	54
(b) Two or more years experience	86	84	87	89	88	99
(c) Training of one day or more	61	55	62	66	70	78
Base: respondents who spent a major part of their time on personnel work						
Unweighted	*1202*	*241*	*205*	*284*	*219*	*253*
Weighted	*835*	*387*	*176*	*152*	*72*	*48*
						Percentages
Personnel/industrial relations specialists						
(a) Some formal qualification	50	48	42	55	54	56
(b) Two or more years experience	89	84	85	88	87	91
(c) Training of one day or more	71	72	69	68	76	73
Base: respondents with personnel job titles						
Unweighted	*828*	*89*	*116*	*203*	*190*	*230*
Weighted	*430*	*125*	*95*	*105*	*61*	*44*

Table V.9 Comparison of formal qualifications, experience and training of respondent and of most recent recruit

Column percentages

	Qualifications			Experience			Training	
	Respondent	Recruit		Respondent	Recruit		Respondent	Recruit
Some formal qualification	61	35[1]	Two or more years experience of personnel work	96	64	Personnel course of one day or more in previous two years	75	68
No formal qualifications	39	64	No such experience	3	35	No course undertaken	24	30
No information	*	*	No information	1	1	No information	*	2
Nature of qualifications			**Locus of experience**			**Type of course**		
Member of professional association only	38	16	Same establishment	46	31	Internal	24	24
Degree/diploma in business/social science	12	10	Same employer/different establishment	15	11	Professional association	26	13
Degree/diploma in personnel/IR	7	4	Different employer	35	21	Commercial/consultancy	19	17
Professional qualification	3	3	No information	*	*	Educational institute	12	14
No information	3	3				Other	3	3
						No information	1	2
Unweighted	499	499		499	499		499	499
Weighted	244	244		244	244		244	244

Base: respondents who had taken on a subordinate in the personnel function

* Fewer than 0.5 per cent
[1] See notes C, D and E

managers. Accordingly, the more people who were employed on site the more likely were respondents involved in personnel work to have formal qualifications in personnel work and to have undergone some recent training in the personnel field (see Table V.8). When, however, analysis was confined to personnel managers, that relationship evaporated. At the same time, there remained differences in relation to type of ownership and industrial sector. Personnel specialists working in central and local government were especially likely to have formal qualifications. In the private sector, overseas owned workplaces and establishments engaged in vehicle manufacture and construction were more likely than others to have personnel specialists with formal qualifications.

The qualifications of recent recruits compared with those of managers

In cases where respondents had support staff and had taken on someone in the personnel function, the recruit tended to be less well qualified, to have had less experience and to have been less likely to have undergone any recent training (see Table V.9). Of course, the pattern is open to a range of possible interpretations. In the context of our findings in this chapter, perhaps the most plausible is that personnel work generally remains a sphere of managerial activity where qualifications are built up through experience on the job. For specialists, that will, in time, contribute to the acquisition of membership of an occupational organisation. There is very little sign indeed of relevant formal qualifications becoming a condition of entry into the occupation.

Comparison between primary and secondary management respondents

As we explain in footnote 5, the information presented so far in this chapter on the characteristics of people doing personnel work has been based upon our primary management respondents. There remained the possibility that the characteristics of secondary management respondents would be substantially different and would alter the overall picture. We explored that possibility and found that in practice it did not prove to be the case. Secondary management respondents were more likely to be personnel specialists and to be better qualified than their primary counterparts in workplaces where both were interviewed. However, secondary respondents were interviewed in only eight per cent of cases and their characteristics were not sufficiently different from those of their primary counterparts to have changed the overall pattern had they been included in the total rather than the primary respondents.

Table V.10   Consultation of outside bodies on personnel/industrial relations matters

Percentages

	All establish-ments	Number employed at establishment				
		Under 100	100–199	200–499	500–999	1000 or more
Outside body con-sulted in previous year	40[1]	33	45	54	66	76
Nature of body consulted						
Employers' associa-tion	13	10	15	21	24	42
Trade union officer	13	10	13	21	28	36
Solicitor/barrister	11	9	9	13	21	28
Personnel manager in other establish-ment	11	9	17	15	15	13
ACAS	9	6	11	16	24	2
Management con-sultant	4	4	3	6	9	1
Accountant	3	3	2	3	3	
Government department/agency	2	2	2	2	2	
No information	*	*	–	–	–	
Base: all estalbishments						
Unweighted	*2040*	*747*	*399*	*378*	*249*	*267*
Weighted	*2000*	*1313*	*347*	*206*	*83*	*51*

*Fewer than 0.5 per cent
[1] See note F

Consulting external bodies or specialists regarding personnel or industrial relations matters

It might have been expected that where establishments did not have their own personnel specialists then they would have been more likely to seek advice or help from outside (Q20). In practice, the use of external advisers on personnel matters operated in the opposite direction. Types of establishment that were more likely to have professional personnel managers were also more likely to use outside advisers or consultants on personnel or industrial relations matters. Table V.10 shows how there was a very strong tendency for establishments to be more likely to use outside consultants the larger the number of people

Table V.11 Comparison of bodies ever consulted on personnel or industrial relations matters with those most recently consulted

Percentages

	Body ever consulted in previous year	Body most often consulted in previous year
Employers' association	13	10
Trade union	13	6
Solicitor/barrister	11	5
Personnel manager in other establishment	11	10
ACAS	9	4
Management consultants	4	3
Accountant	3	1
Government department/agency	2	1
No information	*	1
Base: all establishments		
Unweighted	*2040*	*2040*
Weighted	*2000*	*2000*

*Fewer than 0.5 per cent

they employed. Table V.11 compares the nature of the bodies or specialists who were ever consulted in the previous year with those who were used most often. In view of the way that trade unions are often conceived of as agents of conflict and hostility to management[7], it is of particular interest that full time trade union officers were one of the two outside agents most commonly consulted by managers. That finding is consistent with the results of previous research which has seen trade union officers as lubricants rather than as irritants in the industrial relations system[8].

It is true that full time trade union officers came lower down in the rank order of bodies that were consulted *most frequently* over a period of a year. It is likely that outside trade union officers tend to be consulted more in the event of substantial issues, whereas, for instance, employers' associations might also be consulted on matters of detail relating to routine and day to day issues. The pattern relating to solicitors and barristers was similar to that with regard to full time trade union officers. They ranked relatively high among outside specialists ever consulted over a 12 month period, but lower among those frequently consulted. Again, it is likely that outside lawyers were more likely to be brought in on major issues. It is likely, too, that the growth of legislation concerning employment and industrial relations during the

1970s was one of the reasons why lawyers ranked so high among outside bodies that were ever used. As would be expected, solicitors were the representatives of the legal professions who acted more frequently as advisers to managements.

When managers with responsibility for personnel matters consulted personnel managers in other establishments, they tended overwhelmingly to be personnel managers at the establishment's own head office or divisional office, rather than people located in any other, wider, network.

The Advisory, Conciliation and Arbitration Service was consulted on personnel or industrial relations matters much more frequently than was any other government agency or department. The pattern of consultation, however, resembled that for trade union officers and lawyers rather than that for employers' associations and personnel managers in other establishments. As was the case for such agencies, ACAS was brought in on special occasions, rather than referred to on a continuous basis. It was instructive, though, that ACAS was less frequently involved in establishments that had experienced strikes in the previous 12 months than it was in establishments that had not. That pattern, however, concealed important differences as between establisments of different sizes. Among smaller workplaces that had experienced any industrial action, ACAS had very rarely been consulted, but trade union officers from outside the workplace, employers' associations and management consultants had been used much more than normal. Among workplaces of intermediate size that had had strikes, employers' associations were consulted very much more frequently than was normal and ACAS slightly more frequently. Among the largest establishments, where the use of all types of outside body tended to be more common, there was very little variation indeed in the pattern of usage in relation to whether or not workplaces had experienced strikes or other action.

Membership of employers' associations and their consultation on personnel issues

We have seen that employers' associations of one kind or another were among the bodies external to establishments that were most frequently consulted over personnel or industrial relations issues. At the same time, only 13 per cent of establishments had ever consulted an employers' association in the previous year. To put that figure in perspective, however, it needs to be borne in mind that only just over one quarter of establishments (27 per cent) were members of employers' associations (Q21). Table V.12 shows the details. Employers' associations as such were most relevant to the private sector and in that sector establishments engaged in manufacturing industry or construction

Table V.12 Membership of employers' associations

Column percentages

| | All establishments | All manufacturing | Selected industrial sectors | | | | |
			Construction/ extraction	Finance	Distribution	Professional services	Miscellaneous services
Yes – member	27[1]	56	65	33	18	11	13
No – not member	71	44	33	65	77	86	82
No information	3	–	2	2	5	3	5
Base: all establishments							
Unweighted	*2040[2]*	*775*	*102*	*76*	*189*	*363*	*163*
Weighed	*2000*	*554*	*130*	*95*	*262*	*372*	*243*

[1] See note C
[2] See note H

Table V.13   Representation of personnel/industrial relations function o
governing body of organisation

	All establish- ments	Number employed by organisation			
		25–500	501– 2000	2001– 10,000	10,00 or mor
				Column percentag	
Any representation	67[1]	57	70	75	80
No representation	24	31	26	22	16
No information	8	12	3	4	4
Nature of representation					Percentag
Specialist representation of personnel/industrial relations	34	9	36	45	66
Responsibility for industrial relations specifically, with or without other responsibilities	65	54	69	74	79
Responsibility for personnel specifically, with or without other responsibilities	67	56	68	74	80
Both personnel and industrial relations represented by –					
one member carrying both responsibilities	52	48	50	57	59
two members, one for each responsibility	12	6	16	13	18
Base: all establishments other than government bodies					
Unweighted	*1464*	*393*	*197*	*267*	*517*
Weighted	*1423*	*599*	*169*	*197*	*366*

[1] See note C

were most likely to be members. Those involved in distribution or in
professional or miscellaneous services were least likely to be members.
To that extent membership of employers' associations reflected variations in trade union recognition, so far as industrial sectors were
concerned. Indeed, in the private sector, establishments were substantially more likely to be members of associations where manual trade
unions were recognised.

In cases where establishments did belong to employers' associations,
29 per cent had consulted some association over a personnel or industrial relations issue in the previous year. Interestingly, it remained the
case that larger establishments were very much more likely to have
consulted their association. In places with 1,000 or more employees,

over two-thirds (68 per cent) of members had consulted their association. It is clearly not the case that employers' associations are most frequently used by smaller establishments which do not have the resources to provide their own specialist services.

Representation of the personnel function on the board

One measure of the importance that an organisation attaches to a management function is the extent to which that specialism is represented on the governing body of the organisation. We asked respondents at establishments other than those in central and local government a number of questions about the extent to which the personnel function was represented on their governing bodies (Q18). (Normally, of course, that body will have been the board of directors, but we carried out interviews at such a range of enterprises that we have to use the more general abstraction.) Table V.13 summarises the answers. In two-thirds of cases there was some member of the governing body who had responsibility for personnel or industrial relations matters. That proportion rose to 73 per cent when we discounted the eight per cent who did not have information on the responsibilities of board members. In one third of cases there was someone with specialist responsibililty for personnel matters, industrial relations or both. In 12 per cent of cases responsibility for personnel matters and for industrial relations respectively were separately represented on the board. Normally, however, the same individual carried the two briefs. In consequence, personnel and industrial relations were represented in equal proportions.

So far in our analysis the size of *establishment* has been the chief source of variation in the way that managers organised themselves to deal with personnel matters. In relation to board representation it was *organisation* size that was most important. That was especially the case so far as specialist representation was concerned. In organisations that employed more than 10,000 people, two-thirds had board members whose chief responsibilities were for personnel, industrial relations, or both. In organisations employing 25 to 500 people only nine per cent had such specialists. When, however, we looked at variations in relation to the size of *establishments* among enterprises of similar overall size, we found no consistent trends.

Other sources of variation included form of ownership, sector of industry and level of union membership among manual workers. Nationalised industries and overseas owned companies in the private sector were more likely than were private British companies to have specialist board representation. In terms of industrial sector, the incidence of specialist representation was especially marked in transport and communications, reflecting the extent to which that sector was

Table V.14   Incidence of personnel or industrial relations representation on governing bodes in selected sectors

	Specialist represen- tation	Some represen- tation	*Unweighted base*	*Weighted base*
Transport and communica- tions	72	92	*104*	*90*
Gas, electricity and water	(63)²	(74)	*47*	*29*
Distribution	47	77	*188*	*161*
Bricks, pottery, glass and cement	(46)	(76)	*29*	*17*
Chemicals	43	81	*50*	*30*
Food, drink and tobacco	42	82	*97*	*58*
Vehicles and shipbuilding	35	59	*69*	*28*
Electrical and instrument engineering	34	71	*101*	*49*
Miscellaneous services	32	63	*136*	*204*
Paper, printing and publishing	21	57	*65*	*60*
Metal manufacture	(20)	(62)	*47*	*30*
Mechanical engineering	18	62	*99*	*88*
Construction	14	67	*71*	*96*
Professional services	13	49	*67*	*88*

Base: establishments other than government bodies

¹ See note B

nationalised. Beyond that, it is worth listing the figures for some of the sectors that were of greater interest (see Table V.14).

Of special interest to our inquiry was the extent to which board representation was associated with trade union organisation. In prac- tice, that association was slight. There was some sign that, overall, there was a tendency for specialist personnel or industrial relations representation on the board to be more common where the level of trade union membership at establishments was higher. That association, however, disappeared when we confined analysis to establishments that were part of enterprises of similar size. Of course, it was clear that it was not easy for us to explore sources of variation in board representation, as such representation was principally associated with the character- istics of enterprises rather than those of establishments, while our information related to the traits of establishments and only indirectly to those of enterprises. One feature of labour relations, however, that did appear to be associated with board representation was the most important level of bargaining over periodic increases in rates of pay. Here the most noteworthy contrast was between those establishments where the most important bargaining level over rates of pay for manual workers was the company and those where the most important level was the plant. In cases where company bargaining was the most important level, enterprises were most likely to have specialist representation on the board, while in cases where the most important level was the plant, enterprises were least likely to have specialist representation. Table V.15 summarises the details.

Table V.15   Specialist personnel representation on the board in relation to enterprise size and most important bargaining level over pay

Percentages

Number employed by organisation	All establishments	Company bargaining most important	Plant bargaining most important
25–500	9	21	3
501–10,000	41	46	35
10,000 or more	66	79	57

Base: private sector or trading establishments

The pattern is very striking. It mirrors the relationship between levels of bargaining and board representation found in the Warwick survey of manufacturing industry[9]. The implication of the findings is that enterprises tend to be characterised by either a tendency to centralisation over pay bargaining which is associated with personnel or industrial relations representation on the board or a tendency towards decentralisation which is reflected in importance being attached to plant bargaining but involves lack of personnel representation on the board.

Evidence of change in the extent of specialised personnel management

Analysing our findings in a purely contemporary context, we were struck by the rarity of personnel managers at our establishments and the rarity of formal qualifications among the practising personnel managers that we did identify. Fewer than one half of our respondents spent a major part of their time on personnel work and one half of managers who did spend a major part of their time on personnel work were not personnel specialists. That meant that about one quarter of all our respondents were personnel managers. Moreover, one half of personnel specialists had no formal qualifications for personnel work. Where personnel managers did have qualifications, the most common type was membership of a professional association.

Just as personnel managers were employed at a minority of our establishments, so personnel directors sat on a minority of the enterprise boards that governed our establishments. Where our workplaces were part of organisations that had company boards or equivalent bodies, there was specialist personnel representation on one third of them. Where the board governed an organisation employing 10,000 or more people, the proportion with a personnel director rose to two-thirds.

In contrast with the initial impression we developed from our findings, the Warwick study[10] was clearly impressed by the increase of specialisation in personnel management and the emphasis given to personnel management in the manufacturing establishments that it studied. Indeed, through reference to earlier surveys[11] the Warwick analysis showed that there did appear to have been a substantial increase over the previous decade in the number of manufacturing units employing industrial relations specialists and the number of manufacturing company boards with specialist industrial relations directors. The indications from the Warwick study were that the introduction of major employment legislation during the 1970s gave a considerable boost to the personnel function. Certainly, previous research by PSI also suggested that one of the main effects of employment legislation[12] was to strengthen the influence and impact of personnel managers within the management team. But we are left with the contrast between Warwick's interpretation of its findings and the initial impressions derived from our own. Part of the reason for the difference was that Warwick focused on manufacturing units with 50 or more full time employees, while our industrial coverage was substantially more extensive and included establishments with 25 or more employees, full time or part time. When we identified the sub-sample of establishments that we interviewed that was comparable with those that made up the Warwick sample, we found very little difference in the actual figures, where they referred to the same questioning. With regard to board representation, the results were very similar. Both studies found that there was some industrial relations representation upon boards in about two-thirds of cases and specialist representation in about one third. With regard to specialist personnel management, the position was more complex, owing to different forms of questioning. Warwick found that 46 per cent of respondents said that personnel work was their *main* area of responsibility and took that proportion as its measure of specialist personnel management on site. In manufacturing establishments with

50 or more full time employees, we found that 54 per cent of respondents said that they spent *a major part* of their time on personnel work. But we found, further, that only about one half of such people had job titles which identified them as personnel or industrial relations managers. We adopted a narrower definition of *specialist* than did Warwick and used it to refer to people who both spent a major part of their time on personnel work and had job titles which broadly identified them as personnel or industrial relations managers. Hence the difference between our analysis and that of Warwick resulted partly from our wider coverage, partly from differences in definition of a personnel or industrial relations specialist and partly from differences in perspective. Warwick was impressed by its evidence of an increase in both industrial relations represesntation upon boards and specialist management at workplaces. We were struck by the number of establishments and governing bodies that still lacked personnel specialists despite the growth through the 1970s.

Notes

1. Commission on Industrial Relations, *The Role of Management in Industrial Relations* (HMSO, London, 1973) p. 15.
2   P. Anthony and A. Crichton, *Industrial Relations and the Personnel Specialists* (Batsford, London 1969); S.R. Timperley and M.D. Osbaldeston, 'The Professionalisation Process: An Aspiring Occupational Organisation', *Sociological Review*, Vol. 23, pp. 607–77; A.J. Watson, *The Personnel Managers* (Routledge and Kegan Paul, London, 1977).
3. In this chapter we chiefly use *personnel work* in a general sense to cover both the personnel and industrial relations functions. Where we want to distinguish between these two functions the function is made explicit.
4. W.W. Daniel, *Wage Determination in Industry* (Political and Economic Planning No. 563, London, 1976); William Brown, Ed., *The Changing Contours of British Industrial Relations* (Basil Blackwell, Oxford 1981).
5. In 165 of the 2,040 establishments where interviewing was carried out the senior manager dealing with industrial, staff or employee relations, who was defined as the primary respondent, was *not* able to answer all the questions in the management schedule, and the interviewer was passed on to a colleague who answered the outstanding questions. The colleague was defined as the secondary respondent. In the main the information in this chapter about the characteristics of respondents is based upon primary respondents but we also have a small section which compares the characteristics of secondary with primary respondents.
6. In the rest of the chapter, in order to provide stylistic variation, we refer to people with job titles that identified them as engaged in personnel or industrial relations work as *personnel managers, personnel specialists* or people with *personnel* job titles.
7. Glasgow University Media Group, *Bad News* (Routledge and Kegan Paul, London, 1976); Robert Taylor, *Workers and the New Depression* (Macmillan, London, 1982).
8. W.W. Daniel, *op cit*; W.E.J. McCarthy and S.R. Parker, *Shop Stewards and Workshop Relations* (Donovan Research Paper 10, HMSO, London, 1968).
9. William Brown, Ed., *op. cit.*
10. William Brown, Ed., *op. cit.*
11. Government Social Survey, *Workplace Industrial Relations* (HMSO, London, 1968); A.I. Marsh, 'The Staffing of Industrial Relations Management in the

Engineering Industry', *Industrial Relations Journal*, II. No. 2, 1976; Stanley Parker, *Workplace Industrial Relations 1972* (OPCS, HMSO, London, 1974); British Institute of Management, *The Board of Directors* (BIM, London, 1972).

12.   W.W. Daniel and Elizabeth Stilgoe, *The Impact of Employment Protection Laws* (Policy Studies Institute No. 577, London, 1978).

VI Consultative Committees and Other Channels of Representation

In Chapters II and III we described a number of features of trade union representation at the workplace and extended this in Chapter IV by looking at institutional arrangements on the trade union side. In this chapter we examine other channels of representation, beginning with joint consultative committees and then looking at other committees with employee representatives.

Consultative committees

We asked management and primary worker representatives in all establishments whether at their establishment they had any joint committees of managers and employees primarily concerned with consultation rather than negotiation (Q120a; WQ55a). Health and Safety Committees were excluded and dealt with separately, and interviewers were instructed to exclude committees dealing with specific issues such as canteen, recreation, social or welfare matters.

Table VI.1 shows a very substantial degree of agreement between management and worker representatives about the extent of consultative committees. The slight tendency for managers to report a committee more frequently than worker representatives may have arisen

Table VI.1　Proportion of establishments with consultative committees: the accounts of managers and worker representatives compared

Percentages

| | All management respondents | Establishments where both a manager and a worker representative were interviewed | |
		Managers	Either worker representative
Consultative committee reported	37	51	48
Base: as column heads			
Unweighted	*2040*	*1332*	*1332*
Weighted	*2000*	*1072*	*1072*

Table VI.2 Proportion of establishments where manager reported a consultative committee

Percentages

	Private sector	Public sector
All establishments	33	46
Number employed at establishment		
25–99	25	33
100–499	44	63
500–999	63	72
1000 or more	71	86
Number employed by organisation		
25–500	21	(29)[1]
501–2000	40	43
2001–10000	40	43
1000 or more	50	53
Base: all establishments		
Unweighted 2040		
Weighted 2000		

[1] See note B

from minor uncertainties about the scope of the question, particularly with regard to inactive committees. But the degree of agreement is sufficient to justify using either management or worker representative reports as an adequate indication of existence of committees. The fact that we have management interviews for the whole sample is a strong reason for using them for purposes of general description, and this will be our practice for most of this chapter.

Managers reported the existence of a consultative committee in 37 per cent of establishments overall, a figure that suggests substantial growth, as we shall see later. Establishment size, organisation size and ownership appear to be the main characteristics associated with the presence of consultative committees, establishment size being particularly influential. In workplaces with 1,000 or more employees, nearly 80 per cent of managers said they had consultative committees; only one quarter did so in workplaces with 25 to 49 employees. The contrast between establishments belonging to very large organisations and those which were part of small organisations was quite strong. Table VI.2 shows how both establishment size and organisation size affected the occurrence of consultative committees, with the private sector and public sector shown separately. Committees were more likely to occur

Table VI.3 The overlap between consultative committees and collective bargaining

	All employees	Manual employees	Non-manual employees
As proportion of **establishments**		Column percentages	
(a) **No** JCC and **no** recognised trade unions	26	36	41
(b) **A** JCC and **no** recognised trade unions	7	6	9
(c) **No** JCC **but** trade unions recognised for at least some workers	37	38	30
(d) **A** JCC **and** trade unions recognised for at least some workers	30	20	20
As proportion of **employees**		Column percentages	
(a) **No** JCC and **no** recognised trade unions	10	11	7
(b) **A** JCC and **no** recognised trade unions	5	4	8
(c) **No** JCC **but** trade unions recognised for at least some workers	30	37	40
(d) **A** JCC **and** trade unions recognised for at least some workers	54	48	45
Base: establishments employing categories at column heads			
Unweighted	*2040*	*1899*	*2034*
Weighted	*2000*	*1833*	*1989*

in the public sector: almost one half of public sector establishments had them, compared with one third of private sector establishments. Very little of this difference is explained by different sizes of establishment between the two sectors. In each category of establishment size, public sector establishments were considerably more likely to have committees. Most of the effect of organisation size was accounted for by the greater prevalence of small organisations in the private sector, but in both sectors the tendency to have establishment level consultative committees was markedly greater in establishments belonging to organisations which employed 10,000 or more people.

Until now there has been no extensive evidence as to whether joint consultative machinery is more or less common than collective bargaining machinery in Britain or, indeed, whether the two types of arrangement are more common as alternatives to each other or as complementary to each other. Table VI.3 shows that where there was a single method of representation (rows b and c in the table) that channel was about five times more likely to be through collective bargaining with one or more trade unions than it was to be through joint consultative committees. Where consultative machinery existed, it was about four times more likely to exist alongside collective bargaining than it was to exist on its own. Where a consultative committee was the only method of representation, that tended to be in small establishments: in the private sector 72 per cent of establishments with only a consultative committee had less than 100 employees; 98 per cent had less than 500 employees. Establishments with both channels of representation were more evenly spread in terms of size, although the tendency was for the incidence of both channels to be considerably higher in the larger size bands.

These relationships with establishment size naturally increase the coverage of the various arrangements when we examine the proportion of employees rather than the proportion of establishments. Thus in Table VI.3 we see that more than one half of employees were in establishments with a consultative committee and one or more recognised trade unions (the 'complementary' case), and only 10 per cent of employees were in establishments with neither form of employee representation. Non-manual workers were twice as likely as manual workers to be represented by a consultative committee only, but even so, less than 10 per cent were represented in only this way.

The growth of consultative committees

To establish the extent to which consultative committees were becoming more or less common, where the establishments had a committee we asked, for the two committees covering the most workers (if there were several), when the committee was introduced (Q121c; WQ56c); where no committee currently existed we asked if there had ever been one, and if so when it had last met (Q120b, c; WQ55b, c). The results indicated a clear pattern of growth. Within the three years prior to the survey, consultative committees had been introduced in nine per cent of establishments (seven per cent if the introduction of a second or subsequent committee is excluded), but abandoned in only one per cent. In the two years prior to that (roughly mid-1975 to mid-1977) seven per cent had introduced a committee whereas one per cent reported having abandoned them. In all, only three per cent of managers reported that they had ever had a consultative committee but given it up. These comparisons between 'births' and 'deaths' of consultative committees may, however, overstate the situation. Establishments that had closed down or dropped below 25 employees since 1977 (when our sample was effectively drawn) would not be represented, and there may have been a bias in the recall of our respondents. This was checked as far as possible by comparing the answers on the demise of committees for respondents with varying length of job tenure. From this it appeared that there was no clear tendency for respondents with short job tenure to report less frequently the demise of consultative committees several years ago. In the more extreme cases, they must either have held other jobs in the establishment, and therefore have known about the demise of committees, or must have been drawing on the 'collective memory' of the establishment. Hence, if there was a bias arising from differential recall it was presumably not very pronounced.

Taking these sources of bias together suggests that our results may slightly overstate the growth of consultative committees. Nevertheless, with establishments with newly introduced committees outnumbering those that have abandoned them by about nine to one, we can be sure that some growth has taken place. The findings of previous surveys[1] point in the same direction and strengthen the conclusion.

The results show that the growth in consultative machinery has been a very general phenomenon. Establishments of different sizes were equally affected; there had been slightly more growth in the private sector than in the public sector; and, in industry terms, the services sector, particularly distribution, appeared to have been more active. There were few differences in terms of the pattern of recognition. When, however, we analysed the circumstances of single committees introduced within the previous five years in relation to who was represented on the committee, an important pattern emerged (Q120g; WQ55g). In those cases where only manual workers had recognised unions, about one third of the committees had only manual representatives and nearly two-thirds had both manual and non-manual representatives. In other words, the composition of the newly formed consultative committee included representatives of those sections of the workforce already represented by recognised unions and, possibly, those without recognised unions. It almost never happened that one group was represented by recognised unions only while the other group was represented only on the newly introduced consultative committee. However, these results are for those establishments with a single consultative committee. As we shall see shortly, second and subsequent committees are more likely to be for groups not represented by recognised trade unions.

The structure of joint consultation
Of the 37 per cent of establishments with an extant consultative committee, three-quarters had a single committee for the establishment (28 per cent of all establishments), the remainder having two or more. One per cent had five or more, and those were almost invariably large workplaces (Q120e; WQ55e). Some of them had comprehensive trade

union representation; some had none. It is likely that such establishments had different committees for different departments, with perhaps a super-ordinate committee for the whole establishment. Establishments with more than one committee were generally also those with many recognised trade unions, a characteristic strongly associated with establishment size. Managers were asked whether manual or non-manual or both sections of the workforce had representatives on their consultative committee (Q120g). On the principal committees there were manual and non-manual representatives in about one half of the cases. Of the other half, about two-thirds were cases where the committee had only non-manual representatives. Second committees, where they existed, were much less likely to have both manual and non-manual representatives. (Less than one quarter did so, compared with more than one half for major committees.) Indeed, one half of cases with two consultative committees were cases where manual representatives only were on one committee and non-manuals only were on the other. Hence, a separate committee for manual and non-manual staff goes a long way towards explaining the existence of two or more committees at the same establishment.

The relationship between collective bargaining and consultative machinery is shown in Table VI.4 for the principal consultative committee. Very few of these committees covered a group of workers who were not also covered by collective bargaining arrangements. For example, in only eight per cent of establishments where manual workers were represented by recognised trade unions and non-manual workers were not, was there a consultative committee for non-manual workers only.

In 45 per cent of establishments where there were manual or non-manual trade union members all employee representatives were chosen by the union members[2]. This form of appointment was also strongly related to trade union membership density and, to a lesser extent, the presence of several unions and several negotiating groups (Table VI.5). In nearly 70 per cent of establishments with a full time union representative, managers said that all the consultative committee representatives were chosen by the unions or staff associations (Q121d; WQ56d). The choice of only some of the worker representatives' seats by the unions (11 per cent of establishments with union members present) was not related so clearly to these aspects of trade union organisation, but did appear least likely where there was a comprehensive closed shop. In the remaining 44 per cent of cases, managers reported that none of the worker representatives on the consultative committee was chosen by the unions or staff associations. These were mostly cases where membership density was low or where the unions had members but were not recognised for collective bargaining. This points to the conclusion that

Table VI.4 Composition of principal consultative committee

Row percentages

	Composition of principal consultative committee					
	Manual workers only	Non-manual workers only	Both categories	Not answered	*Un-weighted base*	*Weighted base*
Manual unions recognised but non-manuals not recognised	38	8	45	10	*127*	*118*
Non-manual unions recognised but manual unions not recognised	(3)[1]	(73)	(17)	(7)	*49*	*52*
Both manual and non-manual unions recognised	16	23	52	9	*676*	*383*

Base: establishments where consultative committee reported by manager and both manual and non-manual workers were employed

See note B

consultative committees may tend to become an adjunct to the institutions of collective bargaining where workplace trade union organisation is well established, but provide an alternative channel of representation where it is weak. Further evidence for such a conclusion is given in the next section.

The operation of consultative committees

Only crude indications of the functioning of committees can be obtained from standardised surveys, but they provide a useful supplement to the findings of case studies and other more intensive research methods. We asked about the frequency of meetings, how often senior management attended them and whether discussion at the committee was communicated back to the bulk of employees, in relation to the two committees covering the largest numbers of workers, although most establishments had only a single committee (Q121a, b; Q122; WQ56a, b; WQ58). A prior consideration, of course, is whether a consultative committee is acknowledged to exist. As Table VI.1 showed, there was not universal agreement about the existence of a committee between

Table VI.5   Extent to which trade unions nominated representatives on principa consultative committee

Row percentage

	Trade union nominated					
	All	Some	None	Not answered	*Un-weighted base*	*Weighte base*
All establishments with union members	42	11	42	5	*925[2]*	*640*
Full-time union representation						
Full-time union representative	69	14	13	4	*184*	*49*
No full-time union representative	43	11	41	5	*751*	*591*
Number of recognised unions						
No recognised union	4	5	75	16	*52*	*53*
One or two unions recognised	42	14	42	2	*281*	*274*
Three or four unions	51	9	39	1	*206*	*139*
Five or more unions	50	10	36	4	*396*	*173*
Number of negotiating groups						
One negotiating group	35	12	46	7	*149*	*151*
Two groups	46	10	35	9	*263*	*211*
Three groups	44	9	41	6	*157*	*95*
Four or more groups	54	14	31	1	*302*	*125*
Closed shop arrangements						
Open shop	39	11	47	3	*463*	*347*
Partial closed shop	57	13	28	2	*356*	*190*
Comprehensive manual and non-manual closed shop	51	8	39	2	*64*	*49*
Overall union membership density						
Low (up to 30 per cent)	12	13	59	17	*78*	*64*
Medium (30 per cent to 80 per cent)	34	12	51	3	*312*	*218*
High (over 80 per cent)	63	12	23	2	*370*	*227*
Not known	34	7	50	9	*175*	*131*

Base: establishments with trade union members

[1] See note C
[2] See note H

management and worker representatives. Our analysis therefore takes as its starting point those cases where the manager reported that the major consultative committee covered manual workers or non-manual workers and the relevant worker representative also reported a consultative committee.

Table VI.6   Characteristics of principal consultative committee[1]

	Committee covering manual workers		Committee covering non-manual workers	
	Private sector	Public sector	Private sector	Public sector
Frequency of meetings			Column percentages[2]	
At least once per month	56	21	47	36
At least once per 3 months	36	70	46	56
Less than once per 3 months	6	8	7	6
Not answered	1	1	—	2
				Percentages
All meetings attended by senior managment	88	94	89	91
Base: establishments where a committee was reported by both manager and worker representative				
Unweighted	*262*	*124*	*177*	*175*
Weighted	*149*	*76*	*96*	*119*

Reported by management respondent
See note C

Overall, as Table VI.6 shows, in nearly one half of establishments with a consultative committee managers reported that the principal (or only) committee met at least as often as once a month. In less than 10 per cent of cases did it meet less often than once every three months. Committees covering manual workers met considerably more often in the private sector establishments than in the public sector ones and more often than committees covering non-manual workers. Frequency of meeting showed little variation with other establishment characteristics such as size and industry, except that it was greater where there was a full time union representative. Worker representatives' estimates of the frequency of meetings accorded very closely with those of management respondents. There was also close agreement about the proportion of committee meetings attended by senior management. Between 80 per cent and 90 per cent of both sets of respondents said senior management attended all meetings. Interestingly, although this measure showed little variation, foreign owned establishments reported senior managers attending less frequently. This, of course, might simply reflect different conceptions of 'senior'; or it might reflect the lesser availability of senior managers in foreign owned enterprises.

The great majority of respondents said that discussion at the consultative committee was communicated to other managers, or to the

Table VI.7 Methods of reporting back to management and workforce from principal consultative committee

	Committee covering manual workers		Committee covering non-manual workers	
	Private	Public	Private	Public
Reporting back to management[1]			Column percentages[2]	
Separate meeting	5	2	7	6
Orally/informally	23	14	16	18
Minutes circulated	75	89	80	73
Notice board	19	12	14	10
No communication	2	2	1	8
Reporting back to workforce[3]			Column percentages[2]	
Separate meeting	10	6	3	10
Orally/informally	25	31	24	16
Minutes circulated	55	54	67	60
Notice board	42	40	30	17
No communication	2	1	5	14
Base: establishments where committee was reported by both manager and relevant worker representative				
Unweighted	*262*	*124*	*177*	*175*
Weighted	*149*	*76*	*96*	*119*

[1] Managers' accounts
[2] See note E
[3] Worker representatives' accounts

workforce, but there were significant exceptions, notably with respect to committees covering non-manual employees (Table VI.7). For these, eight per cent of managers in the public sector reported no communication to other managers and 14 per cent of worker representatives reported no communication to fellow non-manual employees. All these cases fell in the local and central government services and not in the nationalised industries. Where the deliberations of consultative committees were communicated back, the most common method for both other managers and the workforce was by the circulation of written minutes. This method was more commonly used for non-manual employees than it was for manual employees, for whom it was more common to use notice boards. In the public sector, informal oral communication was more common for manual employees than for non-manual employees, but there was no corresponding difference in the private sector. Generally, our respondents mentioned only one method of communication. Where more than one occurred, the circulation of minutes and the use of notice boards was the most frequent combination.

Finally, respondents were asked to mention what they thought was the most important matter discussed by the committee in the last year (Q123; WQ59). This open question was coded using a frame of 21 response categories developed from the questionnaire answers, the same frame being applied to both management and worker representative answers. The results show a surprising consistency and suggest that very few consultative committees discussed nothing of substance.

Comparison of manual worker representatives' answers with management ones in the same establishments gave the following results for the major (or only) committee. Three issues were mentioned most frequently by both sets of respondents.

production issues (for example, keeping up production, level of production, increasing productivity, work scheduling)

employment issues (for example, maintaining employment, avoiding redundancy, keeping people in work, coping with reduction in demand, job security)

pay issues (for example, wage/salary reviews, bonus, payment-by-results)

There was also agreement on the next seven issues in terms of their frequency of mention.

working conditions (general or specific, for example, noise, ventilation, heat, dirt, cleanliness)

welfare services

health and safety matters

future trends (for example, plans for future, general company policy)

fringe benefits

financial issues (for example, financial progress, details of company finance)

administrative changes (for example, office/factory reorganisation, relocation of offices, departments)

Thus the same ten issues were most frequently mentioned by both manual worker representatives and managers in the same establishments. Naturally enough there were slight differences in the rank order within the ten, but the only one of any magnitude was in relation to health and safety matters, which worker representatives mentioned more frequently than managers. Surprisingly, the same ten issues were mentioned most frequently by non-manual representatives and their corresponding managers. Again there was accord on the three most frequently mentioned issues, although in this case working conditions replaced pay issues in the top three. No issue stood out as being more frequently mentioned by either non-manual representatives or management. The proportion of respondents who took the view that the major consultative committee never discussed anything important at all was low: three per cent of managers, five per cent of manual worker representatives and eight per cent of non-manual worker representatives.

A number of other issues were coded but were rarely mentioned by any respondent. These included new participation or consultation arrangements/industrial democracy; discipline/dismissals; changes in the distribution of hours of work; employment legislation; grievance and other procedures; training; trade union representation/recognition; the closed shop; energy conservation; a change of ownership; industrial disputes.

Further light can be shed on the overlap between consultative machinery and collective bargaining machinery if we relate responses to those concerning the scope of collective bargaining. The comparison is not a precise one, because the consultative committee question asked only about the most important issue discussed, whereas the bargaining scope question asked about each of ten issues in turn. Also, the bargaining scope question referred to only the largest negotiating group of manual workers, not to manual workers as a whole (Q41; Q72). Nevertheless, if we focus on employment issues (recruitment, manning levels and redundancy) and look only at consultative committees covering manual workers, an impression of overlap can be gained. Where employment issues were negotiated at establishment level, they were more likely to be mentioned as the most important issue discussed at the consultative committee than they were in establishments where employment issues were not negotiated at establishment level (or not negotiated at all). Thus, despite the fact that the form of our questioning was not specifically designed to address this problem, the survey offers some evidence that where consultative machinery and collective bargaining machinery exist together there is some overlap in the issues with which they deal.

The foregoing analysis supports the conclusion of a number of researchers that the practice of joint consultation achieved something of a resurgence in the 1970s. The evidence of other researchers was limited in one way or another – for example, in its industrial coverage, or in its regional coverage or in its use of managerial respondents alone. The results presented here are based upon multiple respondents, with a generally high level of agreement, and extend the evidence on the growth of consultation to the service sectors, both public and private. The evidence shows that joint consultation quite often exists alongside collective bargaining but, less often, may be the sole formal channel of employee representation. In either case, there are several indications that consultative committees were taken seriously by our respondents, most of whom would have been personally involved in the committees, and that the issues dealt with were important.

Other channels of employee representation

So far our analysis of the forms of employee representation other than collective bargaining has focused on joint consultative committees. We also asked about the presence of representative machinery in establishments where manual or non-manual workers were not represented by recognised trade unions, hoping to identify situations where there was a representative committee that had functions other than joint consultation (Q47; Q78). In the event, such committees were relatively rare, and most of the answers obtained to this question referred to the consultative committee. In about one half of the establishments where managers reported both types of machinery we were certain that the same committee was being referred to in both questions, because interviewers recorded the names of those on the committees and these were the same for both answers. There were probably further cases where the same committee was being referred to, but the identity was not established from the recorded names.

Given this overlap and the extensive analysis, already described, on consultative committees, we will restrict our discussion of 'representative committee' cases to that three per cent of establishments where they existed on their own. Almost all of them were in the private sector, divided about equally between the manufacturing and service sectors. Two-thirds of them were in establishments of less than 100 employees. Almost none were in establishments of 500 or more. A very few were in establishments where manual workers had recognised unions and the representative committee provided the channel for non-manual representation in the absence of recognised unions for non-manual workers; almost all were in establishments where there were no recognised unions. A substantial minority were in establishments where the management respondent had refused to answer our question about trade union membership, saying that it was company policy not to have such information. In these cases it is arguable that management had a definite anti-union policy[3] and it is interesting that such establishments were twice as likely to have some form of employee representative structure as establishments where the manager had stated there were no union members. However, the general picture of these committees is that they were a channel for employee representation where collective bargaining, in the sense that we defined it, did not take place, but where something other than consultation did occur.

Health and safety committees

The establishment of joint committees with managers and trade union appointed worker representatives to deal specifically with health and safety at the workplace has been an important development in the last decade. The Health and Safety at Work Act, 1974 contains provisions, brought into force in October 1978, which allow recognised trade unions to appoint safety representatives. Two or more such representatives at a particular workplace may request the formation of a joint committee for health and safety and the request must be met within three months.

To see to what extent these provisions had been used by trade unions, and at the same time to gain a more general picture of health and safety consultation, we asked managers how health and safety matters were dealt with in the establishment (Q125a). Only one per cent of managers said that they had no provision, giving the reason that no health and safety issues had arisen. Where the reply referred to a joint committee specifically for health and safety, managers were asked, in addition, how long the committee had been established (Q126b). We did not ask a further question about whether the committee was established at the request of trade union representatives, but the age of committees is sufficient to indicate that the 1974 Act had a major influence upon their foundation.

Overall, 37 per cent of establishments were reported to have a joint committee specifically for health and safety. Of these, less than one third had been established prior to mid-1975. Nearly one half of the remainder had been set up since mid-1977, when the Regulations had already been laid before Parliament. A further 12 per cent of managers reported the existence of a joint committee which dealt with health and safety among other matters. Another 21 per cent said there were worker representatives for health and safety, but no joint committee. In the remainder of establishments (just over one quarter) health and safety was dealt with by management alone, with no provision for consultation. Thus 49 per cent of establishments had joint committees either dealing specifically with health and safety or dealing with it as part of a larger remit. Such committees were much more likely where there were recognised trade unions – 60 per cent of establishments with recognised trade unions had them – and where trade union membership at the establishment was high. Establishment size was also positively correlated with the presence of health and safety committees (Table VI.8). However, when we controlled for establishment size, with which the presence of recognised unions was positively correlated, it remained the case that establishments with recognised unions, particularly manual unions, were much more likely to have a specific health and safety committee.

	Joint health and safety committee	General committee	Representatives but no committee	No consultation or representation	Other answer	Unweighted base	Weighted base
All establishments	37	12	21	27	3	2040[2]	2000
Number employed at establishment							
25–49	20	11	23	41	5	367	785
50–99	35	11	23	24	7	380	528
100–199	45	14	19	18	4	399	347
200–499	64	13	13	9	1	378	206
500–999	79	10	6	4	1	249	83
1000–1999	81	7	8	3	1	143	34
2000 or more	89	3	8	—	—	124	17
Union recognition							
Any recognised unions	47	12	22	15	3	1585	1335
No recognised unions	17	12	16	51	4	465	665
Manual union density[3]							
Low	31	9	35	18	7	152	174
Medium	46	11	21	16	6	360	295
High	60	14	15	8	3	748	232
Proportion of manual workers in total workforce[3]							
Low	37	10	25	22	6	429	376
Medium	47	12	25	11	5	499	414
High	53	13	19	12	3	647	545

Base: all establishments

[1] See note C
[2] See note H
[3] Base confined to establishments where manual unions were recognised

In relation to the impact of the Health and Safety at Work Act, 1974, it is also noteworthy that about 30 per cent of establishments with no recognised trade unions had such committees. Since the ages of those committees were similar to the ages of committees where there were recognised trade unions, it is arguable that the Act has had a significant impact, in that the setting up of committees has occurred more widely than may be accounted for by statutory requirements. The impact has, however, by no means been even across all types of establishment. Smaller establishments were much less likely to have any formal provision for consultation on health and safety matters (see Table VI.8). Clearly this is partly because they are less often unionised. Indeed, the effect of establishment size is so marked that the overall proportion of employees who were in establishments with no provision for consultation on health and safety was as low as 10 per cent. In very small establishments (those below our threshold of 25 employees) this proportion was substantially greater[4]. Apart from the size of the workforce, other workforce characteristics were clearly also important. Establishments with a predominantly non-manual workforce were nearly one half as likely as other establishments to have a provision for consultation on health and safety. Those with a predominantly female labour force were slightly less likely to have any provision, but where they did it was twice as likely to be individual representatives only, and half as likely to be a specific health and safety committee.

There were also some noticeable industry differences (see Table VI.9) but these were partly a reflection of different sizes of establishment. Overall, 15 per cent of establishments with one or more recognised trade unions had no provision for health and safety consultation (neither a committee nor individual representatives), but this figure rose to 19 per cent in vehicle manufacturing, 29 per cent in distribution, 49 per cent in financial and business services and 24 per cent in construction.

The findings we have shown indicate that there has indeed been a growth in the provision for dealing with health and safety matters at the workplace, although saturation point has by no means been reached. Viewed as a development in formal consultative structures, the growth of joint health and safety committees is significant and is one element of the increasingly complex consultative machinery that characterises large workplaces.

Job evaluation committees

Another type of issue-specific committee involving workforce representatives that we asked about was the kind of committee dealing with the administration of job evaluation schemes. The schemes themselves will be discussed in some detail in Chapter VIII. For present purposes

	Joint health and safety committee	General committee	Representatives but no committee	No consultation or representation	Other answer	Average number employed at establishment	Unweighted base	Weighted base
All establishments	37	12	21	27	3	145	2040	2000
Food, drink, tobacco, chemicals²	57	13	7	23	*	297	141	88
Metals; mechanical engineering; metal goods	55	19	11	13	3	205	205	172
Electrical engineering	61	10	21	7	1	421	102	49
Vehicles	55	11	12	17	5	640	70	28
Textiles; clothing	44	10	17	29	*	142	97	80
All other manufacturing	58	11	12	16	3	185	160	138
Construction	23	12	19	41	5	109	102	130
Gas, electricity, water, transport, communication	54	17	12	12	5	152	191	155
Distribution	25	16	18	37	4	65	189	262
Financial services	16	5	17	59	3	83	76	95
Professional and scientific services	30	7	35	20	8	103	363	372
Miscellaneous services	20	7	25	46	2	55	163	243
Public administration	41	15	30	12	2	193	181	188

Base: all establishments

¹ See note C
² The row labels represent abbreviated descriptions of the sectors covered. See Appendix A for a full account

Table VI.10   The presence of various forms of employee representation

	Proportion of establishments covered		Proportion of employees covered	
	Percentages[1]	Cumulative percentages[1]	Percentages[2]	Cumulative percentage
Recognised trade unions, for at least one group of employees[2]	67	67	84	84
Joint consultative committee[3]	42	75	66	90
Representation committee[3] but no recognised unions	9	77	8	91
Health and safety committee, (or other committee covering health and safety issues)	49	80	75	93
Job evaluation committee with employee representatives	10	81	22	93
Non-trade union respresenta-tives[3]	13	83	13	94
Trade union representatives not recognised for collective bargaining	3	84	3	94
Base: all establishments				
Unweighted	2040			
Weighted	2000			

[1] The first column (percentages) shows what proportion of *establishments* had each of the lis institutions. The second (cumulative percentages) shows the proportion that had that institut or the previous institutions in the list
[2] The first column (percentages) shows what proportion of *employees* were covered by each of listed institutions. The second (cumulative percentages) shows the proportion of *employees* were covered by that institution or the previous ones
[3] As reported by management *or* worker representative respondents

we need note only that in establishments where job evaluation schemes were reported by our management respondent we asked if there was a committee which reviewed the scheme and decided upon the grading of new or changed jobs. If there was, we then asked if this committee contained employee representatives (Q118g, h). Overall, 10 per cent of establishments had such committees, the likelihood of having them being strongly related to establishment size and the presence of recognised trade unions.

The significance of such committees in terms of the overall picture of employee representation is, however, much less than the figure of 10 per cent indicates. Establishments having them were also very likely to have one of the types of representative committee already mentioned or to have recognised trade unions for at least some employees. In fact, as Table VI.10 shows, including establishments with joint job evaluation committees added less than one per cent to the proportion of establishments with some form of employee representation.

Non-union individual representatives

So far we have been discussing channels of representation of a collective nature, as evidenced by the presence of a committee of one sort or another. We knew, however, from previous research that in some workplaces there might well be individual representatives who discussed with management matters affecting the manual or non-manual workforce – or sections or individuals within it – and, accordingly, asked about such representatives in establishments where trade unions were not recognised for collective bargaining (Q48a, b; Q79a, b; WQ45a, b). Our questions distinguished between union and non-union representatives. As can be seen from Table VI.10, individual non-trade union representatives were not uncommon, occurring in 13 per cent of establishments. They were almost all to be found in the private sector, particularly in distribution and miscellaneous service industries. A majority of them represented white collar employees but, surprisingly, they were just as common in large establishments as in small ones.

If we add the establishments having these individual, non-union representatives to the establishments having any of the other forms of representation mentioned previously, this raises the proportion from 81 per cent to 83 per cent (see Table VI.10). Most of the overlap with other forms of representation is with joint consultative committees and health and safety committees.

Trade union representatives not recognised for collective bargaining

The remaining type of representative we asked about was one who was a trade union member, possibly a shop steward, who was recognised by management for dealing with a limited range of issues but not for collective bargaining about pay and conditions of employment (Q46a; Q77a; WQ43a). Again, we asked about such representatives only in establishments where no part of the manual or non-manual workforce had representatives recognised for collective bargaining. This type of union representative was rare, being reported by management in only three per cent of establishments. This occurrence was most common in the financial services sector, and, generally, in smaller establishments. Again, such representatives add very little to the proportion of establishments having any of the forms of representation we have previously mentioned.

Taking the presence of any of the forms of representation shown in Table VI.10 as an indication that at least some sections of the workforce have formal representatives who deal with management on their behalf, the overall picture is of widespread representation in the British economy. Over four-fifths of establishments had some form of employee representation. Most of these forms of representation were more common in larger establishments – the proportion rose from 74 per cent in workplaces with under 50 employees to 99 per cent in those with over 500 employees.

Disclosure of information

We attempted to learn something of the context in which machinery for consultation at workplace level operated by asking questions on the information about their establishment given by management to worker representatives[5]. We first asked both management and worker representatives to assess the amount of information given on each of three broad topics: pay and conditions of service; manpower requirements; and the financial position of the establishment (Q124; WQ60a). Secondly, we asked about requests for information under the provisions of the Employment Protection Act, 1975 (Q125; WQ61). Worker representatives were also asked how useful they found the information received from management in discussions or negotiations with them (WQ60b).

Managers clearly assessed rather differently the amount of information they gave on the three broad topics. Pay and conditions of employment were the subject of more communication to the workforce than manpower requirements, which in establishments with stable or even growing workforces (about 70 per cent of establishments) could be argued as requiring less communication. The financial position of the establishment was the subject of least communication out of the three topics, a reflection of the extent and scope of collective bargaining, as we shall show shortly.

We asked the question of all managers, including those in establishments with no worker representatives. In such establishments managers must have answered in terms of the workforce as a whole. There is, however, substantial interest in establishments with worker representatives and particularly in those (the great majority) where at least one worker representative was interviewed. In such cases managers' assessments of the amount disclosed were higher than in establishments where no worker representative was interviewed – partly due to the exclusion of small establishments which more often did not have worker representatives – but the relative assessments of the three types of information remained the same.

Worker representatives assessed the amount of information they received a good deal lower than managers assessed the amount they gave. (See Table VI.11). The differences were substantial for all three

Table VI.11 Information about establishment given to worker representatives by management

	Managers' accounts[1]	Manual representatives' accounts	Non-manual representatives' accounts
			Column percentages[2]
Pay and conditions of service			
A great deal of information	55	30	30
Quite a lot	19	23	23
A fair amount	12	22	19
Very little	7	15	16
None	6	8	9
No information	1	1	3
			Column percentages
Manpower requirements			
A great deal of information	33	18	18
Quite a lot	25	23	21
A fair amount	16	18	21
Very little	13	24	26
None	13	16	12
No information	1	1	2
			Column percentages
The financial position of the establishment			
A great deal of information	23	16	15
Quite a lot	18	14	16
A fair amount	20	16	21
Very little	16	23	26
None	22	30	19
No information	2	1	3
Base: as column heads			
Unweighted	*1332*	*1040*	*1016*
Weighted	*1072*	*770*	*722*

In cases where a worker representative was interviewed
See note C

topics and occurred with both manual and non-manual worker representatives. Since these were legitimate differences of opinion, our approach in the rest of this analysis is to look at each set of respondents separately, noting patterns of variation with other establishment characteristics.

Management responses
Managers in larger establishments, and particularly in those with a full

time worker representative such as a convenor, assessed more highly the amount of information disclosed on all three topics. The assessments were also higher where the top governing body of the organisation had a personnel or industrial relations specialist. This could be interpreted as part of a rather general effect of having a professional personnel function in the organisation or, perhaps, the result of a deliberate policy favouring greater disclosure. The highest assessments on all three topics came, however, from managers in nationalised industry establishments, perhaps a reflection of statutory obligations to consult and bargain with trade unions. (When some interviews which were conducted entirely at regional or head offices were eliminated, the difference remained almost as great.) Even in the nationalised industries, however, one quarter of all managers reported that management gave worker representatives very little or no information about the financial position of the establishment. In the private sector, managers' assessments tended to be slightly higher in foreign owned establishments than in UK owned establishments, but this appears to be entirely explicable as a size effect. When we compared foreign and UK owned plants of similar sizes there were no discernible differences.

It was reasonable to suppose that in the private sector the amount of information disclosed might vary according to the recent financial performance of the establishment[6]. It turned out that managers who assessed their establishment's performance as below average also rated lower the amount of information disclosed on pay and conditions and manpower requirements than was the case in better-performing establishments. There was no difference, however, in the assessments of the amount of information given about the establishment's financial performance. Thus there was a greater emphasis on financial information, as against other kinds, when performance was poor – a matter of some significance in the context of collective bargaining.

A clear difference appeared in managers' ratings of the amount of information disclosed according to the proportion of women employed. When this proportion was high (over 70 per cent), the amount of information given, according to managers themselves, was considerably less, even when we controlled for establishment size. This was particularly the case for information about pay and conditions and manpower requirements. This seemed to be at least partly because establishments with a high proportion of women had a less developed representative structure: for example, they were much less likely to have senior stewards or representatives.

There was a noticeable difference in the amount of information that management claimed to give worker representatives about pay and conditions according to the location of pay negotiations. Managers' highest assessments were given when pay negotiations took place at establishment level, for both manual and non-manual employees. It o la also the case that assessments of the amount of financial information disclosed were higher when the establishment was the locus of pay negotiations, indicating the range of information brought to bear on local negotiations about pay. This type of difference, however, did not appear for employment issues: when these were negotiated locally for the largest manual negotiating group, managers' assessments of the amount of information given to worker representatives were no higher than when employment issues were not negotiated locally.

Worker representative responses
The pattern of worker representative responses shows some similarities with the pattern of management responses. The general tendency for the amount of information given to be assessed more highly in larger establishments was repeated in worker representative responses, but in the largest establishments the amount was often assessed lower than it was in establishments in the middle of the size range. As was the case with managers, the presence of a full time worker representative was associated with a higher assessment, so some other factor must have been responsible for the lower assessments in the largest establishments. We have as yet done insufficient analysis to identify this factor. Worker representatives in nationalised industries consistently assessed more highly the amount of information they received about all three types of issue than did their counterparts elsewhere, and the differences were often very substantial. Finally, managers' lower assessment of the amount of information given to worker representatives where the workforce was predominantly female was reflected in the assessments of worker representatives. This was particularly the case for manual worker representatives, and applied for all three kinds of issue. It appears, therefore, that it was workforces that were predominantly female and manual that received the least amount of information from management.

When we asked worker representatives how useful they found the information that management gave them, we did not attempt to distinguish between the three kinds of issue mentioned earlier, but by cross tabulating the two questions a judgement can be made about which kind of issue was having most effect on responses. It appeared that manual worker representatives found information on manpower requirements more useful than did non-manual worker representatives. Non-manual worker representatives, however, appeared to find financial information of greater use than did manual representatives. Otherwise there were no differences. The general tendency was that the higher the assessment of the amount of information given, the more useful was the information regarded.

A further indication of the importance which worker representatives attached to information received from management was given by their assessments of the general state of relations between management and the workforce at the establishment (WQ74). For both manual and non-manual worker representatives there was a strong relationship between high assessments of the amount of information received from management and a favourable assessment of their establishment's industrial relations. For example, only five per cent of manual representatives saying they received 'quite a lot' or a 'great deal' of information on pay and conditions rated their establishment's industrial relations climate as quite bad or worse. On the other hand, 27 per cent of representatives receiving 'very little' or 'no information' on pay and conditions rated their establishment's industrial relations climate at that level. Similar differences occurred for non-manual representatives, and rather less sharply for the other two information topics. This pattern was repeated when we compared managers' assessments of the amount of information given and their assessments of the general state of industrial relations in the establishment (Q146). Hence where managers give little or no information to worker representatives the general industrial relations atmosphere is likely to be regarded as poor.

Disclosure of information requests under the Employment Protection Act, 1975

Both managers and worker representatives were asked whether worker representatives had made requests for disclosure of information under the provisions of the Employment Protection Act, 1975 (Q125; WQ61). Nine per cent of managers in establishments with recognised unions reported having received such a request (six per cent of all establishments). Compared with this, 20 per cent of manual worker representatives and 14 per cent of non-manual representatives reported making requests. When responses were compared establishment by establishment there was agreement in 70 per cent of cases between the manager and the worker representative about reporting or not reporting a request. Most of the cases of disagreement were where a worker representative reported a request under the provisions of the Act but the manager did not. This may have been because the worker representative did not mention his statutory right to the information and the manager might well not have known the request had statutory backing unless he initially refused to provide the information.

It is noticeable that requests for disclosure of information came more frequently from manual worker representatives than from non-manual representatives. However, the ratio of requests was very similar to the ratio of manual to non-manual representatives in all establishments, so there was no difference in their rate of making requests. That is very

Table VI.12   Proportion of establishments where either worker representative had requested information from management under the Employment Protection Act

Percentages

	Number employed at establishment		
	25–99	100–499	500 or more
Establishments with a joint consultative committee	17	29	54
Establishments without a joint consultative committee	9	20	43
Base: establishments with recognised trade unions and where a representative was interviewed			
Unweighted	*1243*		
Weighted	*988*		

different from what happens when the legal appeal machinery is invoked. Of the 134 references made to the Central Arbitration Committee (CAC) by the end of 1980 under section 19 of the Act, nearly two-thirds were brought by white collar trade unions[7]. The preponderance of cases brought by white collar unions (notably ASTMS) appears to be more a reflection of their determination to enforce their rights, or the greater reluctance of the employers they deal with, than any greater use of the provisions at workplace level. But clearly the provisions are used to support requests for information much more extensively than the references to the CAC suggest.

The incidence of requests, as reported by worker representatives, shows a number of variations with establishment characteristics. Requests were more likely in larger establishments, even when analysis was confined to establishments with recognised unions. In addition, the number of trade unions recognised at the workplace, and indeed the number of separate negotiating groups, increased the likelihood of a request. So did the presence of a full time shop steward or convenor. What is more, requests by manual worker representatives were much higher when they said they received no information from management about pay and conditions. These relationships suggest that requests for disclosure were related to what trade union representatives at the workplace thought they needed in the way of information, rather than made in pursuit of a headquarters policy for some reason unrelated to individual workplace circumstances. Requests for disclosure were considerably more common in establishments where collective bargaining was supplemented by formal consultative machinery. This remained true when the effect of establishment size was controlled, as Table

Table VI.13   Accounts of changes made by management with the aim of increasin employee involvement

Column percentage

| | All managers | Cases where any employee representative interviewed | |
		Managers	Employee representative
Any initiative to increase involvement	25	28	23
New consultative committee	6	7	4
New health and safety committee	1	1	1
New joint meetings	4	5	4
Any structural innovation	10	13	9
Improvements to existing committee	1	1	1
More two-way communication	5	5	5
More information to employees	4	4	5
Participation scheme – unspecified	1	1	1
Suggestion or share scheme	1	1	1
Autonomous working groups	1	1	1
Management training for employee participation	1	1	1
Any other conventional participation initiative	13	14	11
Other initiative	4	4	6
Base: as column heads			
Unweighted	*2040*	*1332*	*1332*
Weighted	*2000*	*1072*	*1072*

[1] See note F

VI.12 shows. It cannot be argued from this result that the existence of consultative committees directly stimulates requests for information, but an alternative type of relationship – that the existence of consultative committees reduces the need to request disclosure of information – seems distinctly less plausible in the face of this evidence.

Initiatives to increase employee involvement
To round off our questions on consultation, we asked all respondents if management had made any major change in the last three years with the aim of increasing employees' involvement in the running of their establishment (Q143a, b; WQ71a, b). Answers to these questions were coded using a list of codes built up from the interviewers' written notes, the list being common to management and worker representatives. Some 25 different codes were used, representing a broad range of

initiatives that respondents considered might be designed to increase the involvement of employees. These 25 different responses have been grouped into three broad categories: *institutional innovations*, such as a new joint consultative committee; *other conventional participation initiatives*, such as moves to improve communications, a new suggestion scheme, a share ownership scheme, or the introduction of autonomous working groups; and *other initiatives*, not included in the first two groups, which did not fit into the more commonly held conceptions of 'participation' and 'employee involvement'. Table VI.13 shows the results in aggregate.

As can be seen, the only notable difference between respondents was that managers were more likely than worker representatives to report the introduction of a new joint consultative committee as an initiative to increase employee involvement. Overall, some sort of intitiative was reported in about one quarter of establishments, just under one half of those initiatives being 'institutional innovations' and a further one quarter being what we have termed 'other conventional participation initiatives'. The remaining one quarter of responses referred to the introduction of incentive payment schemes, new pension arrangements, staff status for manual workers and the recognition of trade unions which, although viewed in this light by respondents, are not widely regarded as central to the aim of increasing employees' involvement in the operation of their place of work.

There is some interest in what was left out in response to this question. For example, only one third of managers who reported a joint consultative committee of three years standing or less mentioned a new consultative committee in their response to our question about changes in the last three years to increase employee involvement. Clearly, some of the remaining two-thirds may be accounted for by inaccurate recall over such an extensive period as three years, but it seems that there were some cases where the introduction of a joint consultative committee was not seen as a major change, or was not made with the specific aim of increasing employee involvement, as opposed to serving another purpose, such as facilitating changes in production methods. The same kind of point applies to the introduction of other kinds of committee. Less than five per cent of managers reporting a recently established joint health and safety committee included mention of these committees in their reply to our question on employee involvement initiatives. A similar result obtained for share ownership schemes. It does not follow from this, however, that the introduction of such committees may not have had the effect of increasing the amount of worker participation or involvement: it is necessary to distinguish between the aims of setting up a committee, which may be many and varied, and the effects, which may include increasing the involvement of employees.

Considerable numbers of managers and, more important perhaps, worker representatives reported changes of both structural and qualitative kinds (particularly more information and communication) which can more surely be interpreted as increasing employee involvement, both in intention and effect. Against this must be set the fact that we asked no question about changes introduced by management with the aim of reducing the influence of employees upon decisions concerning the way their establishment was managed. This imbalance of evidence suggests

Table VI.14   **Accounts of changes made by management with the aim of increasin employee involvement in relation to establishment size and owne ship**

Percentag

		All establish- ments	Number employed at establishment		
			25–99	100–499	500 or mo employee
A. All managers					
All private sector	(a)[1]	26	21	35	44
	(b)	10	7	14	23
Nationalised industries	(a)	29	(18)[2]	33	51
	(b)	16	(14)	15	31
Public administration	(a)	24	24	21	31
	(b)	10	8	9	24
B. Managers where employee representatives were interviewed					
All private sector	(a)	30	25	33	43
	(b)	15	13	15	21
Nationalised industries	(a)	31	(21)	34	50
	(b)	17	(17)	13	20
Public administration	(a)	25	29	19	32
	(b)	11	11	6	25
C. Employee representatives					
All private sector	(a)	27	24	28	42
	(b)	10	8	11	17
Nationalised industries	(a)	37	(39)	34	43
	(b)	14	(14)	9	28
Public administration	(a)	14	10	17	31
	(b)	6	5	8	8
Bases: as described by A, B and C					

[1] (a) Any change with the aim of increasing employee involvement reported
(b) Structural change to increase involvement reported
[2] See note B

further caution in the interpretation of the results discussed above.

There are, however, one or two patterns in the results that have a clear interpretation (Table VI.14). As one might expect, large establishments, which on most measures have more formalised and elaborate industrial relations institutions, were much more likely than small establishments to have made an 'institutional innovation' to increase employee involvement. But they were not more likely to have made any other sort of change. When larger establishments did report other changes it was more commonly an improvement in communications. Autonomous working groups and management training to foster greater employee participation were reported in only two per cent of establishments and almost all of these had less than 500 employees. Both managers and worker representatives were more likely to report 'institutional innovations' where there was a personnel or industrial relations specialist present at the establishment. However, when size of establishment, to which the presence of specialist management is strongly related, was controlled for, this correlation disappeared. Nor was there any clear pattern when establishments with a personnel spcialist on their top governing body were compared with those not having such a specialist.

A number of other characteristics of establishments were explored to see if they cast light on the extent to which initiatives to increase employee involvement were reported, including ownership, the presence of recognised unions, the composition of the workforce, the industrial relations 'climate' and financial performance. Of these, the only one showing any consistent pattern was ownership. Although the private and public sectors showed similar patterns, there was a discernible difference within the public sector between nationalised industry establishments and those in public administration. As Table VI.14 shows, nationalised industry establishments were more likely to report initiatives to increase employee involvement, of any type, than other public sector establishments. The commonest innovation in the nationalised industries was a new joint consultative committee. Yet these are the types of establishment where joint consultative committees are most common anyway: two-thirds of such establishments had them. It was also more common for them to have multiple committees.

We can, therefore, characterise the initiatives taken by management in the nationalised industries to increase employee involvement as extending or elaborating their structure for joint consultation. Changes of this nature were rather less common in the rest of the public sector, as were other initiatives for this purpose. Both 'institutional innovations' and qualitative changes such as better communication were also quite often reported in the private sector. But any sectoral differences were small compared with the differences shown by establishments of varying sizes. Larger establishments were more likely to report any change to increase employee involvement – one half of those with 1,000 or more employees did so – and the changes they reported were more likely to be institutional. Small establishments were just as likely as large ones to report changes that did not involve the creation of formal consultative machinery.

Notes

1. W.R. Hawes and C.C.P. Brookes, 'Joint Consultation in British Industry', Department of Employment *Gazette*, April 1980, pp. 353–61; William Brown, Ed., *The Changing Contours of British Industrial Relations* (Basil Blackwell, Oxford, 1981); Peter Cressey, John Eldridge, John MacInnes and Geoff Norris, 'Participation Prospects: some Scottish evidence', Department of Employment *Gazette*, March 1981, pp. 117–24.
2. The overall figure of 45 per cent given here excludes the 'not answered' cases in Table VI.5.
3. In establishments with a neutral policy to trade union recruitment, the normal response where membership numbers were not known would have been 'don't know'. The alternative, and much less common response, 'no information – company policy', was allowed for in the main survey after pilot interviewers had identified cases where managers stated that it was management policy not to know about union membership among the workforce.
4. See 'Safely Appointed', Department of Employment *Gazette*, February 1981.
5. Disclosure of information has recently been the subject of a Social Science Research Council sponsored research initiative. Researchers at the Universities of Edinburgh, Kent and Oxford and at the Anglian Management Centre were funded, and research reports are to be published soon.
6. See, for example, R. Walton and R. McKersie, *A Behavioral Theory of Labor Negotiations* (McGraw-Hill, New York, 1965).
7. Central Arbitration Committee, *Awards*, Vols. LVII to LXI (HMSO, London, 1976–81).

VII Industrial Relations Procedures

Formal procedures for dealing with the recurrent problems of management–employee relationships are widespread. In this chapter we explore their extent among workplaces in Britain and some of the ways in which they vary. Some procedures, for example, are determined solely by management; others are agreed with trade unions; some have provision for third party intervention. We also present results on the growth of procedures, how important procedures were in the resolution of disputes and how satisfied respondents were with the way they worked.

The extent of the main types of procedure

In common with previous writers[1] we distinguished three main types of issue for which establishments might have procedures. These issues were: individual grievances; issues concerning discipline and dismissal; and disputes over pay and conditions of employment. The extent of each of these three types of procedure, as reported by managers, is shown in Table VII.1 (Q83). Worker representatives reported very similarly and their results, as they are for only part of the sample, are not shown.

The most common types of procedure were for dealing with discipline and dismissals (reported by management in 83 per cent of establishments) and individual grievances (80 per cent of all establishments). These issues were often dealt with under a single, general procedure: in just over one half of establishments which had a discipline and dismissals procedure this was the case. But where establishments had separate procedures for these two types of issue, or only a single procedure, it was most commonly one dealing with discipline and dismissals (Q104).

Procedures for dealing with disputes over pay and conditions were substantially less common, being reported by management in 59 per cent of establishments overall. Part of the reason for this lower incidence may be that we focused the question on collective disputes: individual grievances over pay may well have been conceived as falling within the general procedure for individual grievances. More important, however, pay disputes – certainly those involving industrial action – most commonly arose in the context of collective bargaining and hence where trade unions were recognised. Since trade union recognition for even a minority of employees existed in only about two-thirds

Table VII.1 Formal industrial relations procedures in relation to various characteristics of establishments

Percentages

	Discipline and dismissals	Individual grievances	Pay and conditions disputes	Any of the three procedures	Unweighted base	Weighted base
All establishments	**83**	**80**	**59**	**86**	**2040**	**2000**
Number employed at establishment						
25–49	75	70	48	79	367	785
50–99	83	79	58	86	380	528
100–199	87	88	64	91	399	347
200–499	96	95	79	97	378	206
500–999	98	97	83	99	249	83
1000 or more	99	99	90	99	267	51
Number of recognised unions						
No recognised unions	74	66	41	77	465	665
One or more recognised unions	88	87	68	91	1575	1335
Manual and non-manual unions recognised[1]	89	91	72	92	1077	761
Union density						
No union members present[2]	70	63	42	74	240	390
Low (under 30 per cent)	85	76	52	88	169	202
Medium (30–79 per cent)	86	83	66	89	598	560
High (80–100 per cent)	88	88	74	92	610	456
Ownership						
Public sector[1]	85	85	58	88	710	656
Nationalised industries	96	95	74	96	134	79
Central and local government	83	84	55	88	542	550
Private sector	83	77	59	85	1330	1344
Independent establishments	71	57	44	74	276	382
Part of larger organisation	87	85	66	90	919	962

Base: all establishments

of establishments, the proportion of establishments which had procedures related to pay disputes was naturally lower.

As Table VII.1 shows, the presence of each of the three types of procedure was strongly related to size of establishment. However, as can be seen from the remainder of the table, this relationship is clearly in part the outcome of other factors which are related to size. Those relating to the degree of trade union organisation at the workplace are particularly relevant. Both the absence of any recognised trade unions and the absence of trade union members significantly reduced the likelihood that an establishment would have formal procedures of any of the three types we mentioned. These factors remained important sources of variation even when we controlled for establishment size. Ownership and organisational size generally appeared to have little influence upon the existence of procedures if the factors of workplace size and trade union organisation were taken into account. However, one combination of ownership and organisation size gave a particularly low figure for the presence of procedures. This was the small firm (independent, private sector establishments with between 25 and 49 employees). Managers in these small firms reported discipline and dismissal procedures in 63 per cent of cases and individual grievance procedures in 45 per cent of cases.

The patterns of variation for the three types of procedure had important differences and similarities. Disciplinary and individual grievance procedures (usually present together in the same establishments) varied in their extent in similar ways. In workplaces with no recognised trade unions, however, individual grievance procedures were significantly less common than disciplinary procedures. This difference was most marked in the case of small firms, mentioned earlier, which very rarely recognised trade unions. This could perhaps be a reflection of the impact of recent legislation on the extent of disciplinary and dismissals procedures but not on other types of procedure. We will return to this in looking at the date of introduction of procedures.

The extent of procedures for disputes over pay and conditions varied substantially with trade union recognition, as might have been expected. Sixty-eight per cent of establishments with recognised unions had a disputes procedure for pay issues (72 per cent where both manual and non-manual unions were recognised), compared with 41 per cent of workplaces where unions were not recognised. Even so, the figure where unions were recognised may be regarded as relatively low. The existence of such procedures became nearly universal in only the largest establishments. Substantial numbers of establishments in both the private and public sectors appeared to have no formal procedure, whether agreed with the trade unions or not, for resolving issues at establishment level about pay and conditions of employment. In the public sector this may well reflect the prevalence of nationally determined pay scales and of issues arising mainly at the national level. In the private sector the explanation appears less obvious.

On the other hand, it may be regarded as surprising that in 41 per cent of establishments where unions were not recognised managers reported procedures for dealing with pay and conditions issues. Even where there was no formal worker representation of any kind the proportion was 32 per cent. However, as we shall show later, procedures in these types of workplace were less likely to be written down and were also less structured in other ways. These 'procedures' were presumably routine ways in which successive levels in the management hierarchy dealt with informal pressures from the workforce when pay and conditions were the focus of a collective grievance.

Characteristics of procedures
We turn now to examine some of the main characteristics of the procedures themselves, as reported by managers. We begin with disciplinary procedures.

The nature of disciplinary procedures
In the great majority of establishments that had a disciplinary and dismissals procedure (83 per cent) managers reported that substantially the same procedure applied to all employees covered (88 per cent gave this answer (Q93)). Hence 73 per cent of all establishments had a uniform disciplinary procedure. This need not mean that all employees at an establishment would have the same access to a disciplinary procedure or be treated similarly within it – for example, members and non-members of a trade union might have different rights of representation at disciplinary hearings. We made no attempt to investigate this aspect, as this is more appropriately done by case study methods and documentary analysis. But the small minority of cases where managers reported that different groups of employees were treated differently under the procedure gives a hint of the bases of differentiation. The most common basis was broad occupational group, manual and non-manual employees having different procedures in seven per cent of cases where there were procedures. Other types of occupation added a further one per cent. Different procedures for different unions or groups of unions were reported in less than one per cent of cases, but it seems likely, given that representation is normally by different unions for manual and non-manual employees, that many of the seven per cent of cases where procedures were different for manual and non-manual workers may equally have fallen under the head of different procedures for different unions. Earlier research[2] indicated that disciplinary procedures commonly had varying applicability to different groups of employees. The present evidence indicates that disciplinary procedures

have become more standardised and universal in their application since the early 1970s, probably under the impact of unfair dismissals legislation.

The growth of formal disciplinary procedures

According to managers, disciplinary procedures were written down in 91 per cent of establishments which had them (Q94). The most common exception was the small independent establishment in the private sector but, even so, the procedure was written down in 73 per cent of these cases. Generally speaking, the factors associated with the presence of a procedure were also associated with the likelihood of that procedure being a written one: union recognition, union membership density, the presence of senior or full time shop stewards, size of workplace and, in addition, public ownership. However, a notable divergence was that establishments where only manual trade unions were recognised and those with a predominantly manual workforce were less likely to have written disciplinary procedures. This was also the case with establishments employing homeworkers or outworkers, as might have been expected.

The high proportion of disciplinary procedures that were set out in a written document is very much a recent development in Britain. Evidence from an unpublished Government Social Survey report[3] of research carried out in 1969 was that only eight per cent of private sector establishments had a formal procedure of this kind. Our equivalent figure for 1980 was over 80 per cent. The Warwick study has documented the growth of procedures in the manufacturing sector up to 1978[4]. By asking managers when the disciplinary procedure was first set out in a written document we were able to update this picture to 1980, and to extend it to the service sectors. Table VII.2 contains the overall results.

The introduction of written disciplinary procedures appears to have been most common in the mid-1970s. By the late 1970s the bulk of establishments already had such procedures and the rate of introduction slowed down. Only 17 per cent of establishments with written disciplinary procedures had introduced them since mid-1977 (four per cent since mid-1979) and very few of these were recently created establishments. Recent introductions were more common in small firms but, as elsewhere in the private sector, the rate of introduction appeared to have slowed down. Comparisons with the Warwick survey for manufacturing industry show very similar proportions of establishments which had written disciplinary procedures for 1977/78 and reinforce the suggestion that the rate of introduction has slowed down but is still significant. In the rest of the private sector, the pattern of introduction appeared to be similar to that in manufacturing. In

Table VII.2 Characteristics of procedures for (a) discipline and dismissals and (b) pay and conditions disputes

	All establishments		Private Sector		Public Sector	
	Discipline and dismissals	Pay and conditions disputes	Discipline and dismissals	Pay and conditions disputes	Discipline and dismissals	Pay and conditions disputes
	Column percentages					
Coverage						
Similar for all workers	88	87	93	88	79	84
Different for manual/non-manual	7	9	4	7	14	11
Different for other groups	2	3	0	2	6	5
Not answered	3	1	3	3	1	*
Set out in written document	91	89	87	85	98	97
	Column percentages[2]					
Within last 3 years[1]	17	12	19	16	14	6
3 to 5 years	23	17	25	21	18	11
6 to 10 years	31	30	33	31	26	26
Over 10 years	27	37	21	30	38	51
Not answered	2[2]	5	2	3	4	6
	Column percentages					
Applicability						
Sampled establishment only	20	21	28	30	4	3
Own organisation only	36	31	37	32	35	30
Other employers within same industry	3	5	4	6	1	3
Whole industry	38	40	27	29	58	64
Not answered	3	3	4	4	2	1
Base[1]: establishments with procedures specified in column heads						
Unweighted	1829	1430	1188	949	641	481
Weighted	1665	1182	1109	799	556	383

[1] The base for the proportions that introduced procedures in the specified periods changes to establishments with written procedures

the public sector, written procedures were much older and almost universal.

A further aspect of the formality of disciplinary procedures is the degree to which they specify a system of warnings prior to the ultimate sanction of dismissal. In almost all establishments procedures were reported as having a system of warnings. In nine out of ten cases, the procedure contained provision for oral then written warnings, as recommended for some years in official codes of practice[5]. That proportion was even higher where the procedure was jointly agreed between management and unions and the subject of written agreement.

Internal and external procedures

In general, managers said that their disciplinary procedure was not exclusive to their own establishment (Q95). In the public sector the procedure applied more widely than to the establishment in over 95 per cent of cases, but in the private sector there was much more variation. In about one quarter of cases the procedure applied to the whole industry; a further one quarter were 'internal' procedures, applying only to that establishment; the remainder were nearly all enterprise wide procedures. Enterprise wide procedures were particularly common where the dominant level of pay bargaining was enterprise wide. Most of the internal procedures were in single independent establishments: such procedures were reported in only 19 per cent of establishments that were part of larger, private sector enterprises. Of the private sector establishments affiliated to an employers' association, only one third had disciplinary procedures described by management as industry wide. Broadly speaking, in three-quarters of cases the dominant level of pay bargaining (establishment or higher in the organisation) coincided with the level to which the disciplinary procedure applied. This was so when both manual and non-manual bargaining levels were examined. In the private sector, industry wide bargaining was less likely to coincide with industry wide disciplinary procedures. The association was still apparent, but as many as one half of establishments with industry wide bargaining had internal disciplinary procedures.

Agreed procedures

So far our description of the extent and nature of procedures has covered both those introduced unilaterally by management and those subject to agreement between management and worker representatives, most commonly through trade unions or staff associations. In establishments where employees covered by the procedure were represented by trade unions or staff associations, managers reported that the procedure had been agreed with those bodies in the great majority of

Table VII.3 Establishments with joint procedures of various types

	All establishments		Private Sector		Public Sector	
	Discipline and dismissals	Pay and conditions disputes	Discipline and dismissals	Pay and conditions disputes	Discipline and dismissals	Pay and conditions disputes
						Percentages
Agreed with unions or staff associations	91	93	87	91	96	96
Base: establishments with the specified procedures and where workers covered by them are represented by trade unions or staff associations						
Unweighted	*1434*	*1198*	*818*	*735*	*616*	*463*
Weighted	*1134*	*869*	*605*	*501*	*529*	*368*
						Column percentages
Joint signing of document						
Agreed – and subject of jointly signed document	80¹	84	78	82	82	88
Agreed – not subject of jointly signed document	15	13	19	17	11	9
Not answered	4	2	3	1	7	4
						Column percentages
Level of agreement						
Agreed at establishment	26	27	42	43	9	8
Agreed at higher level	70	71	52	56	90	91
Not answered	4	1	6	1	1	1

Base: establishments where the specified procedures are agreed with unions or staff associations

¹ See note C

cases (91 per cent of those with unions, which amounted to 64 per cent of all establishments; see Table VII.3). The proportion was even higher where there were recognised unions for both manual and non-manual employees (95 per cent) and where there were other indications of strong trade union organisation. Where employee representation existed, in the majority of cases the procedure was set out in a document signed by both parties (80 per cent in the private sector, 88 per cent in the public sector). The exceptions were frequently private sector establishments where only manual trade unions were recognised, indicating that some of the traditional reluctance of some manual unions to become involved in joint disciplinary proceedings[6] still exists (Q96).

Jointly signed disciplinary procedures were normally agreed and signed at a level in the organisation higher than the individual establishment. This was so in 90 per cent of public sector establishments with jointly signed agreements (95 per cent in the nationalised industries, lower in the remainder; but about one tenth of respondents in educational services and central government did not know). In the private sector, nearly one half of procedures were agreed locally. Thus the level at which procedures were agreed followed quite closely the sector-by-sector pattern of pay bargaining and, as we shall see shortly, the distribution of procedures for dealing with pay and conditions disputes. Hence, while the various legislative initiatives of the last fifteen years have influenced the extent of dismissal procedures and their formality, the levels at which they were agreed, where this was so, largely followed existing patterns of collective bargaining.

Outside intervention
When procedures at establishment level do not lead to the resolution of an issue over discipline there is frequently provision within them to invoke an 'external' procedure or go to a higher level in the organisation. Such a provision was reported in over 80 per cent of public sector establishments and in nearly 60 per cent of private sector establishments with procedures (Q97). It was more common when the procedure was jointly agreed with trade unions, when it applied to other establishments of the same organisation and when it was agreed at higher levels in the organisation. The body or person most commonly specified was higher level management, in most cases at the organisation's head office (see Table VII.4). This provision was reported in nearly 40 per cent of establishments with a procedure, and particularly widely in private sector services and the public sector. The Advisory, Conciliation and Arbitration Service was specified in nearly one third of cases where a disciplinary procedure contained provision for conciliation or arbitration (in most cases both forms of intervention were specified). Private sector establishments, particularly independent or

Table VII.4   **Provision for and use of third party intervention**

Column percentages

	Discipline and dismissals	Pay and conditions disputes
Provision in procedure for third-party intervention	Column percentages	
Provision made	67	72[1]
No provision made	29	23
Not answered or known	4	4
Use of third-party intervention in previous year	Column percentages	
Yes	13	15
No	84	82
Not answered or known	3	2
Bases: establishments with procedure specified at column heads		
Unweighted	*1829*	*1430*
Weighted	*1665*	*1182*

[1] See note C

foreign owned ones, were more likely than others to specify ACAS in the procedure. The remaining bodies specified included a great variety of employer and trade union bodies, either on their own or jointly, and arbitrators independent of the employers, the unions and ACAS.

Such provisions were by no means unused. In 13 per cent of establishments with a disciplinary procedure managers reported that a body or person outside the establishment had been brought in to help settle a disciplinary dispute during the past year (Table VII.4)[7]. Large establishments, where presumably more disciplinary cases arose, were more likely to have used an outside body or person. Intervention was only half as likely to occur where there was no provision for it within the procedure. Where an intervention during the year was reported it was usually a single occurrence; two or more interventions were common only in large establishments (Q98).

Managers were asked the identity of the body or person asked to help settle the most recent dispute during the past 12 months. With two important exceptions the pattern of use was similar to the pattern of provision (Table VII.5). Management at a higher organisational level was still most frequently mentioned; joint bodies were relatively rare. However, trade union officials from outside the establishment were asked to help settle disputes much more commonly than they were mentioned in the formal procedure in this role. In consequence, all

Table VII.5   Provision for or use of persons or organisations for third party intervention

	Discipline and dismissals	Pay and conditions disputes
Person or organisations specified	Column percentages	
Management at higher level	36[1]	23
Employers' association	9	11
Union official	7	7
Joint management or employers' association and union(s)	12	17
ACAS	29	36
Other answers	10	10
Not known, not answered or not specified in procedure	18	17
Base: establishments with procedure specified at column heads which contained provision for third party intervention		
Unweighted	*1253*	*1117*
Weighted	*1109*	*855*
Person or organisation used to help settle dispute in previous year	Column percentages	
Management at higher level	31	15
Employers' association	5	16
Union official	23	30
Joint management or employers' association and union(s)	8	15
ACAS	17	12
Other answers	13	9
Not known, not answered or not specified in procedure	5	5
Base: establishments with procedure specified at column head and where third-party intervention was used		
Unweighted	*322*	*360*
Weighted	*215*	*183*

[1] See note E

other bodies, including ACAS, were used proportionately less often. This different pattern of provision for, and use of, third parties in disciplinary cases suggests that even relatively formal procedures are used flexibly and that trade union officials may be brought in frequently by management before the final stages of a formal procedure are reached.

Disciplinary procedures in use
Both management and worker representatives were also asked, first, about the extent to which disciplinary procedures were adhered to and, secondly, how satisfied they were with the way the procedures worked.

In 85 per cent of cases where there were procedures, managers reported that most matters in respect of disputes over discipline and dismissals were dealt with under the procedure laid down (Q102). In the remainder of cases the procedure was either not normally used if there was a dispute or else there had been no disputes, but we cannot confidently distinguish these cases. However, in large establishments the distinction is irrelevant – over 99 per cent of managers in establishments of 500 or more employees replied that most cases were dealt with under the procedure. Worker representatives were slightly less likely than managers in the same establishments to say that most disputes went through the procedure.

Managers were much more likely than worker representatives to be satisfied with the working of the disciplinary procedures at their establishment: 61 per cent of managers were 'very satisfied' and only five per cent were 'not very' or 'not at all' satisfied (Q103). The corresponding figures for manual worker representatives (WQ52) were 39 per cent 'very satisfied' (non-manual representatives 35 per cent) and 13 per cent 'not very' or 'not at all' satisfied (non-manual representatives nine per cent). Dissatisfaction was expressed most frequently by managers and worker representatives in the public sector, particularly in local and central government services. For all types of respondent, dissatisfaction with the working of their disciplinary procedure was strongly associated with a less favourable assessment of the establishment's general state of industrial relations. But there appeared to be no clear connection with recent experience of dismissals or with cases having gone to industrial tribunals[8].

A wide variety of reasons was given for dissatisfaction, where it existed, with disciplinary procedures, but two reasons were dominant. The length and complexity of the procedure was the reason most frequently given by both managers and worker representatives. The other main reason was that the procedure favoured the other party. There was no general tendency for any set of respondents to be more dissatisfied with disciplinary procedures where the procedure was long-established[9]. This, together with the large number of different reasons for dissatisfaction – and the wide variety of procedures in existence – suggests that the defects are specific rather than general and hence not amenable to general remedies.

Dismissals and disciplinary deductions from pay
Before leaving the subject of industrial discipline we make brief men-

tion of two related matters: establishments' recent experience of dismissals and management's use of disciplinary deductions from pay. In both cases managers only were asked the relevant questions (Q107a; Q111b, c).

Managers in less than one half (42 per cent) of the surveyed establishments reported that an employee had been dismissed for reasons other than redundancy during the previous year. Where there had been a dismissal it was often an isolated occurrence. In only nine per cent of establishments were more than five dismissals reported; in only two per cent had there been more than twenty dismissals. As would be expected, the absolute number of dismissals reported by larger establishments was higher; but the rate of dismissal relative to the number of employees was lower. Establishments with less than 100 employees had dismissed 18 employees per 1,000 employed. The corresponding figure for establishments of 1,000 or more was four per thousand. Overall the average was 11 per 1,000. This pattern is generally consistent with research on dismissal rates in the late 1970s (for example, the work of Daniel and Stilgoe[10] and the Warwick survey[11]). Daniel and Stilgoe compared their findings for 1977 with those of the previously mentioned Government Social Survey report[12] and showed that the reduction in dismissal rates within manufacturing industry was largely due to the reduced incidence of very high dismissal rates. Our comparision with the Government Social Survey results shows that the same change is apparent for the manufacturing and service sectors between 1969 and 1980. Whether some of this occurred after 1977 has still to be investigated.

The second of our questions on disciplinary practice concerned the use of deductions from pay. Some deductions from wages are allowed for in the Truck Acts in relation to 'workmen', broadly equivalent to manual workers in the terms of our survey. Non-manual workers are not covered by the Truck Acts and for them disciplinary deductions from pay are a matter for agreement between employer and employee. Our question to management respondents referred specifically to three types of deduction from pay: deductions for bad work, for loss or damage to the employers' property and for other disciplinary offences. Where any of these deductions had been made in the past year, managers were asked to estimate the number of employees affected.

Managers in 12 per cent of establishments reported the use of one or other of the three types of deduction. There was substantial variation across establishments of different sizes. Seven per cent of the smallest establishments (25 to 49 employees) were reported to have used them, compared with 40 per cent of the largest establishments (2,000 or more employees). There was little variation across industrial sectors. Even in sectors with almost entirely non-manual workforces managers reported their use: for example, seven per cent of managers in the financial and business services sector did so. Of those establishments in the survey which employed only non-manual workers, seven per cent reported making disciplinary deductions from pay. It is clear, therefore, that these deductions were made within and without the sectors of employment covered by the provisions of the Truck Acts. A further point of interest is that managers were much more likely to report their use where they assessed the general state of industrial relations at the establishment to be poor. In the small minority of establishments where assessments were 'quite bad' or worse, 41 per cent reported the use of disciplinary deductions.

The most common type of deduction from pay was for 'other disciplinary offences' which were reported in three-quarters of cases where deductions were reported. These dominated the pattern for all types of deduction, reported above. It is noteworthy, however, that deductions for bad work were nearly as common in the service industries as they were in manufacturing and construction. The correlation between disciplinary deductions and managers' low assessment of the general state of the establishment's industrial relations was evident for each of the three types of deduction. Managers found it difficult to estimate the number of employees subject to each of the three types of deduction. Where estimates were given, deductions for bad work were reported as affecting the highest number of employees.

Procedures for disputes over pay and conditions
At the beginning of this chapter we described the extent of procedures for dealing with matters of pay and conditions and a number of factors associated with their presence or absence in sampled establishments. We now turn to an analysis of some of the characteristics of those procedures and their sources of variation. To a large extent the results are similar to those we have just discussed for dismissal procedures. The analysis is therefore briefer, and highlights differences between the two kinds of procedure.

As Table VII.2 shows, the same pay and conditions procedures applied to all employees in establishments to about the same extent that disciplinary procedures had applied to all (87 per cent). However, there were sectoral variations. In the private sector, pay and conditions procedures were more often different for different groups than were disciplinary procedures. In the public sector, disciplinary procedures were more likely to be different for different groups than were pay and conditions procedures (Q85). In both sectors, pay and conditions procedures were almost as likely to be written down (89 per cent overall) as were disciplinary procedures (Q86).

Written pay and conditions procedures tended to have existed for longer, particularly in the public sector (Table VII.2). This suggests that the development of written pay and conditions procedures, particularly in the decade up to 1980, was slower than the development of written disciplinary procedures. For example, comparing the two types of procedure in the three years prior to the survey, six per cent of all establishments had introduced a written pay and conditions procedure, while 13 per cent had introduced a written disciplinary procedure. Evidence of the position prior to 1970 is imprecise and there is no firm survey evidence with which to compare, as there is for disciplinary procedures. It is possible, however, to make rough comparisons within manufacturing between the end of 1977 and mid-1980 using the results obtained by the Warwick survey[13]. In that survey the question of whether or not the procedure was written down was asked only where the procedure contained provision for third party intervention. If we restrict our comparison to such cases, the Warwick results indicate that in 79 per cent of manufacturing establishments pay and conditions procedures were written, while the corresponding figure from our 1980 survey is 92 per cent. It may be that this merely reflects the emphasis in our 1980 survey question on formal procedures, so that informal and unwritten procedures would already have been omitted. If this is not so, then a further growth in procedural formality seems to have taken place in the late 1970s, at least in manufacturing.

In terms of their applicability to the establishment only or to other establishments also, pay and conditions procedures followed a similar pattern to disciplinary procedures (Q87). Pay and conditions procedures exclusive to the establishment were again largely a feature of independent private sector establishments (single plant firms). In only about one fifth of establishments that were part of large, private sector enterprises were the procedures internal. In that sector they were slightly less likely to be enterprise wide and more likely to be multi-employer than were disciplinary procedures. Moreover, the same relationship with the level of pay bargaining as had appeared for disciplinary procedures was apparent: the proportion of establishments where the most important level of bargaining coincided with the level at which the pay and conditions procedure applied was also about three-quarters. It is surprising that the match was not higher, since pay and conditions procedures are directly related to pay bargaining whereas disciplinary procedures are not. Given that they have been introduced more recently, the implication seems to be that disciplinary procedures are introduced to a large degree into the framework of collective bargaining.

When procedures for settling disputes over pay and conditions of employment are subject to formal agreement between management and worker representatives, then they may be considered to be *negotiating procedures* (Q88). Overall, 62 per cent of establishments with recognised trade unions had such negotiating procedures, the remaining 38 per cent presumably either relying upon informal understandings or perhaps having little experience of disputes over pay. In only a few cases were written negotiating procedures not jointly signed: 59 per cent of establishments with recognised unions (39 per cent of all establishments in the sample) had a jointly signed negotiating procedure. As with disciplinary procedures, it was mainly in private sector establishments where only manual unions were recognised that negotiating procedures were not jointly signed. The level at which negotiating procedures were agreed also followed closely the pattern for disciplinary procedures, with nearly three-quarters of them having been agreed above establishment level.

In terms of provision for third party intervention, managers reported such a provision rather more frequently for pay and conditions procedures (Q89) than for disciplinary procedures (72 per cent overall, compared with 67 per cent). Again such a provision was more likely in the public sector than the private sector, more likely when the procedure was jointly signed and, also, when it was agreed and applied more widely than the establishment. However, the specified third party varied between the two types of procedure (Table VII.4). ACAS and joint bodies were more frequently mentioned. Management at higher levels featured less often, in part presumably a reflection of the fact that pay and conditions procedures tended to be concentrated in establishments with recognised trade unions and thus pay was more often a negotiated issue than were disciplinary cases.

The pattern for pay and conditions disputes was again similar to that for disputes over disciplinary matters so far as the use of outside intervention was concerned (Q90). If any intervention had occurred (as had happened in 15 per cent of establishments with a procedure) a single intervention during the previous year was the general rule; more than one intervention tended to be reported only in larger establishments. Multiple interventions were more common in the public sector, presumably reflecting the difficulties of reaching agreement on public sector pay in 1979/80.

As with disciplinary procedures, the identity of the body or person brought in to help settle pay and conditions disputes broadly followed what was specifed in the procedure but there was even more use of trade union officials. Employers' associations also featured more prominently in practice than was provided for in the procedure – the opposite of the pattern for disciplinary disputes. ACAS was less frequently used, particularly in the public sector, where it was, in any case, less often specified in the procedure.

Both managers and worker representatives reported that most disputes about pay and conditions were dealt with under the formal procedure (Q91), as had been the case with disciplinary disputes. The pattern of evaluation was also similar. Dissatisfaction with pay and conditions procedures (Q92) was registered more often by worker representatives than by managers, and more often by non-manual worker representatives. However, sectoral differences were much more marked than they were for disciplinary procedures. In the public sector, some nine per cent of managers and 20 per cent of non-manual worker representatives expressed dissatisfaction with the working of their pay and conditions procedures, compared with two per cent and 11 per cent respectively in the private sector. Again, a wide variety of reasons was given for dissatisfaction with the procedures. In contrast to disciplinary procedures, however, managers almost never mentioned that the procedure favoured the employees. Worker representatives, particularly non-manual ones, occasionally reported that the negotiating procedure favoured management. However, since dissatisfaction was expressed in a minority of cases and the reasons were so varied, it is not practical to analyse these results in much detail. Where procedures were regarded as unsatisfactory the remedies would again appear to be specific rather than general.

Notes

1. N. Singleton, *Industrial Relations Procedures* (HMSO, London, 1975); William Brown, Ed., *The Changing Contours of British Industrial Relations* (Basil Blackwell, Oxford, 1981).
2. S.D. Anderman, *Voluntary Dismissals Procedure and the Industrial Relations Act* (Political and Economic Planning No. 538, London, 1971); A.W.J. Thomson and V.V. Murray, *Grievance Procedures* (Saxon House, Farnborough, 1976).
3. Government Social Survey, *Disciplinary and dismissal practices and procedures* (1969, unpublished).
4. William Brown, Ed., *op. cit.*
5. ACAS, *Disciplinary practice and procedures in employment* (ACAS, London, 1977).
6. K.W. Wedderburn and P.L. Davies, *Employment Grievances and Disputes Procedures in Britain* (University of California Press, London, 1969).
7. Managers who reported the absence of a procedure at their establishment were also asked about the use of bodies or persons outside the establishment to help settle disputes over pay and conditions or discipline and dismissals. Such outside intervention was rare and the addition of these cases would make little difference to the results presented (Q84).
8. The survey included a question to managers, 'Has any employee or ex-employee in the last year started a tribunal action against the employer at this establishment'. There seems to be some confusion in the results between 'no' and 'not answered' responses. For this reason no presentation of these data are given in this book. However, the affirmative responses appear to be reliable and were used to test the relationship with respondents' satisfaction with the disciplinary procedure at their establishment.
9. The argument for periodic review and reform of disciplinary procedure is often made in the literature. See, for example, A.W.J. Thomson and V.V. Murray, *op cit.*
10. W.W. Daniel and Elizabeth Stilgoe, *The Impact of Employment Protection Laws* (Policy Studies Institute No. 577, London, 1978).

11. William Brown, Ed., *op. cit.*
12. Government Social Survey, *op. cit.*
13. William Brown, Ed., *op. cit.*

VIII Pay Determination

A distinctive characteristic of the methods of pay determination that result from the British system of labour relations is the diversity and multiplicity of levels at which there is collective bargaining that influences rates of pay. There are negotiations between employers' associations and trade unions at the national or industry level. There is bargaining at the company level between a particular employer and the trade unions he recognises. Within nationalised industries, national or industry bargaining and company or corporation bargaining tend to be one and the same. At lower levels, multi-employer bargaining sometimes takes place at regional or district levels and company bargaining at divisional levels. Beyond that there is often a further stage of negotiations at the workplace. Such plant bargaining still takes the form of formal periodic negotiations over rates of pay. Frequently there remains a final level of bargaining at shop floor level which is concerned with day to day negotiations over grading, bonuses, overtime, special payments or rates for the job under payment-by-results. The number of different levels of bargaining that have a direct or indirect influence upon the pay of workers, and their relative importance, vary from workplace to workplace, as does the relative importance of the different levels in terms of the comparative influence that they have over pay. As we show in this chapter, there are sharp differences between the public and private sectors generally. Even within the private sector there are very marked differences in, first, the extent to which rates of pay are directly influenced by collective bargaining and in, secondly, the level of bargaining which has most influence. All this diversity creates very substantial problems for any national strategy or policy to change industrial relations or influence the level of pay settlements. In particular, it has been widely seen as creating problems for national incomes policies[1]. That which is possible or appropriate in the public sector may be impossible or inappropriate in the private sector. Policies designed to bring about desirable changes in the engineering industry may be irrelevant to the construction industry or to personal services. Complicating the picture still further, rates of pay in a large part of the private sector are not subject to collective bargaining at all. Some sectors in that part are required to pay minimum rates established by wages councils. Others neither recognise trade unions nor come under wages councils.

For purposes of describing and analysing in our present study the

formal institutional structures that influenced rates of pay, we distinguished between three main types of workplace. First, there were the
establishments that recognised trade unions. We asked them what
levels of bargaining had either led directly to increases in rates
or formed the basis of subsequent negotiations on the most recent
occasion that rates had been increased (Q39a; Q70a; WQ14a). We also
asked which of these levels had had the greatest impact on the size of the
increase (Q39b; Q70b; WQ14b). Secondly, we attempted to identify
those establishments where pay increases were determined by wages
councils. The third category was composed of establishments where
rates were neither regulated by wages councils nor subject to collective
bargaining. We asked such establishments how their most recent
increases in rates of pay had been arrived at.

In addition, in establishments where there was trade union recognition, we explored differences between the largest and second largest
negotiating units in cases where there was more than one unit, and we
covered the same ground for non-manual workers as we did for manual
workers. Similarly, we asked many of the same questions of both
manual and non-manual representatives as we did of managers.
According to our general practice, our starting point is the account by
managers of arrangements for the largest group of manual workers.
Then, where appropriate, we subsequently pick up any contrasts with
the corresponding worker representative account, or with the second
largest negotiating group or with the largest negotiating unit for non-
manual workers.

The overall pattern
By way of introduction to this chapter, Table VIII.1 shows the overall
pattern revealed by our results regarding the institutional mechanisms
through which pay increases were reached. In over half the establishments, increases for manual workers were the result of collective bargaining at some level. Among these, the national or industry level was
most commonly cited as being the most important. The company level
was the second most important. Perhaps surprisingly, in only ten per
cent of establishments was plant bargaining the most important institution for determining pay increases for manual workers. As we shall
show, however, there were major variations in the relative importance
of different levels and these differences meant that plant bargaining was
a much more important institution than might appear from Table
VIII.1. First, greater importance was attributed to plant bargaining in
larger workplaces. Accordingly, that level of negotiations was most
important for a larger proportion of employees than the proportion of
establishments for which it was the most important level. Secondly,
as we show later in the chapter, there were parts of manufacturing

Table VIII.1 **Basis for most recent pay increase: manual and non-manual workers compared**

Column percentages

	Manual workers	Non-manual workers
Direct result of collective bargaining	58	50
Most important level		
National/regional	34	30
Company/division	13	12
Plant/establishment	10	6
Other answer	1	2
Not result of collective bargaining	39	49
Wages council[1]	6	4
Other method[2]	33	45
No information	3	1
Base: establishments employing workers in column headings		
Unweighted	*1899*	*2034*
Weighted	*1833*	*1989*

[1] The percentages exclude cases where the activity of the establishment was not in an industry (Minimum List Heading of the Standard Industrial Classification, 1968) where any workers were judged to be within the scope of a wages council

[2] The percentages include cases where the response was 'statutory wages councils', but it was judged that no worker came within the scope of a wages council

industry where plant bargaining was judged to be the most important level in the majority of workplaces. Those parts may properly be regarded as among the key sectors of the British economy.

In that proportion of establishments where pay increases were judged not to be the result of collective bargaining, one third of managers reported that pay for manual workers was regulated by wages councils. In fact, that proportion certainly exaggerates the influence of wages councils. As we show later in the chapter, in cases where respondents said that pay was regulated by wages councils, we distinguished at the coding stage between those establishments that were in sectors of the economy covered by councils and those that were not. That coding was necessarily very crude because wages councils are not neatly organised to fit in with definitions of industrial sectors, even at Minimum List Heading level. Nevertheless, the exercise showed that there was a substantial number of cases where managers said that they were covered by wages councils but where they operated in sectors that did not come within the ambit of councils. Indeed, in the majority of cases where managers reported that pay increases for manual workers were regulated by wages councils, establishments were in sectors that fell outside the ambit of wages councils. There appeared to be two possible explanations of these mistaken accounts by managers of how pay levels were regulated at their establishments. First, it was clear that some managers erroneously took negotiating bodies like Whitley Councils or joint industrial councils to be wages councils. That was clear, for example, from the extent to which establishments in public administration that did not recognise unions said that they came under wages councils. Secondly, it is possible that some establishments that did not recognise unions adopted the rates specified by some wages council (or indeed perhaps some negotiating council that was sometimes confused with a wages council) as the basis for their rates of pay, even though formally they were not bound by those rates.

Table VIII.1 shows that the overall pattern for the largest group of non-manual workers differed markedly, although not dramatically, from that for the largest group of manual workers. The main difference was that in a substantially higher proportion of establishments non-manual pay was neither subject to collective bargaining nor regulated by a wages council. In this chapter we follow our normal practice of referring to the pattern for non-manual workers only where it differed from that for manual workers. Accordingly we will be paying more attention to non-manual pay increases when we consider the basis for increases in rates in establishments where they were not directly constrained by collective bargaining or wages councils. Meanwhile, in our analysis of variations in the pattern of institutional arrangements for regulating pay, we shall concentrate on arrangements for the largest group of manual workers. As far as the overall pattern was concerned, the variations largely followed the pattern relating to trade union recognition already identified in Chapter II. Accordingly, it is of more interest to explore the variations within the three main institutional arrangements, as these supplement the picture regarding recognition that has already been described. Before doing that, however, it is worth summarising the overall pattern in relation to different types of employer, which was one of the main sources of contrasts.

Table VIII.2 summarises the overall pattern and confirms the diversity that characterises institutional arrangements for pay determination in the British economy. In the public sector, the pay of manual workers was largely subject to collective bargaining and bargaining was largely centralised. In manufacturing industry, collective bargaining still covered the majority of establishments but, in marked contrast, there was a much greater tendency for bargaining to be decentralised. In most establishments in the personal services sector the rates for manual workers were not subject to collective bargaining; but it was clear that

Table VIII.2   Basis for most recent pay increase (manual workers)

Column percentages

	All Public sector	Nationalised industries	Public administration	All private sector	Manufacturing	Construction	Miscellaneous services
Direct result of collective bargaining	76[1]	98	73	50	68	(71)[2]	19
Most important level							
National/regional	57	50	58	23	28	(24)	10
Company/division	18	47	13	11	11	(32)	4
Plant/establishment	*	1	*	15	28	(13)	4
Other answers	1	–	1	1	1	(2)	1
Not result of collective bargaining	19	–	23	48	31	(27)	81
Wages council[3]	*	–	*	*	1	(–)	27
Other method	19	–	23	47	30	(27)	54
No information/ answer	5	2	4	2	1	(2)	–
Base: establishments employing some manual workers							
Unweighted	644	130	514	1255[4]	736	46	131
Weighted	588	75	513	1245	542	48	198

[1] See note D
[2] See note B
[3] See notes 2 and 3 to Table VIII.1
[4] See note H

wages councils played a substantial part in the sector, although for reasons already emphasised we were not able to establish how substantial a part.

Comparison of management accounts with those of worker representatives

Two qualifications must be made at this point to the information that has been presented so far on critical levels of bargaining. First, the idea

Table VIII.3   **Comparison of answers by management and worker representative over levels and areas of collective bargaining**

	Manual workers		Non-manual workers	
	Management representative	Worker representative	Management representative	Worker representative
A. Most important level of bargaining over pay			Column percentage	
National/industry	50[1]	49	60	59
Regional/district	4	2	*	1
Company – some or all establishments	22	22	21	23
Plant/establishment	23	24	15	13
Other answer	2	3	3	4
B. Proportion saying item was subject to negotiation at the establishment			Percentage	
Physical working conditions	73	72	66	72
Redeployment within estab.	72	69	64	61
Manning levels	58	56	40	41
Redundancy	55	50	41	41
Changes in production methods	55	47	38	36
Recruitment	50	52	40	38
Holiday entitlement	19	23	15	22
Length of working week	18	19	14	18
Capital investment	19	10	13	9
Pensions	13	17	7	12
Base: cases in which both union and management representatives were interviewed				
Unweighted	*947*	*947*	*895*	*895*
Weighted	*690*	*690*	*638*	*638*

[1] See note C

of the most important level of bargaining was, in principle, open to a range of different interpretations. It could have meant the level of bargaining at which the largest proportion of any increase was agreed or it could have meant the level at which it was most difficult to get agreement or the level which contributed the most significant marginal element or the level which was most important from the perspective of the particular respondent. We foresaw those possibilities and made it clear in our instructions to interviewers that we intended the *most important level* to be the level at which the largest proportion of the pay increase was agreed. There remained the possibility, however, that some managers may have placed their own interpretation upon the phrase. Secondly, the pattern we have presented so far has depended upon the answers of managers to questions principally concerned with the largest groups of manual workers. In view of the range of different interpretations that different respondents might have placed upon *important* there was clearly very considerable scope for inconsistencies between the answers of management and union representatives. With that background, the figures shown in Part A of Table VIII.3 are remarkable. For both manual and non-manual groups, the answers of management and union representatives were very close. Indeed, in survey research terms they could reasonably be regarded as the same. Similarly, as part B of the table shows, there was also remarkable congruence between the independent accounts of management and union respondents as to which different aspects of employment were the subject of negotiations at the establishment level. Again, the congruence was especially striking, given the scope there was for different interpretations of what constituted *negotiations*, as we point out later in the chapter.

Comparison between pattern for largest negotiating unit and second largest negotiating unit

Certainly so far as managers' judgements of the most important level of bargaining over pay were concerned, it was also the case that the pattern for the second largest negotiating group was very similar to that for the largest group (see Table VIII.4). That was true for both manual and non-manual workers (Q44a, b; Q75a, b). Indeed, the only difference appeared to be that managers were less likely to feel that they could make judgements in relation to the second largest groups. That overall pattern, however, did conceal differences among particular categories of establishment. For instance, so far as manual workers were concerned, managers in the largest establishments tended to report that company and establishment level bargaining was more important in relation to the second largest negotiating group than in relation to the largest. For the largest group, national or industry bargaining was seen

Table VIII.4   Comparison between largest and second largest negotiating groups of most important bargaining levels over pay

Column percentages

	Manual		Non-manual	
	1st group	2nd group	1st group	2nd group
National/industry regional	64[1]	57	68	61
Company – all or some establishments	19	19	21	19
Plant/establishment	15	17	8	8
Other answer	*	1	1	2
Not stated	1	6	1	10
Base: all establishments that had more than one bargaining unit				
Unweighted	*470*	*470*	*635*	*635*
Weighted	*260*	*260*	*434*	*434*

[1] See note C

to be more important than for the second group. That pattern was not reflected in the picture for non-manual grades.

Different bargaining levels and their relative importance
This section focuses upon those sectors of the economy where pay was subject to collective bargaining and analyses answers to the questions about levels of bargaining that directly resulted in increases in rates or formed the basis for subsequent negotiations. Table VIII.5 shows separately the answers that emerged for the largest groups of manual and non-manual workers. The only substantial difference between the systems for the two main groups of employee was that plant or establishment level bargaining was less common for non-manual workers. Again, however, as will have already become apparent, differences between different types of employer were of more interest than the overall pattern. Table VIII.6 summarises those differences for the largest negotiating group of manual workers. In the public sector it was rare for collective bargaining over rates of pay to take place at all at establishment level. Formal collective bargaining over rates was confined to the national or enterprise level which, in the nationalised industries, for instance, was often the same thing. In the private sector, by contrast, plant bargaining was much more common. The majority of establishments in the manufacturing sector that recognised trade unions engaged in plant bargaining, and in engineering, metal working and vehicle manufacture the large majority did so. It also tended to be the case that where plant bargaining was more common so also was the

Table VIII.5 **Levels of negotiation that resulted in pay increases: manual and non-manual compared**

Percentages

	Manual	Non-manual
National/regional	68[1]	63
National/industry	64	62
Regional/district	9	6
Company/enterprise	31	34
All establishments	26	30
Some establishments	6	6
Plant/establishment	26	15
Other answer	3	4
No information	1	1
Base: establishments recognising appropriate unions		
Unweighted	*1344*	*1250*
Weighted	*1070*	*988*

[1] See note F

tendency for bargaining to be reported at more than one level. For instance in engineering, metal working and vehicle manufacturing the average number of levels reported was nearly one and one half, whereas for nationalised industries it was just over one. Even these figures are likely to understate the position. Only one half of the establishments that recognised unions in the engineering, metal working and vehicle building sector reported that collective bargaining at the national level had directly resulted in pay increases or formed the basis subsequently negotiated. It may be that national engineering agreements were seen by many establishments in this sector to play such a small part in influencing rates of pay compared with their own company or plant agreements that they discounted the role of national agreements. At the same time, it is unlikely that so many as one half were not bound by national agreements and did not take them into account in their own domestic bargaining. For instance, a substantial minority of establishments that belonged to employers' associations did not mention national or industry bargaining as having an influence over pay levels, while the majority of establishments that were not members of associations said that national bargaining resulted in pay increases for manual workers or became the subject of further bargaining that led to increases (see Table VIII.7). Apart from the expected difference between members and non-members of employers' associations in the extent to which importance was attached to national agreements, there was a second important contrast. Members were substantially more likely to

Table VIII.6 Levels of bargaining that influenced pay increases (manual workers)

Column percentages

	All public sector	Nationalised industries	Public administration	All private sector	Manufacturing	Construction	All private services
National/regional	79[1]	52	84	60	61	(46)[2]	59
National/industry	77	51	83	54	54	(46)	55
Regional/district	11	5	12	8	8	(5)	7
Company/enterprise	34	51	30	29	21	(61)	39
All establishments	30	48	26	22	16	(52)	37
Some establishments	5	6	5	7	6	(9)	9
Plant/establishment	6	6	6	40	55	(21)	18
Other	3	–	3	4	2	–	7
No information	*	–	*	1	*	–	1
Base: establishments that recognised manual unions							
Unweighted	*528*	*128*	*400*	*816[3]*	*570*	*35*	*222*
Weighted	*448*	*74*	*375*	*621*	*370*	*34*	*246*

[1] See notes D and E
[2] See note B
[3] See note H

Table VIII.7 **Levels of bargaining that influenced increases in pay for manual workers in the largest bargaining unit**

Column percentages

Level of bargaining	Member of employers' association	Not member of employers' association
Multi employer total	83[1]	60
National/industry	78	56
Regional/district	12	8
Company total	22	36
Company – all establishments	16	30
Company – some establishments	7	6
Establishment/plant	32	22
Other answer	1	4
Not stated	1	*
Base: all establishments that recognised manual unions		
Unweighted	*476*	*848*
Weighted	*362*	*685*

[1] See notes E and F

mention plant bargaining, while non-members were substantially more likely to mention company bargaining.

The most important level of bargaining

The variations among sectors were shown more clearly when we focused upon the level that managers judged to be most important (see Table VIII.8). In private manufacturing industry, 41 per cent of managers reported that plant bargaining was the most important level of negotiations that influenced rates of pay for manual workers in the largest bargaining unit. In private services as a whole that proportion fell to 13 per cent. In the public sector hardly any managers took that view. Nothing could show more clearly the diversity of practice systems that characterise different sectors of the British economy. Similarly nothing could show more clearly the dangers of focusing upon just one sector or sub-sector and taking that as the model for the whole economy. For instance, the Warwick study concluded 'single employer bargaining has become the most important means of pay determination for two-thirds of manual workers'[2]. In fact, while this may have been true for manufacturing industry employing 50 or more full time workers, it is clearly not the case for the economy as a whole. Of course, as far as the nationalised industries and government are concerned, the

Table VIII.8   Most important level of bargaining influencing most recent pay increase in relation to type of employer (manual workers)

Column percentages

services	All public sector	Nationalised industries	Public administration	All private sector	All private manufacturing	Engineering/ vehicles	Construction	All private services
National/regional	75[1]	51	80	46	41	34	(34)[2]	54
National/industry	73	50	78	41	36	32	(30)	49
Regional/district	2	1	2	5	5	2	(5)	5
Company/enterprise	23	48	18	22	16	23	(46)	28
All establishments	22	46	17	16	12	17	(37)	22
Some establishments	2	2	2	6	4	6	(9)	6
Plant/establishment	*	1	*	30	41	39	(19)	13
Other answer	1	—	1	2	1	3	—	4
No information	*	—	*	1	1	2	(1)	1
Base: establishments that recognised manual unions								
Unweighted	528	128	400	816[3]	590	196	35	222
Weighted	448	74	375	621	370	77	34	246

[1] See notes C and D
[2] See note B
[3] See note H

distinction between a national agreement and a single employer agreement is largely metaphysical. But leaving aside that kind of consideration, it is clear from Table VIII.8 that among establishments where unions were recognised for bargaining over pay and conditions, the multi-employer agreement remained the most important level for large and important industries among both private and public services.

Here it should be stressed that when we confined analysis to manufacturing establishments employing 50 or more full time workers, the sub-sample which was equivalent to the Warwick sample, our findings on the most important level of bargaining were consistent with those of Warwick, especially as there were slight differences in the design of the questions. For instance, we found, for the critical sub-sample in our survey, that, where unions were recognised, 39 per cent of managers said that multi-employer agreements had most influence upon pay. The comparable figure for Warwick was 40 per cent. Forty-six per cent of managers said that plant bargaining was most important, compared with 42 per cent in the Warwick survey. Clearly any differences in the picture presented by our findings compared with that painted by Warwick did not emerge as a result of different types of finding in relation to the same types of workplace. The point we wish to stress is that there is so much diversity in the British system of pay determination that the picture depends very much upon the sector or sectors studied.

Apart from industrial sector and form of ownership, size had an independent influence upon levels of bargaining that were judged to be most important (see Table VIII.9). The larger the number of people employed on site, the greater was the importance attached to plant bargaining. At the same time, the larger the number of people employed by the enterprise, the greater was the importance attached to company or corporation bargaining. The independent influence of establishment size was shown more clearly when the pattern for establishments of different size was compared within enterprises of similar size (see Table VIII.10). It was also the case that establishment size had an impact even within different sectors and forms of ownership. Table VIII.11 shows that in the private sector generally, and in the manufacturing sector in particular, there was a strong tendency for the proportion describing the establishment as the most important level of bargaining to increase the greater the number of people on site. Even in the nationalised industries there were signs that some importance was attached to plant bargaining when the number employed at the establishment rose to 1,000 or more. Local and central government, however, remained impervious to the influence of size.

Table VIII.9 Most important level of bargaining influencing most recent pay increase (manual workers)

Column percentages

	All establishments	Number employed at establishment					Number employed by enterprise			
		25–99	100–199	200–499	500–999	1,000 or more	25–500	501–2,000	2,001–10,000	10,001 or more
National/regional	58[1]	61	56	57	50[2]	39	62	57	54	49
National/industry	54	57	53	55	46	38	56	56	51	46
Regional/district	4	4	3	2	3	*	6	1	3	3
Company/enterprise	22	22	24	18	24	20	9	22	22	35
All establishments	18	19	21	13	21	15	8	18	19	28
Some establishments	4	4	4	5	3	5	8	18	19	28
Plant/establishment	17	13	18	22	26	29	27	16	22	13
Other answer	2	2	1	2	—	2	2	2	2	2
No information	1	1	1	1	*	—	*	2	1	*
Base: establishments that recognised manual unions										
Unweighted	1344	399	251	290	218	246	172	179	275	574
Weighted	1070	578	214	157	73	48	229	140	192	349

[1] See note C
[2] See note D

Table VIII.10 Most important level of bargaining for manual workers in relation to establishment and organisation size

Percentages

Number employed by organisation	Number employed at establishment			
	25–99	100–499	500–999	1000 or more
A. Plant bargaining most important level				
501–10,000	12	24	28	38
Over 10,000	2	16	26	42
B. Company bargaining most important level				
501–10,000	25	19	27	14
Over 10,000	43	31	25	24

Base: establishments in specified size bands that recognised manual unions

Collective bargaining over pay for non-manual workers

A striking feature of our findings was the extent to which the pay of non-manual workers was regulated by collective bargaining. The fact that the pattern for non-manual grades was so similar to that for manual workers has meant that we have tended to neglect them for fear of boring the reader through repetition. The similarity of the pattern, however, also represents a finding of substance and importance. We have seen in this chapter that the pay of non-manual employees is less likely than that of manual groups to be the subject of collective bargaining and where the pay of non-manual groups was jointly regulated, negotiations were more likely to be centralised. But the striking feature was how close were the patterns for manual and non-manual grades. On the other hand, it was also true, as would be expected following the analysis of patterns of recognition in Chapter II, that the contrast between manual and non-manual groups was more marked in the private sector (see Table II.27).

Extent of consultation about pay increases

In cases where managers reported that a level of bargaining higher than the establishment had had most influence upon the most recent pay increase, we asked whether local managers were consulted before the increase was agreed. Where managers said that the establishment was the most important level, we asked whether managers at higher levels had been consulted before increases were agreed (Q40a, b; Q71a, b). We also asked union representatives whether members were consulted before the agreement of their most recent pay increase (WQ15a, b).

Table VIII.11   **Proportion of establishments where plant bargaining had the most important influence on pay settlement (manual workers) in relation to type of ownership**

Percentages

Number employed at establishment	Nationalised industries	Central/ local government	All private sector	Manufac- turing industry
25–99	(—)[1]	—	22	35
100–499	—	—	34	41
500–999	(3)	—	44	45
100 or more	(24)	—	58	63

Base: all establishments that recognised manual unions

[1] See note B

Table VIII.12 shows the pattern of consultation between different levels of manager concerning the most recent pay increases for manual workers in the largest bargaining unit. Local managers were consulted in only 30 per cent of cases and such consultation was least frequent in the smallest establishments. Where 1,000 or more people were employed at the establishment, the proportion of cases where local managers were consulted rose to about one half. On the face of it those figures appear low and suggest that much national and company pay bargaining takes place without the benefit, on the management side, of

Table VIII.12   **The extent of consultation between different levels of management in relation to the most recent pay settlement**

Percentages

		Number employed at establishment				
	Total	25– 99	100– 199	200– 499	500– 999	1000 or more
(a) Most important level of bargaining was higher than the establishment						
Higher-level managers consulted local management	30	26	31	37	40	51
Base: as specified at (a)						
(b) Plant level bargaining was most important level						
Higher-level managers consulted by local managers	58	(46)[1]	(51)	66	77	73
Base: as specified at (b)						

[1] See note B

Table VIII.13   The extent to which stewards and members were consulted over the most recent pay settlement (largest bargaining unit of manual workers)

	Total	Number employed at establishment				
		25– 99	100– 199	200– 499	500– 999	1000 or more
						Percentages
Consultations held	72	65	71[1]	80	88	93
with members and stewards	64	58	61	73	82	87
with stewards only	8	7	11	7	6	6
Form of consultation					Column percentages	
show of hands	72	72[2]	75	70	72	66
workplace ballot	15	11	12	20	23	24
postal ballot	7	8	6	6	2	5
other method	6	8	5	4	4	2
Base: establishments where manual union recognised and manual representative interviewed						
Unweighted	955	206	174	209	166	200
Weighted	694	343	142	113	56	39

See note D
See note C

the views of local operating managers. In cases where most importance was attached by managers to national bargaining, local managers were consulted in only 28 per cent of cases. Where most importance was attached to bargaining for the company as a whole, only 30 per cent were consulted. Of course, it may be that management engaged in pay negotiations at higher levels than the workplace had established systems of communication through which they could be well informed about local developments and requirements on a continuous basis. Our question on whether local management was consulted about the most recent pay settlement may have been interpreted as asking whether there had been any special consultation over and above such normal communications. That same reasoning, however, could be applied to our corresponding question asked in circumstances where the most important level of bargaining was described as being the establishment; that is to say, whether management at a higher level had been consulted before the most recent settlement. In such circumstances, higher level management was consulted almost twice as frequently about local settlements as local managers were consulted about settlements at higher levels. Consultations of both types were more common in relation to larger workplaces.

In about three-quarters of all cases manual workers reported that constituent stewards or members or both were consulted over the most recent pay settlement for the largest bargaining unit of manual workers (see Table VIII.13). In about two-thirds of the cases it was reported that the membership was consulted. Where such consultations took place, the most common means whereby manual workers expressed their views was through a show of hands. Workplace ballots took place in 15 per cent of establishments where there were consultations and postal ballots occurred in seven per cent of cases. Those figures, though modest, are higher than might have been expected. The consultation of members were more frequent in larger establishments. It was also more frequent, as might be expected, where settlements were local; that is to say, where the most important level of bargaining was described as being the establishment, the district or region or the division. Where national bargaining or company bargaining was felt to be most important, the membership was consulted much less frequently.

Non-manual representatives reported substantially less frequently that constituents were consulted than did manual counterparts (see Table VIII.14). Where consultations did take place among non-manual groups, however, the workplace ballot was the method most frequently used. Ballots were carried out in 61 per cent of instances where there was consultation.

Table VIII.14 **Extent of consultation over most recent pay settlement – accounts of manual and non-manual representatives compared**

	Manual representative	Non-manual representative
		Percentages
Consultations held	72	64
with members and stewards	64	52
with stewards only	8	12
Form of consultation		Column percentages
show of hands	72	10[1]
workplace ballot	15	61
postal ballot	7	14
other method	6	12
Base: establishments where the appropriate representatives were interviewed		
Unweighted	*955*	*900*
Weighted	*694*	*639*

[1] See note C

Basis for increase in pay where trade unions were not recognised
We discussed earlier in the chapter how, in cases where pay was not
subject to collective bargaining, a substantial number of management
respondents said that pay at their establishment was regulated by wages
councils when, in fact, they operated in sectors that did not come within
the ambit of wages councils. We also explained how that was likely to
have occurred. Table VIII.15 focuses upon those establishments where
pay was not regulated by collective bargaining. It summarises the
answers of managers to questions asking how the most recent increase
in pay had been brought about and identifies (Q49a, b; Q80a, b), first,
those who said rates of pay were regulated by wages councils and came
within appropriate sectors; secondly, those who were not in appro-

Table VIII.15 Basis for most recent pay increase where trade unions were
not recognised (manual and non-manual compared)

		Percentages
	Manual workers	Non-manual workers
Statutory wages council (correct MLH)[1]	13	8
Statutory wages council (incorrect MLH)	17	9
Other method		
Body taking decision		
Head office	21	28
Board/chairman/management	14	22
Discussion – management/employees	10	8
Negotiation – employers/unions	3	1
Not specified	19	22
Considerations in decision		
Merit/individual performance	5	15
Inflation	6	9
Market rates	10	8
Geared to other internal increase	1	8
Geared to formal external settlement	10	7
Ability to pay	4	5
Industry published norms	4	3
Fixed proportion of sales revenue	3	1
Not specified	30	37
Base: establishments where unions were not recognised		
Unweighted	*524*	*757*
Weighted	*738*	*987*

[1] As explained earlier in the chapter, there were a number of establishments where
managers said that their pay levels were regulated by wages councils but where the
establishments were in sectors not covered by wages councils. The table distinguishes
between wage-council answers that fell into appropriate and inappropriate sectors

priate sectors but said that wages councils settled their rates; and thirdly, the various explanations given by those who reported that they were outside the ambits of both collective bargaining and wages councils. Managers interpreted the question in different ways. Some managers answered the question asking how the pay increase had come about by explaining who had made the decision, while others did so in terms of how the decision had been taken. Some did both. This means that the answers give an indication of the range of influences over pay increases in the unorganised and unregulated sectors of employment but provide a poor basis for systematic comparisons. So far as comparisons between manual and non-manual groups are concerned, individual evaluations of performance were more important for non-manual than for manual workers, as was the gearing of the increase to some other internal settlement, presumably manual. There was some tendency for wages councils to be more important the larger was the size of enterprises but the smaller was the size of establishments. In consequence, wages councils were attributed special importance in small establishments that belonged to large organisations. This reflected the way in which distribution dominated that sector.

In some ways the structure of our interview schedules may have created a misleading impression of a clear cut distinction between two completely different systems for pay determination, depending upon whether or not trade unions were recognised. In our interview routing, we established crucially whether unions were recognised for bargaining about pay and conditions and, as far as pay determination was concerned, we asked completely different questions at workplaces where unions were recognised and at those where they were not. If unions were recognised we asked about levels of bargaining and so on. If unions were not recognised we explored how the most recent increase had come about. The fact that we asked different questions inevitably gives the impression that quite different influences were at work. In fact many of the major influences upon pay increases, including the increase in the cost of living, comparisons with the earnings and increases of other groups of worker, the ability of the employer to pay, the state of the labour market and so on will be common to situations where unions are recognised and those where they are not[3]. The distinction between the two situations is that, in the latter, management often makes a unilateral judgement about the considerations, their relative importance and inter-relationship. In the former, that judgement is constrained by what is acceptable to trade union representatives. In practice, there may sometimes be little difference in either the considerations or the outcomes depending upon whether the judgement is unilateral or jointly agreed. Our present study was not designed to explore the extent of such similarities or differences, but we need to

Table VIII.16 Extent to which different issues were the subject of collective bargaining by manual and non-manual groups (a) being negotiated at the establishment and (b) being negotiated at any level (establishment or enterprise)

Percentages

		Manual workers	Non-manual workers
Physical working conditions	(a)	65	58
	(b)	92	88
Redeployment within establishment	(a)	64	57
	(b)	80	79
Manning levels	(a)	49	35
	(b)	76	73
Redundancy	(a)	48	36
	(b)	88	84
Major changes in production methods	(a)	45	33
	(b)	65	56
Recruitment	(a)	43	35
	(b)	67	68
Holiday entitlement	(a)	15	12
	(b)	96	94
Length of working week	(a)	15	12
	(b)	95	92
Capital investment	(a)	15	11
	(b)	39	36
Pensions	(a)	11	6
	(b)	76	84
Base: establishments where appropriate unions were recognised			
Unweighted		*1344*	*1250*
Weighted		*1070*	*988*

make sure that the structure of our interview schedule does not give a misleading impression.

Bargaining over non-pay issues
In establishments where unions were recognised, we asked managers how a range of issues was resolved in relation to the largest bargaining units of both manual and non-manual workers and sought to establish, in particular, whether they were negotiated at a higher level or whether they were not subject to collective bargaining at all (Q41; Q72). We asked a corresponding set of questions of worker representatives. The answers of managers appeared to show that a surprisingly large range of

issues was subject to joint regulation with the largest manual union, especially at the workplace, which in many ways is the most important level. For instance, in nearly two-thirds of cases where trade unions were recognised management respondents reported that they negotiated with representatives of manual workers at the workplace about issues concerning physical working conditions and the redeployment of labour within the establishment (see Table VIII.16). In nearly one half of the cases, issues concerning manning levels, redundancy, major changes in production methods and recruitment were negotiated at the workplace. It was relatively rare for the length of the working week, holiday entitlement, capital investment and pensions to be subject to collective bargaining at establishment level. But, apart from capital investment, such issues did tend to come within the ambit of union negotiations at a higher level. Even in the case of capital investment, 39 per cent of managers said that it was subject to collective bargaining at some level. Moreover, the pattern in relation to the largest bargaining unit for non-manual workers was surprisingly little different, especially when the comparison was confined to workplaces that recognised both manual and non-manual trade unions.

Of course we cannot be sure what management respondents meant by negotiations. At one extreme it might mean that no changes in, say, physical working conditions or the deployment of staff could be made without the consent of local union officers. Alternatively, it might mean that union officers occasionally raised with managers complaints, demands or suggestions concerning physical working conditions or redeployment. Equally it might simply have meant that managers normally discussed with union officers any changes in working conditions or in the deployment of staff before they were made, but that such discussions took place in an implicitly joint consultative framework rather than a bargaining framework. In short, it is likely that what managers meant by negotiation will have varied from workplace to workplace and from sector to sector. At the same time, the answers of union representatives to the corresponding questions about negotiations over non-pay issues were remarkably consistent with those of managers (as shown by Table VIII.3 earlier in the chapter). That consistency suggests that there was genuine scope for union officers to influence decisions over a wide range of issues in large sectors of industry.

These findings refer, of course, to only those workplaces where unions were recognised but, as we have continuously stressed, they tended to be the larger workplaces and therefore accounted for a large proportion of the workforce. Moreover the larger was the workplace the more likely were managers to report that issues were negotiated at the workplace level. By contrast, there was a slight tendency for issues

Table VIII.17   Extent to which different issues were negotiated at the establishment (manual workers)

Percentages

	Central/local government	Nationalised industries	Manufacturing industry	Construction	Miscellaneous services
Physical working conditions	51	73	84	49	63
Redeployment within establishment	52	71	77	49	57
Manning levels	30	46	66	48	40
Redundancy	22	44	75	45	40
Major changes in production methods	31	21	72	30	36
Recruitment	31	34	55	46	45
Holiday entitlement	1	3	36	1	6
Length of working week	3	2	32	6	6
Capital investment	11	2	24	19	13
Pensions	*	*	25	11	9
Base: establishments that recognised manual unions					
Unweighted	*274*	*128*	*619*	*67*	*58*
Weighted	*355*	*74*	*376*	*79*	*71*

to be less likely to be subject to workplace bargaining the larger was the size of the enterprise. The overall impact of these divergent sources of variation was that plant bargaining was most common at the larger establishment belonging to a relatively small enterprise. Bargaining at a higher level was most common for the small establishment that belonged to a relatively large enterprise. In general terms, there tended to be little variation in relation to size in the extent to which negotiations over the various issues were said to occur at some level. The chief variation was the level at which bargaining occurred.

Analysis in relation to type of employer and industrial sector showed that the decentralisation of collective bargaining over the different issues was most marked in the manufacturing sector (see Table VIII.17). The pattern persisted even when differences in size were taken into account. Surprisingly, the pattern revealed for construction and miscellaneous services was not dramatically different from that which characterised national or local government.

Systems of payment and control

In the early part of this chapter we examined the levels of collective bargaining that influenced pay through formal, periodic negotiations over rates. As we stressed initially, however, there is a further level of negotiations that has a substantial impact upon pay. That is the shop floor level. There the chief targets for bargaining are job grading and rates for the job under systems of payment-by-results (PBR). Accordingly, for purposes of exploring the different sources of pressure on pay, it is important to know how far employers operate systems of payment-by-results, how far the application of such systems is based upon work study and how far job grading is carried out on a systematic basis subject to joint regulation. Accordingly we included in our study questions on payment-by-results, work study and job evaluation (Q108a, b, c; Q118a, b, c, d, e, f, g, h, i, j, k).

As well as being of relevance to sets of issues concerned with pay determination, these questions were also relevant to methods of bureaucratic control. Traditionally in British employment, especially in manufacturing industry, there have been strong class divisions in the system of control used by employers in relation to different levels of employee. There has been a tendency for direct sanctions and incentives to be brought to bear upon manual workers. For example, they have been required to clock on in the morning and clock off in the evening in order to control their hours of work. Control over their output has been sought through piecework or direct payment-by-results. Absenteeism has been discouraged by loss of pay when absent, and so on. By contrast, it has been assumed that non-manual workers are much more inclined to meet employers' requirements without needing direct incentives and sanctions. Accordingly, linked to our questions about PBR we also asked about methods of controlling time keeping and arrangements for payment when sick.

Table VIII.18 shows that there remained very sharp differences in the extent to which the majority of people in different job categories were paid according to results. Skilled manual workers and semi-skilled or unskilled male manual workers were the groups paid by results most frequently. Female workers were subject to rather less PBR than their male counterparts at the semi-skilled or unskilled level. By contrast, PBR was relatively rare among all levels of non-manual worker.

For manual grades there was a strong tendency for the proportion of establishments that operated PBR to increase the larger the number of people employed on site. Among middle and senior managers there was a very slight trend in the opposite direction. In consequence, the gap between manual workers and the higher occupational levels was most marked in the largest establishments. As PBR was more common in the

Table VIII.18 Extent to which the majority of workers in different categories were paid by results

Percentages

	Total	25–99	100–199	200–499	500–999	1,000 or more
		Number employed at establishment				
Unskilled/semi-skilled male manual						
PBR	23	18	24	37	38	48
PBR based on work study	11	5	14	25	27	31
Unskilled/semi-skilled female manual						
PBR	16	11	15	33	33	42
PBR based on work study	8	4	8	22	22	29
Skilled manual (male and female)						
PBR	26	23	26	33	33	39
PBR based on work study	12	6	16	20	24	23
Clerical/administrative/secretarial						
PBR	4	4	4	3	6	3
PBR based on work study	1	1	2	–	*	1
Foremen/supervisory						
PBR	11	13	10	8	11	7
PBR based on work study	3	3	4	4	3	4
Technical/professional						
PBR	7	8	7	4	9	5
PBR based on work study	1	1	2	—	—	1
Middle and senior managers						
PBR	8	9	7	4	4	3
PBR based on work study	1	1	2	1	—	1

Base: for each pair of rows the base is all establishments that employed the particular category of workers; consequently the base varies for each occupational category

Table VIII.19   Extent to which the majority of skilled manual workers were paid by results in relation to size and type of employer

Percentages

	Number employed at establishment			
	25–99	100–499	500–999	1,000 or more
All public sector				
PBR	15	28	30	33
PBR based on work study	7	21	27	13
Nationalised industries				
PBR	(31)[1]	14	(14)	(22)
PBR based on work study	(15)	11	(11)	(10)
Central/local government				
PBR	12	32	36	39
PBR based on work study	5	26	33	15
All private sector				
PBR	25	30	35	41
PBR based on work study	6	16	22	28

Base: establishments that employed skilled manual workers

[1] See note B

larger workplaces, the coverage of PBR among manual workers will have been wider than that suggested by the 'Total' column in Table VIII.18. Our findings on the extent of PBR also suggest that it was less common than some other sources because we asked whether the *majority* of specified occupational groups were paid by results, while other surveys have tended to ask whether *any* workers of specified groups were paid by results. We discuss that difference again later in the chapter where we compare our findings with others. Here the important point about Table VIII.18 is that it gives the impression that managers were more inclined to take the view that direct financial incentives were necessary to control the output of manual workers the larger was the size of the workplace. It will also be the case, of course, that larger workplaces are more likely to have the resources necessary to operate PBR and the division of labour that makes it appropriate.

There were also major differences in the extent of PBR in relation to type of employer. Systems of payment-by-results for the job levels principally involved were most common in the private sector generally, and in manufacturing industry and construction in particular. Establishment size and type of employer were independent influences upon the incidence of PBR. When we looked at establishments of similar size, the differences in relation to type of employer persisted (see Table VIII.19). Equally, when we confined our analysis to particular types of employer it remained the case that PBR for manual workers was more common in larger establishments.

Among manual workers PBR was based upon work study in about half the cases where it was operated. As far as size was concerned, there was some tendency for work study to be more frequently used in the operation of PBR in the larger workplaces. In consequence, there was an even more marked difference between the largest and smallest workplaces in the extent to which PBR based upon work study was used than there was in the extent to which PBR in any form was used. The type of difference, however, was not reflected in the variations according to type of employer. Indeed, there were many fewer contrasts in the use of work study between the public and private sectors, and within those two sectors, than there were in the operation of some form of PBR.

Trend in the coverage of payment-by-results

In order to provide some indication of the trend over time in the application of PBR, we asked managers in those establishments which operated PBR for some category of their employees whether more or fewer employees were paid by results than had been the case three years previously. Of course, that questioning meant that we missed those establishments that had totally abandoned PBR in the previous three years. Among those who were operating some PBR, slightly more judged that its coverage had grown over the previous three years than reported that it had declined. There were, however, divergent patterns as between different types of employer. In the public sector there was a consistent tendency for the coverage of PBR to have grown. In the private sector, there were reports of relatively extensive growth of PBR in construction. At the same time it was reported that fewer people were paid by results in manufacturing and in personal services. We consider our findings in relation to other sources of information about the trend in relation to PBR after briefly considering the extent of job evaluation.

The extent and nature of job evaluation schemes

A substantial proportion of disputes that arise on a day to day basis at the shop floor level result from disagreements over differentials or the pay of one individual or group compared with that of another. Job evaluation offers a systematic and often jointly regulated basis for establishing relative pay levels within establishments and organisations. Table VIII.20 summarises the extent to which job evaluation is practised in Britain generally, and the forms that it takes, according to our results. Nearly one quarter of establishments reported that some

Table VIII.20   Incidence and details of job evaluation schemes

Percentages

	All establishments	Number employed at establishment				
		25–99	100–199	200–499	500–999	1,000 or more
Job evaluation scheme	23	17	24	40	53	57
Base: all establishments						
Two or more schemes	25	18	17	26	45	64
Less than 3 years' old[1]	33	33	33	34	31	36
Review body in existence	63	55	64	70	82	73
Based on points system	47	41	44	55	63	50
Base: establishments with job evaluation						
Worker representation on review body	65	63	62	65	73	74
Base: establishments with a review body						
Operated in other establishments	80	95	76	64	65	57
Base: establishments that had job evaluation and were part of larger organisations						

[1] Refers to most recent scheme if more than one

employees at the establishment were covered by a job evaluation scheme. There was a strong tendency for the incidence of schemes to increase in line with increases in the size of the establishment. Over one half of workplaces with 500 or more workers reported that they had a scheme.

In most cases where establishments had schemes there was only one scheme, but in one quarter of all establishments there were two or more different schemes. That proportion rose to about two-thirds in establishments with 1,000 or more people. There were strong indications that many schemes were recent. One third had been introduced within the previous three years and there was little difference in that proportion among establishments of different size. Innovation in job evaluation did tend, however, to be more common in the private sector generally, and in manufacturing industry in particular.

In nearly two-thirds of instances where there were schemes, there was a review committee that oversaw the scheme and was responsible for the grading of new or changed jobs. Again, schemes tended more frequently to come under such bodies in larger workplaces. In about two-thirds of the cases where there were such job evaluation committees, employee representatives sat upon them. In most cases (72 per cent) these representatives were appointed by trade unions or staff associations. The larger was the size of the establishment the more likely were staff to be represented on job evaluation committees and the more often was the union or staff association the medium of representation.

Where establishments were part of a larger organisation, it was normally the case that the job evaluation schemes they operated were also used by other establishments in the enterprise. That practice, however, was slightly less common for larger establishments.

The most common type of job evaluation scheme was based on the points system and that was especially the case for the larger establishments. The simpler grading and ranking systems were more common in smaller workplaces and in sectors like construction, distribution, and textiles and clothing.

So far as different types of employer were concerned, job evaluation was concentrated in the private sector and manufacturing industry in particular. Within manufacturing industry, schemes were most common in engineering, vehicle manufacture and food, drink or chemicals. It was also the case, however, that schemes were relatively common in nationalised industries. Indeed, the pattern for nationalised industries with regard to job evaluation had much more in common with the private sector than with other parts of the public sector. Generally, though, it was manufacturing industry that led the way as far as job evaluation was concerned. Schemes were most common and, as has already been mentioned, likely to have been introduced most recently in that sector.

Perhaps the strongest influences upon the existence of job evaluation schemes, however, were size and, importantly, the proportion of the manual workforce who were women. There was a strong tendency for workplaces to be *less* likely to have job evaluation schemes the *larger* was the proportion of women who were employed. It is clear that systematic job evaluation was markedly less common in circumstances where a relatively large proportion of the workforce was female. Two-thirds of establishments with 1,000 or more people had job evaluation schemes where fewer than 30 per cent of the workforce were women. Only one quarter of such establishments had schemes when the female proportion of the workforce rose to over 70 per cent[4].

The relationship between job evaluation and payment-by-results

Traditionally the purpose of PBR systems of pay has been to encourage workers to increase effort and output. In principle, if they achieved their aim, this would result in a wage range of different levels of earnings among a group of workers with varying skills and aptitudes. In practice, there has been a tendency for PBR to become more an instrument of management control designed to ensure consistency of

Table VIII.21   **Relationship between payment by results and job evaluation**

Column percentages[1]

	All establishments	\multicolumn{7}{c}{Number employed at establishment}					
		25– 49	50– 99	100– 199	200– 499	500– 999	1000– 1999	2000 or more
Job evaluation and PBR	9	4	9	9	18	28	32	35
Job evaluation but no PBR	14	11	10	16	22	25	21	27
PBR but not job evaluation	23	20	27	22	26	18	26	16
No job evaluation or PBR	53	64	53	53	33	28	20	20
Base: all establishments that employed manual workers								
Unweighted	*1899*	*323*	*347*	*363*	*355*	*246*	*142*	*123*
Weighted	*1833*	*704*	*486*	*317*	*194*	*82*	*34*	*17*

[1] See note C

output[5]. The main purpose and effect of systematic job evaluation is to promote equity in levels of earnings and, in contrast with effects of traditional piecework, one of the main consequences of its introduction has been to reduce the distinctions among jobs and to simplify the structure of wage rates[6]. Accordingly, in principle, it might be expected that in their pure forms job evaluation and PBR would be alternatives. We carried out the analysis shown in Table VIII.21 to explore how far workplaces which practised job evaluation also operated PBR and *vice versa*. It is apparent that PBR and job evaluation could and did co-exist and that co-existence was common in our largest workplaces, where around one third of workplaces had both. At the same time, it was substantially more common for workplaces to have either one or the other than to have both of the management tools. In 37 per cent of all workplaces there was either PBR but no job evaluation (23 per cent) or job evaluation but no PBR (14 per cent), while only nine per cent of all establishments had both. Even in the largest workplaces, where job evaluation combined with PBR occurred most frequently, it remained the case that it was more common for establishments to use just one of the two tools. It may be assumed, moreover, that, where PBR co-existed with job evaluation, it was a substantially more refined form of PBR than traditional piecework.

Trend in the coverage of payment-by-results and job evaluation

The Warwick survey[7] found that some manual workers were paid by results in 64 per cent of establishments, while we found that the majority of some category of manual workers was paid by results in 32 per cent of establishments. Similarly, the Warwick study found that systematic job evaluation was practised for manual workers in 43 per cent of establishments. We found that just under one quarter of establishments operated job evaluation schemes.

Our present findings suggest that previous comparable surveys of workplaces have tended to give an exaggerated impression of the extent of PBR and job evaluation for two main reasons. First, they have concentrated upon manufacturing industry, where both PBR and job evaluation tend to be most common. Secondly, they have tended to concentrate upon larger workplaces and we found that there was also a strong tendency for both PBR and job evaluation to be more common in larger workplaces. In addition, as far as PBR was concerned, previous surveys have tended to ask whether *any* group of manual workers was paid by results, while we have focused upon whether a *majority of specified occupational groups* was paid by results.

When we identified the sub-sample in our survey that was comparable with the Warwick sample we found that the two sets of findings were consistent. So far as job evaluation was concerned, the correspondence was remarkable. Warwick found that 43 per cent of establishments had job evaluation schemes. We found that 42 per cent of manufacturing establishments with 50 or more full time employees had one or more job evaluation schemes. Warwick found that *some* manual workers were paid by results in 64 per cent of establishments. The comparable sub-sample in our survey revealed that a *majority* of some group of manual workers was paid by results in 52 per cent of workplaces. Accordingly, the differences between the overall findings for the two surveys did not arise from inconsistency in the answers of managers when like establishments were compared with like establishments. The contrasts resulted from the differences in the sectors covered by the two surveys.

In view of the way that the measurement of change was made very much more difficult by the tendency for different surveys to look at different sectors of industry, and, indeed, to ask different questions, a better measure of the trend in PBR over the past 10 years or so is provided by the New Earnings Survey (see Table VIII.22)[8].

It is apparent that there has been a steady long-term tendency for PBR earnings to make up a lower proportion of total earnings despite a contrary tendency for the coverage of PBR schemes to fluctuate. One of the reasons for those fluctuations in Britain has been the cyclical operation of national incomes policies that have encouraged them. For

Table VIII.22   **Payment by results in Britain, 1968–82**

Source: annual reports of the *New Earnings Survey*.

		1968	1970	1973	1975	1977	1979	1982
All industries	(a)	11.4	10.4	9.6	8.5	8.0	9.4	7.6
	(b)	–¹	–	39.3	41.2	36.8	44.0	44.5
Manufacturing industry	(a)	15.7	13.9	11.6	9.5	9.2	9.7	7.5
	(b)	–	–	43.3	40.9	39.5	47.0	–¹
Non-manufacturing industry	(a)	7.4	6.8	7.4	7.4	6.9	9.0	7.7
	(b)	–	–	35.5	41.5	34.3	41.1	–

(a) Percentage of total earnings from PBR
(b) Percentage of full-time men aged 21 or over receiving PBR
Base: full-time manual men aged 21 or over

---

¹ Proportion of full-time men aged 21 or over receiving PBR was not available in a comparable form for the year before 1973 and was not yet available for 1982 at the time of writing

instance, White has shown that the increase in the incidence of PBR that occurred towards the end of the 1970s owed much to the incomes policy operating at the time[9]. It is also important to note that many of the PBR schemes encouraged by that policy tended to be of the collective rather than of the individual type, using White's terminology. Within the collective category he included group and plant wide schemes and negotiated productivity rates.

It is also apparent from the table that in the most recent year for which figures are available, nearly one half of adult men (45 per cent) were paid by results. That figure suggests a wider coverage of PBR than our own findings. Again, however, the apparent inconsistency arose, first, because our figures refer to proportions of establishments rather than proportions of employees covered by PBR: as PBR was very much more common in larger establishments, our figure of one third of establishments where a majority of some group of manual workers was paid by results would have converted into a substantially higher proportion of employees covered by PBR, had the conversion been possible. But, secondly, as we asked simply whether a majority of a number of specified groups was paid by results and did not identify actual numbers, the conversion was not possible.

The checking of starting and finishing times
There were stark differences in the extent to which starting and finishing times of workers at different job levels were checked and in the manner in which they were checked (Q109c). Practice also varied markedly in establishments of different size and in those belonging to

Table VIII.23 Extent to which starting and finishing times were formally checked (manual and non-manual workers compared)

Percentages

	All establishments	All public sector	Nationalised industries	Central/local government	All private sector	Manufacturing	Construction	Miscellaneous services
Manual workers checked in some way	54	45	63	42	59	76	(46)[1]	50
Non-manual workers checked in some way	13	17	26	16	12	9	(19)	15
Methods of checking								
All clocked:								
manual	32	7	12	7	43	71	(16)	22
non-manual	2	2	6	1	3	3	(–)	4
All checked in:								
manual	13	19	17	18	10	4	(28)	11
non-manual	6	8	8	8	5	3	(11)	6
All sign in:								
manual	10	19	34	15	6	2	(6)	16
non-manual	5	7	12	7	4	3	(8)	4

Base:[2] establishments that employed manual workers and non-manual workers respectively

[1] See note B

[2] The base numbers differ slightly for the manual and the non-manual percentages and so the figures are not shown

different types of employer. For instance, nearly three-quarters of establishments in manufacturing industry required all manual workers to clock both in and out. It was very rare for all non-manual workers to be required to clock in and out, whatever the nature of the employer (see Table VIII.23). Where there was any formal check on non-manual workers it was more common for them to be checked in or to sign in.

Variation in the extent of clocking for manual workers also provided the most striking source of difference in relation to establishment size. Just over one half of all establishments with 2,000 or more employees required all manual workers to clock on and off. The same was true in only about one fifth of establishments with 25 to 49 employees.

Arrangements for payment when sick

The pattern of variation revealed in relation to clocking was in many ways mirrored in the responses of managers to questioning on arrangements for payment when people were away sick (see Table VIII.24; Q110). In the private sector, establishments were substantially more likely to pay non-manual workers in full when they were off sick than they were to continue paying manual workers in full. The gap was especially marked in manufacturing and construction. In the public sector generally, manual workers fared very much better, and, indeed, the gap between practices relating to manual and non-manual employees was relatively slight.

Share option schemes

A final aspect of the financial reward system at which we looked was the provision of share option schemes (Q112a, b, c, d). These have received some legislative and fiscal encouragement in recent years and we wanted to gain an indication of their coverage and possible growth[10]. Table VIII.25 shows that 14 per cent of all commercial establishments reported that they did have schemes and that they were very much more common in the financial services than in any other sector. They were least common in manufacturing. The prominence of financial services was even more apparent when variations in relation to the size of establishments were taken into account. Financial services were characterised by small establishments and smaller establishments were generally less likely to have schemes. Hence, the extent to which that sector was so much more likely than others to operate share option schemes was even more remarkable and the gap between it and other sectors was even wider when establishments of similar size were compared. There was clear evidence of recent activity, as one half of the schemes had been introduced in the previous three years, and it is probable that at least some of this was encouraged by tax advantages in the Finance Act, 1978[11]. The rate of introduction was accelerating prior

Table VIII.24 Arrangements for payment when sick

Percentages

	All estab-lishments	All public sector	Nation-alised industries	Public administra-tion	All private sector	Manu-facturing	Miscellan-eous services
Practice for manual workers when sick							
All receive full pay	41	60	70	59	32	23	36
None receives full pay	35	15	10	16	45	53	43
Base: management respondents in establishments employing manual workers							
Unweighted	1899	644	130	514	1255[1]	736	131
Weighted	1833	588	75	513	1245	542	198
Practice for non-manual workers when sick							
All receive full pay	62	69	75	68	58	58	49
None receives full pay	15	12	6	13	16	16	22
Base: management respondents in establishments employing non-manual workers							
Unweighted	2034	706	133	573	1328	746	133
Weighted	1989	650	78	572	1339	548	200

[1] See note H

Table VIII.25   Details of share option schemes

Percentage

	All commercial establishments	Manufacturing	Distribution	Financial services
Share option scheme operated	14[1]	11	21	45
Recency of introduction:				
Within previous 3 years	6	5	(9)[2]	(22)
3–10 years previously	4	3	(7)	(13)
Over 10 years previously	2	2	(2)	(9)
Proportion of employees who qualify (average per cent)	61	57	(74)	(83)
Proportion of those who qualify who take up (average per cent)	48	38	(60)	(67)
Base: commercial establishments[3]				
Unweighted	*1464*	*771*	*188*	*75*
Weighted	*1423*	*553*	*261*	*95*

[1] The percentages who had introduced schemes in the specified periods do not add to the proportion that had schemes because some managers could not recall when schemes were introduced

[2] See note B

[3] For the proportion of qualifiers and participants the base is described in the row label

to 1978 and there has been some fluctuation in recent years. In proportionate terms, relative to the previous incidence of schemes, the extent to which schemes had been recently introduced was common to all sectors. Generally, it appeared that schemes tended to be introduced when firms were doing well. They were more common where product demand was rising, where the size of the workforce was increasing and where managers gave a favourable rating to the financial performance of the establishment. Where schemes existed they tended to be available to the majority of employees. There were clear indications, however, that eligibility and take-up were most widespread in those sectors where schemes were most common. In concluding this section it is important to emphasise that the overall coverage of these schemes is not great. About five per cent of employees in the private sector were reported to be participants in share option schemes.

Notes

1.   D.C. Smith, *Incomes and wage-price policies* (Queen's University, Kingston, Ontario, 1967); Hugh Clegg, *How to run an Incomes Policy and why we made such a*

mess of the last one (Heinemann, London, 1974); F.T. Blackaby, 'The Reform of the Wage Bargaining System', *National Institute Economic Review*, August 1978, pp. 49–54; F.T. Blackaby, Ed., *The Future of Pay Bargaining* (Heinemann, London, 1980).

2. William Brown, Ed., *The Changing Contours of British Industrial Relations* (Basil Blackwell, Oxford, 1981).

3. See Table VIII.1 of W.W. Daniel, *Wage Determination in Industry* (Political and Economic Planning No. 563, London, 1976), compared with Table VIII.15 of the present study.

4. That pattern may well have implications for the achievement of equal pay at establishments and the possibility is currently under study at the Policy Studies Institute as one of the follow-up projects arising from our present survey.

5. Keith Carby and W.W. Daniel, *Consolidated report on wage payment systems by results* (European Foundation for Living and Working Conditions, Dublin, 1982).

6. Michael White, *Payment Systems in Britain* (Gower, in association with PSI, 1981).

7. William Brown, Ed., *op cit*.

8. Michael White, *op. cit*.

9. Michael White, *op. cit*.

10. The Finance Act, 1978 introduced special tax advantages for new profit sharing schemes that satisfied specified conditions. The advantages were enhanced and the conditions relaxed in the Finance Act, 1980.

11. That analysis is consistent with the picture presented in a review of employee financial involvement in Britain which argued that there was a tendency for share option schemes to increase throughout the 1980s. See Stephen Creigh, Nigel Donaldson and Eric Hawthorn, 'A stake in the firm', *Department of Employment Gazette*, May 1981.

IX Industrial Action

The forms and extent of collective conflict behaviour
Most discussions of industrial relations in Britain include some reference to industrial conflict. Strikes tend to be the centre of attention, partly because they are the most newsworthy manifestations of conflict but also because they are the one form for which extensive statistical material is available. With few exceptions[1], industrial relations researchers have taken the official records of strikes as their starting point in the investigation of industrial conflict.

We sought in this survey to broaden the available picture to include all manifestations of collective conflict behaviour. Thus we investigated the incidence of overtime bans, go-slows and so on, whereas individual manifestations of withdrawal from work such as absence, accidents and labour turnover, were excluded. The starting point for our analysis is therefore to look at the extent of the various forms of collective action, based upon responses to our question about the forms, if any, of industrial action which had taken place among workers in the establishment during the previous 12 months. Similar questions were put to both management and worker representative respondents and Table IX.1 shows how their reports compared (Q127a; Q128a; WQ62a). These results are confined to establishments with worker representative respondents.

In broad terms, about one quarter of establishments were reported as having experienced some form of industrial action amongst manual workers in the year up to mid-1980. The proportion was similar for non-manual workers. Manual workers, however, were more likely to take strike action, whereas non-manual workers were more likely to take non-strike action. Where non-strike action was taken, overtime bans were most frequent among both groups of workers, although less markedly so for non-manual workers, who often are not paid additionally for overtime.

There were, however, distinct differences when the responses of managers were compared with those of worker representatives. Management respondents appear to have reported industrial action, especially strike action, among manual workers, more often than did manual worker representatives. On the other hand, non-manual worker representatives more frequently reported industrial action, especially non-strike action, than did management respondents. These differences are too large to ignore. Moreover, the fact that they are in

Table IX.1 Comparison of responses by manager and worker representatives on whether there was any type of industrial action in the establishment in the previous year in relation to manual and non-manual workers.

Percentages

	Manual		Non-manual	
	Manager	Worker representative	Manager	Worker representative
Any type of industrial action	28	24	19	24
Strike/lockout	19[1]	17	8	9
Strike less than one day	6	5	3	5
Strike one day or more	14	12	6	5
Lockout	1	2	*	*
Other industrial action	15	15	12	17
Overtime ban or restriction	11	12	8	9
Work-to-rule	5	5	4	7
Go-slow	2	1	*	*
Blacking of work	4	3	5	8
Other	1	1	1	2

Base: establishments where both management and worker representatives specified in column head were interviewed

Unweighted	1040	1040	1016	1016
Weighted	779	779	722	722

[1] See note F

different directions for the two groups of workers makes it even less defensible to ignore them and continue the analysis using a single type of respondent. Indeed, if we compare responses establishment by establishment it is clear that there were many cases where industrial action had been reported by one respondent and not by his counterpart. Table IX.2 summarises these comparisons. All four comparisons show substantial levels of agreement but it is clear that there is less agreement about the occurrence of non-strike action.

That of itself is not surprising. First, there is a serious problem over the definition of industrial action and its various forms[2]. In consequence, estimates of the extent of industrial action which rely upon the recollections of a single informant must be suspect. For example, if we took only managers' reports of strikes among manual workers we would have 280 establishments (27 per cent) in Table IX.2 whereas there are 358 establishments (34 per cent) with strikes reported by either the

Table IX.2 **Variations in reports of industrial action in the previous year** ⁱ
management and worker representatives

Percentage

	Worker representative	Manager	Both respondents	Either respondent	Degree of Agreement
Manual workers					
Strike/lockout	24	27	17	34	0.87
Non-strike action	21	22	11	32	0.74
Base: establishments where managers and manual worker representatives were inter viewed					
Unweighted	*1040*	*1040*	*1040*	*1040*	
Non-manual workers					
Strike/lockout	12	11	6	17	0.91
Non-strike action	20	15	8	27	0.79
Base: establishments where managers and non-manual worker representatives were interviewed					
Unweighted	*1016*	*1016*	*1016*	*1016*	

¹ All percentages and measures of agreement use unweighted data.
² As measured by Yule's Q for dichotomous variables

manager or the manual worker representative. Secondly, there are two main sources of error in response to well-defined factual questions: errors of omission, owing to incomplete recall; and the 'telescoping' of events whereby events outside the reference period are reported as being within it. For relatively long reference periods, such as the year that was used in this question it is considered that the effects of incomplete recall are dominant³. Moreover, our subsequent question about the month in which any reported action began is likely to have reduced the telescoping error. In consequence, the balance of possible errors is in the direction of under-reporting industrial action. And reliance upon a single respondent's account will almost certainly lead to underestimation of the extent of industrial action.

A further conclusion that can be drawn from Table IX.2 is that reliance upon management reports would particularly underestimate the extent of non-strike action by non-manual workers. This type of action was reported by one third more worker representatives than managers. Some of the discrepancy undoubtedly arose from lack of awareness or errors of recall on the part of managers, but there are probably other factors besides these that contributed to so large a difference.

In view of these considerations we describe the extent of industrial

Table IX.3 Establishments where any industrial action in the previous year was reported by manager or worker representative

Percentages

	Manager and worker representative interviewed		No worker representative interviewed
	Either respondent	Manager	Manager
Industrial action by manual workers reported	47	38	15
Base: establishments with manual workers			
Unweighted	*1040*	*1040*	*859*
Weighted	*779*	*779*	*975*
Industrial action by non-manual workers reported	35	23	6
Base: establishments with non-manual workers			
Unweighted	*1016*	*1016*	*1018*
Weighted	*722*	*722*	*1267*

action using the combined reports of managers and worker representatives. Such a measure has the inherent disadvantage that in some cases only a manager was interviewed. The possibility of under-reporting will remain in these cases; but they are only a minority, as Table IX.3 indicates. The better measurement for the majority of cases must surely outweigh this.

Sources of variation in industrial action by manual workers
The period covered by our survey data was one of exceptionally widespread strike activity, the number of workers involved in officially-recorded strikes being 40 per cent higher than the annual average for the period since 1966[4]. The combined reports of managers and worker representatives showed that 24 per cent of survey establishments had been affected by some kind of industrial action in the year up to mid-1980. In all, 18 per cent were affected by strikes or lockouts and 19 per cent were affected by one or more of the forms of non-strike action. The use of the different forms of industrial action varied considerably between manual and non-manual employees and so in this section we deal with manual workers only, beginning with the relationship between structural or organisational features of establishments, such as numbers employed and payment systems, on the incidence of industrial action. We deal with non-manual employees in a separate section.

Table IX.4   Establishments in which different types of industrial action by manual workers in the previous year were reported (by manager or worker representatives) in relation to number of manual workers

Percentage

	Total	1–9	10–24	25–49	50–99	100–199	200–499	500–999	1000 or more
Any type of industrial action by manual workers	**18**	**2**	**8**	**13**	**27**	**33**	**50**	**74**	**77**
Strike/lockout	12¹	2	5	8	18	21	40	53	67
Strike less than one day	5	1	2	3	7	9	15	25	4
Strike more than one day	8	1	3	5	12	14	31	38	5
Lockout	1	–	–	1	1	1	1	1	
Other industrial action	11	*	4	8	18	21	27	57	55
Overtime ban or restriction	8	*	3	6	11	14	22	45	4
Work-to-rule	4	–	3	3	6	7	13	16	1
Go-slow	1	–	1	*	1	2	5	8	
Blacking of work	3	–	*	2	4	6	9	18	2
Other	1	–	–	1	1	1	1	4	
Base: all establishments with manual employees									
Unweighted	*1899*	*162*	*244*	*336*	*280*	*293*	*306*	*140*	*138*
Weighted	*1834*	*223*	*424*	*522*	*282*	*197*	*127*	*38*	*21*

¹ See note F

Numbers employed

Table IX.4 shows the extent of the various types of industrial action by manual workers and its variation with the number of manual workers employed. Clearly there is a strong relationship between the occurrence of every type of industrial action and the number of manual workers at the establishment. There is no surprise in this. The relationship has been observed before and there are several plausible lines of explanation for its existence[5]. Some writers have argued that the greater number of communication links between individuals and groups provide more sources of conflict in large establishments. Others have argued that larger establishments are more bureaucratically managed and that this produces a lower level of commitment to the employing unit by employees. A third line of theorising has stressed the greater division of labour and fragmentation of tasks in larger units and hence a more alienated workforce. Adjudicating between these explanations would itself be a substantial analytical task, beyond the scope of this book. But two observations can be made at this stage, before we proceed to examine other variables. The first is that the effect of size is so strong that we should obviously control for size in examining other variables, which may or may not be correlated with size. The second point is that there is a hint in some of the results of non-linearity and, in particular, that some forms of industrial action are subject to a 'threshold effect', becoming feasible only in establishments with a minimum number of manual employees. On the other hand, it is surprising that establishments with as few as ten or twenty manual employees should be affected by industrial action to the extent shown by these results.

Union density, recognition and representatives

In considering other factors besides workforce size which might be expected to help explain differences in establishments' experience of industrial action we turn first to those which represent the ability of a workforce to organise such collective behaviour. The indicators of the presence and strength of workplace trade union organisation that we have used are, first, the proportion of the workforce who were union members (union density[6]); secondly, the presence of trade unions recognised by management for negotiating pay and conditions; and thirdly, the presence of shop stewards or other representatives. All these indicators are based on management reports.

For manual workers, both strike and non-strike industrial action were clearly related to union membership density, as Table IX.5 shows. These relationships persisted when establishment size was held constant. Indeed, the occurrence of industrial action showed marked variation with both union density and establishment size. However, there was possibly an exception. In establishments with less than 25 manual employees the tendency to experience industrial action was low and affected very little by the proportion of workers who were union members. This suggests that the relationship is not a simple one and may be subject to threshold effects. Recognition by management and the presence of shop stewards may provide such an effect, since both are discrete advances in union organisation at the workplace. As Table IX.5 shows, recognition and the presence of representatives increased the likelihood of an establishment being affected by industrial action – again irrespective of establishment size, to which both of these factors were positively related.

Table IX.5 **Establishments where strike and non-strike action by manual workers were reported (by managers or worker representative) in relation to workplace trade union organisation**

Percentages

	Total	Number of workers in establishment			
		1–24	25–99	100–499	500 or more
Strike					
No union members	*	–	1	(2)[1]	§[2]
Low union density[3]	5	5	4	10	§
Medium union density	16	7	13	28	52
High union density	29	8	24	39	64
No manual union recognised	2	1	3	6	§
One or more manual unions recognised	19	6	16	24	58
No manual union representative	4	3	4	12	(33)
Union representative at establishment	26	8	21	33	62
Senior representative	37	§	30	39	58
Non-strike action					
No union members	*	–	–	(2)	§
Low union density	5	3	5	8	§
Medium union density	13	6	11	22	45
High union density	25	9	22	31	60
No manual union recognised	2	1	3	7	§
One or more manual unions recognised	21	7	15	30	59
No manual union representative	4	2	3	11	(65)
Union representative at establishment	23	8	20	27	55
Senior representative	32	§	28	31	55
Base: establishments with manual workers					
Unweighted	*1899*				
Weighted	*1833*				

[1] See note B
[2] See note A
[3] See Appendix A for definitions of union density categories

These findings are in accordance with common sense expectations and are at variance with some surprising results from the Warwick survey of manufacturing establishments in 1977–8[7]. That report quotes 45 per cent of establishments with low manual union density (0–20 per cent) as having had a strike within the previous two years, compared with 21 to 40 per cent for plants with higher union density. If the results reported here are confined to manufacturing establishments within the same size range as those of the Warwick survey, the plants with low manual union density still have considerably lower strike experience than plants with higher density, no matter whose reports of manual strike activity we take.

A further step in the development of workplace trade union organisation is the development of some sort of hierarchy among representatives. Such a hierarchy, it might be argued, would increase their ability to mount collective action. This argument received some support from the results in Table IX.5, but it appears not to be as important as the presence at all of shop stewards. Moreover, the presence of senior stewards appeared to have no effect in the largest workplaces with 500 or more manual employees.

Workforce composition
Another source of explanation for the pattern of industrial action is the differing composition of establishment workforces. We have already distinguished between manual and non-manual workforces and seen that they used the various types of industrial action in varying degrees (see Table IX.1). Other characteristics that are often held to be associated with frequent disputes are a high proportion of males and a high proportion of full time workers, these characteristics themselves being associated with high trade union membership, as our results in Chapter II confirm. Table IX.6 gives some support to these suggestions in respect of manual workers.

The table shows clearly that at low levels of trade union density there was no difference in experience of industrial action between establishments with a predominantly male workforce and those with a predominantly female one. At high levels of union density, however, a high proportion of male employees increased substantially the likelihood of industrial action. Similarly, it was only at high levels of union membership density that the proportion of full time workers made a marked increase to the likelihood of industrial action.

These results indicate a complex set of relationships between the proportions of male and full time employees, union density and the tendency to industrial action. When union density was not controlled for in the analysis there appeared to be reasonably strong correlations between the proportion of the workforce which was male and the

Table IX.6   Establishments where industrial action by manual workers was reported (by manager or worker representative) in relation to union density, sexual composition of workforce and percentage of workforce which was full time

Percentages

| | | Union density among manual workers | | |
	Total	Low	Medium	High
Percentage of workforce which was male				
Up to 30 per cent	10	9	21	(15)[1]
30 to 70 per cent	17	8	24	32
More than 70 per cent	26	8	23	44
Percentage of workforce which was full-time				
Up to 60 per cent	6	9	10	§[2]
60 to 95 per cent	13	5	26	28
More than 95 per cent	31	15	24	46

Base: establishments where management estimates of trade union membership among full-time manual workers were reported
    Unweighted   *1364*
    Weighted   *1137*

[1] See note B
[2] See note A

proportion which was full time and the likelihood of industrial action. However, the rest of IX.6 shows that the correlation was largely confined to establishments with high union density. This may explain why previous analyses have often failed to find a very strong relationship with these workforce characteristics[8]; both non-linearity and interactions between the variables appear to be involved.

Level of pay negotiations and payment system
The complicated pattern of pay determination revealed by our survey was discussed in Chapter VIII. As in our analysis of other material, we have extracted a small part of those results, focusing on what the management respondent considered was the most important level at which the last pay increase was settled for the largest group of manual workers. Table IX.7 shows how this related to industrial action, controlling as before for the effects of workforce size.

As we expected, there was a much greater likelihood of manual workers taking strike action where they negotiated at establishment level. This relationship was apparent at all sizes of the manual workforce. We thought that at least part of the reason for this was likely to be that payment-by-results schemes were considerably more common

Table IX.7 **Establishments reporting¹ industrial action by manual workers in relation to level of pay bargaining**

Percentages

	Total	Number of manual employees in establishment			
		1–24	25–99	100–499	500 or more
Most important level of pay bargaining for largest group of manual workers					
Strike					
National, industry or regional	16	7	14	26	52
Single employer but multi-establishment	19	(6)²	15	28	50
Single establishment	46	§³	42	50	71
Non-strike action					
National, industry or regional	15	3	15	26	46
Single employer but multi-establishment	17	(12)	11	22	52
Single establishment	37	§	35	32	73
Base: establishments with recognised unions for manual workers					
Unweighted	*1314*				
Weighted	*1043*				

¹ The percentages represent those establishments where either manager or worker representative reported industrial action
² See note B
³ See note A

where pay negotiations took place at establishment level. Indeed, the effect of payment-by-results upon the likelihood of an establishment experiencing industrial action was quite profound, as Table IX.8 shows. Many writers have observed this connection before, particularly when explaining inter-industry differences in strike behaviour. However, such observations have normally been based upon industry level data on the coverage of payment-by-results – and the strike frequencies of those industries – with no possibility of controlling for establishment size, union density and so on⁹. We have in Table IX.8 direct evidence of the effect of payment-by-results systems. These differences were most apparent in the engineering industries but also existed to a lesser degree in the rest of manufacturing, the private sector and the nationalised industries. They occurred whatever the main level of pay determination, although the differences were greatest when the plant was the main locus of bargaining. The same kind of result appeared for non-strike action: such action was strongly associated with establishment

Table IX.8   **Establishments reporting¹ industrial action by manual workers in relation to payment by results**

Percentages

	Total	Number of manual employees in establishment			
		1–24	25–99	100–499	500 or more
Strike/lockout					
Some manuals covered by PBR	26	(5)²	17	42	61
No group of manuals where majority covered by PBR	9	4	10	16	54
Non-strike industrial action					
Some manuals covered by PBR	22	(8)	16	30	62
No group of manuals where majority covered by PBR	8	2	9	18	46
Base: establishments with manual employees					
Unweighted	*1899*				
Weighted	*1833*				

¹ The percentages represent those establishments where either manager or worker representative reported industrial action
² See note B

level pay bargaining and the presence of payment-by-results. Piece-work bargaining certainly appears to involve a high incidence of industrial disputes.

Complexity of representation and negotiating arrangements
Two other factors which are sometimes held to lead to disputes are the complexity of representation and negotiating arrangements. As indicators of these factors we have taken the number of unions representing manual workers and the number of negotiating groups into which they combined (if there were two or more unions). Both these factors were positively related to the size of workforce, as we saw in Chapter II, and so again we controlled for workforce size in the analysis.

There appeared to be a rather weak tendency for strikes to be more frequent among manual workers where there were more unions representing the manual workforce (Table IX.9). What looks like a very strong relationship in the 'Total' column is much less definite when workforce size is controlled for. The same was true for industrial action other than strikes. Multi-unionism does not appear to be the culprit for Britain's industrial relations record that some commentators have suggested it is[10], at least if we take industrial action as the criterion.

Table IX.9 Establishments reporting[1] industrial action by manual workers according to complexity of representation

Percentages

	Total	Number of manual employees in establishment			
		1–24	25–99	100–499	500 or more
Strike/lockout					
One recognised manual union	15	7	16	17	(24)
Two recognised manual unions	24	(11)[2]	23	27	(55)
Three recognised manual unions	23	§[3]	(14)	28	(76)
Four recognised manual unions	47	§	§	48	71
Five recognised manual unions	53	§	§	51	64
One negotiating group	19	8	18	29	53
Two negotiating groups	26	§	18	31	64
Three negotiating groups	28	§	§	(35)	(64)
Four negotiating groups	58	§	§	(64)	(63)
Non-strike action					
One recognised manual union	12	5	12	22	(54)
Two recognised manual unions	22	(19)	26	15	(56)
Three recognised manual unions	27	§	(25)	29	(65)
Four recognised manual unions	42	§	§	44	63
Five recognised manual unions	43	§	§	44	54
One negotiating group	16	7	15	24	71
Two negotiating groups	24	§	22	23	83
Three negotiating groups	30	§	§	31	(80)
Four negotiating groups	41	§	§	(40)	(77)

Base: establishments with recognised unions for manual employees
Unweighted 1375
Weighted 1095

[1] The percentages represent those establishments where either manager or worker representative reported industrial action
[2] See note A
[3] See note B

The presence of agreed procedures
The relationship between institutional arrangements such as the presence of agreed procedures for dealing with disputes and the incidence of industrial action is an open question. On the one hand, it may be held that the existence of such procedures should reduce the likelihood of industrial action by providing rules for the resolution of disputes. On the other hand it may be argued that the introduction of formal

procedures becomes necessary or desirable only when there is a potential for industrial action, or some recent experience of it, and therefore that the existence of such procedures indicates a tendency to industrial action. To make an initial examination of these suggestions, we took the presence of an agreed procedure, written down and signed by management and trade union representatives, covering disputes about pay and conditions or discipline and dismissals, as our definition of the circumstances where formal procedures existed. Such procedures were common: management respondents reported them in 46 per cent of establishments. Such establishments turned out to be those with a greater chance of experiencing manual industrial action; 27 per cent of establishments with procedures had experienced action: only 10 per cent without procedures had done so. However, both the occurrence of industrial action and the presence of procedures were strongly related to establishment size, and controlling for establishment size made the positive correlaton between the presence of formal procedures and experience of industrial action disappear, even when only establishments with recognised trade unions were considered. What is clear is that there was certainly no tendency for establishments with formal, agreed and signed procedures to be less prone to industrial action. To make the test a more appropriate one, however, we would have to control, in a statistical sense, the level of underlying disputes which the agreed procedure might help prevent leading to industrial action. One possibility for doing this lies in respondents' perceptions of the general state of industrial relations at the establishment, poor assessments being interpreted as an indication of incipient unrest. Unfortunately, restricting the analysis in this way leaves us with too few cases to carry out the analysis. The most we can say is that recent industrial action and the existence of formal industrial relations procedures are largely independent.

Joint consultative arrangements

We tested for any association between the presence of joint consultative arrangements and the incidence of industrial action. Again the comparisons were confined to establishments with at least one recognised trade union and are given for different sizes of establishment. As Table IX.10 shows, there was a clear tendency in small establishments for industrial action to occur more commonly where there was a joint consultative committee – the reverse of any suggestion that joint consultative arrangements might, in general, reduce overt conflict between managements and unions. For establishments with over 500 employees, however, there appeared to be no difference. A similar pattern emerged when analysis was confined to manual employees. The explanation for small establishments with consultative committees

Table IX.10 Establishments reporting[1] any industrial action in relation to presence of consultative committees

Percentages

| | Total | Number employed in establishment | | | | | |
		25–49	50–99	100–199	200–499	500–999	1000 or more
Consultative committee	46	30	37	45	59	63	76
No consultative committee	26	18	27	30	34	(74)[2]	(74)

Base: establishments where any respondent reported the presence of a recognised trade union

Unweighted	*1576*
Weighted	*1336*

[1] The percentages represent those establishments where any respondent reported industrial action
[2] See note B

being more likely to experience industrial action is not obvious. In the absence of a direct link between the presence of consultative committees and the occurrence of industrial action, it must be the case that both these characteristics are themselves influenced by other variables such as the degree of union organisation. Complex multi-variate analysis would be required to unravel an explanation of this finding.

Share ownership schemes
A factor which might be expected to lessen the likelihood of industrial action is the presence of a share ownership scheme with at least a modest degree of participation. The argument here is that when a significant proportion of the workforce have an equity interest in their employing organisation they more readily perceive a commonality of interest with management and are less likely to resort to action which is financially damaging to the firm[11]. In subjecting such a proposition to empirical test we faced some difficult problems, the most serious being that only a few establishments of any considerable size had a share ownership scheme with a significant proportion of the workforce participating in it. If we take a minimum participation rate of 10 per cent (in other words, at least 10 per cent of the establishment's workforce participated in the share ownership scheme), then only seven per cent of private sector establishments were above the minimum. This arbitrary cut-off excludes what are mainly management-only schemes, five per cent of the workforce on average being classified as middle or senior

management, but is otherwise a generous one for defining 'widespread' financial participation. If the comparison is confined to establishments with recognised unions and within the 25 to 99 employee size band (industrial action being highly size-related and larger establishments with schemes being too few), then three per cent of establishments with 'widespread' share ownership among the workforce had experienced industrial action, compared with 26 per cent of establishments with no share ownership scheme or low participation in one. (These figures are on unweighted bases of 22 and 198 respectively.) Given the small numbers involved in the comparison and the variety of other factors which might also be involved, not too much should be made of this result. But it is probably the best evidence available so far and does at least suggest a connection between widespread share ownership and industrial peace.

Industrial sector
It may be thought remiss that we have only at this point introduced industrial sector into our analysis, as it is one of the most common variables for analysing strike behaviour. This has been deliberate. Inter-industry analyses of strikes have generally incorporated some of the variables that we have already mentioned, although often relying upon less satisfactory evidence[12], in order to explain the different strike records of different industries. With data on individual establishments it is preferable to explain their individual strike records directly rather than to aggregate them initially into industries. There is, in any case, plenty of information about the industrial distribution of strikes[13]. What has been missing from this picture until now is the corresponding picture for non-strike industrial action, and this is provided by our analysis. Our final table in this section, therefore, shows how the industrial distribution of strikes compared with that for non-strike action.

Over most of the broad industry groups shown in Table IX.11 there is close correspondence between the extent of strikes and the extent of other forms of industrial action. Industries which had extensive strike experience also had extensive experience of the other collective sanctions. Such a result would be expected from our foregoing analysis because, generally speaking, the factors that we have found to be associated with one type of action have also been found to be associated with the other. However, there are two important exceptions to this overall correspondence: local and national government, where non-strike action was much more widespread than strike action and vehicle manufacturing, where strikes were the more common form. Part of the explanation for these divergences from the general pattern is likely to lie in the main factor that distinguished the extent of strikes from the

Table IX.11 Establishments reporting[1] various forms of industrial action in relation to industry sector[2]

Percentages

	All establishments	A	B	C	D	E	F	G	H	I	J	K	L	M
Any industrial action	25	19	46	40	63	14	35	22	31	6	7	26	13	48
Strike or lockout	16	13	37	31	53	7	26	14	21	3	2	14	9	21
Strike of one day or more	11	7	31	30	48	4	13	11	16	2	3	8	6	10
Non-strike industrial action	19	13	31	29	41	8	28	17	19	3	5	19	7	44
Base: all establishments														
Unweighted	*2040*	*141*	*205*	*102*	*70*	*97*	*160*	*102*	*191*	*189*	*76*	*363*	*163*	*181*
Weighted	*2000*	*88*	*172*	*49*	*28*	*80*	*138*	*130*	*155*	*262*	*95*	*372*	*243*	*188*

Key to column labels
A Food/chemicals
B Metals/Mechanical engineering
C Electrical engineering
D Vehicles
E Textiles/Clothing
F Miscellaneous manufacturing
G Construction/Extraction

H Utilities/Transport
I Distribution
J Financial services
K Professional/Scientific services
L Miscellaneous services
M Public administration

[1] The percentages represent those establishments where any respondent reported industrial action
[2] The column labels represent abbreviated descriptions of the sections coverd. See Appendix A for a full account

extent of non-strike action, namely, the proportions of manual and white collar employees in the workforce. Public administration is predominantly a white collar sector (only 18 per cent of establishments had 70 per cent or more manual workers, compared with 40 per cent for all sectors). Vehicle manufacturing has high concentrations of manual workers.

The picture of industrial action presented by the Department of Employment official records of strikes can be compared with the more complete picture covering all forms of action provided by our results. The survey questions identified separately strikes of one day or more and these correspond approximately to strikes within the official recording limits. The first and third rows of Table IX.11 compare the proportion of establishments having such strikes with the proportion where any industrial action was reported. It shows that there was a wide variation in the degree to which strikes of a day or more are a good indicator of the extent of industrial action of all types. In the engineering industries there were few establishments affected by industrial action that were not also affected by strikes of one day or longer. On the other hand, strikes of one day or more are a very inadequate indicator of the extent of industrial action in sectors as varied as food and chemicals, textiles and clothing, miscellaneous manufacturing, professional and scientific services and public administration. So far as we know, this is the first time that the extent of non-strike action in the non-manufacturing sectors of the economy has been revealed.

Technology
Technology, or the nature of the production system, has often been regarded as being related to industrial disputes, although the relationship has never been very firmly established. The core of the argument has been that manufacturing systems which approached the stereotype of the single-product, mass-production assembly line were most vulnerable to effective work stoppages and also employed workers in the most alienating conditions. Our measure of technology aimed to capture the first of these two features but, as with previous attempts, was forced to focus upon the 'main' production system if there were several. Thus our technology measure may have ignored the most critical parts of an establishment's production technology while our measure of strike-affectedness covered the whole establishment. Perhaps our test was, therefore, an inadequate one, but it is still worth reporting that we found no clear connection between a manufacturing establishment's production technology and its likelihood of being affected by industrial action among manual workers. A similar result was reported by the Warwick team and by Edwards[14], both of whom used the more conventional measure of production technology.

Economic cycle and method of labour force contraction

Many analyses of strike behaviour have revealed the tendency for strike activity to fluctuate with the general economic cycle. Our survey, being a cross-sectional study of establishments in mid-1980, could shed light on this only indirectly. But a plausible implication of the economist's time series model is that establishments in economic difficulties would be less likely to experience industrial action. We used several indicators of economic difficulties to test this proposition: the contraction of the establishment's workforce at several levels of severity; the introduction of short time working; and the manager's assessment of the state of demand for the establishment's products or services. None of these appeared to affect the likelihood of industrial action. What did appear to affect the incidence of industrial action was the method of implementing workforce reductions. Establishments which had reduced their workforces by using both voluntary *and* compulsory redundancies were much more likely to have had a strike or an overtime ban than establishments which had used only voluntary or only compulsory methods for reducing the workforce, or had made no reductions. And this difference was apparent for all sizes of establishment. Thus it seems that is the means by which workforce reductions are carried out by management – rather than their existence or severity – that is associated with disputes.

Finally, the generality of the foregoing results must be addressed. So far as statistical representativeness is concerned, the cautious approach that we have adopted to cross-tabulation is unlikely to have produced freak results[15]. But a further question that may be asked is how typical are the results of this survey, based as they are on reports about a 12 month period ending in mid-1980. The most obvious candidate for a major national dispute which could be dominating the results for a particular sector during the period was the protracted engineering industry dispute which began in August 1979 and consisted of a series of intermittent one day strikes. When we isolated establishments that were affected only by that dispute[16] they came to less than 10 per cent of the survey sample in that sector and less than one quarter of the strike-affected establishments. This strongly suggests that our analysis has not been greatly distorted by a single, widespread dispute and that the relationships reported will apply to other periods besides the one to which the survey data specifically refer.

The comparative pattern for non-manual workers

The foregoing analysis has concentrated upon industrial action by manual workers and associated characteristics of the manual workforce. We now turn to the corresponding picture for non-manual workers, bearing in mind their greater use of non-strike industrial

Table IX.12   **Establishments where industrial action by non-manual workers wa reported (by manager or worker representative) in relation to wor place trade union organisation**

Percentage

	Total	Number of non-manual workers i establishment			
		1–24	25–99	100–499	500 or more
Strike					
No union members	–	–	–	–	§[1]
Low union density	5	(3)[2]	2	11	(26)
Medium union density	11	5	10	14	32
High union density	10	5	9	20	50
No non-manual union recognised	1	*	1	*	§
One or more non-manual union recognised	10	5	9	17	36
No non-manual union representative	1	1	2	1	§
Union representative at establishment	13	7	11	17	35
Senior representative	20	§	14	22	38
Non-strike action					
No union members	*	–	1	–	§
Low union density	5	(2)	2	14	(24)
Medium union density	18	5	18	26	47
High union density	22	11	24	44	62
No non-manual union recognised	1	*	1	2	§
One or more non-manual union recognised	19	9	17	33	48
No non-manual union representative	3	2	3	4	§
Union representative at establishment	24	13	20	35	44
Senior representative	30	§	17	40	50
Base: establishments with non-manual workers					
Unweighted	2034				
Weighted	1989				

[1] See note A
[2] See note B

action, particularly work-to-rules and blackings of work, and their less frequent use of other sanctions. All types of industrial action were, however, closely associated with workforce size, as was the case with manual employees. The patterns in relation to union density and recognition were similar to those for manual workers (Table IX.12) but, unlike the results for manual workers, there was no tendency for high union density and a high proportion of male non-manual

Table IX.13 Establishments reporting[1] industrial action by non-manual workers in relation to level of pay bargaining

Percentages

	Total	Number of non-manual workers in establishment			
		1–24	25–99	100–499	500 or more
Most important level of pay bargaining for largest group of non-manual workers					
Strike					
National, industry or regional	10	5	7	19	31
Single employer but multi-establishment	11	7	12	12	34
Single establishment	15	§[2]	10	17	53
Non-strike action					
National, industry or regional	24	12	22	45	51
Single employer but multi-establishment	13	7	12	19	39
Single establishment	15	§	9	18	54
Base: establishments with recognised unions for non-manual workers					
Unweighted	*1205*				
Weighted	*943*				

The percentages represent those establishments where either manager or worker representative reported industrial action
See note A

employees to coincide with a greater likelihood of industrial action. Apart from this curious exception, the greater the proportion of males the greater was the likelihood of industrial action.

Unlike the case of manual workers, there was no tendency for non-manual strike experience to be greater when pay determination was at establishment level (Table IX.13). The explanation for this difference between manual and non-manual workers is likely to be the presence of payment-by-results systems, which were considerably more common for manual workers than for non-manual workers (Chapter VIII). Industrial action other than strikes was, for non-manual workers, more prevalent where bargaining was at a national level. Other than the fact that non-strike action was more commonly about issues other than pay, so that the level at which pay bargaining took place was a less relevant factor, there was also an indication that this tendency was largely confined to the public sector. However, taking the results for manual and non-manual workers together, it is clear that features of the bargaining system have some relevance in explaining the patterns of industrial action.

The characteristics of reported industrial action

We asked a number of questions about the types of industrial action, if any, that had taken place in the previous 12 months, including questions about the numbers of different incidents, the main reasons for the dispute, the groups of employees involved and the duration of the action.

Extent of different kinds of incident

Taking all strikes, both long and short, as a single category, only three per cent of establishments had had two or more strikes by manual workers during the year, according to management reports (Q127b). The equivalent figure for non-manual workers was one per cent (Q128b). These proportions were too small to carry out any worthwhile analysis of strike frequency or strike frequency per worker. Such analysis would generally require a much larger sample or a longer reporting period than the one year that we selected. In any case, given the greater unreliability of recollections over longer periods, we doubt whether the survey method is appropriate for examining characteristics associated with strike frequency. The same argument applies with even greater force to the other forms of industrial action, since individually they affected even smaller numbers of establishments, at least as reported by managers.

We therefore turn to look at features of the most recent strike or other industrial action reported at the establishment, these being the subject of further separate questioning. Although our questions, for practical reasons, were confined to the most recent dispute, that dispute can nevertheless be said to be typical of all the disputes that affected our sampled establishments in the year in question in that most respondents, whether management or worker representatives, reported only a single incident of any of the eight types of action we classified. In consequence, the characteristics of the most recent dispute must be close to, in aggregate, the characteristics of all disputes in the year up to mid-1980. However, the number of cases where we have information is quite small, especially in the case of non-strike action, because the data are spread out over each of the five types identified, although only overtime bans, work-to-rules and blackings are numerically important. Our questions referred to strikes and other action separately and strikes of less than one day were excluded. This exclusion must be borne in mind when the characteristics of strikes are being discussed.

Workforce characteristics

Fifty-seven per cent of management respondents reported (Q129b) that the most recent strike of a day or more at their establishment concerned only manual employees, more than three times the proportion reporting a strike involving only non-manual employees (18 per cent). In only one quarter of establishments did the strike involve both manual and non-manual employees, most of these cases being strikes involving all sections of the workforce (Q129g). Worker representatives were asked the questions only in relation to their own part of the workforce, either manual or non-manual, and so no direct comparison between respondents is possible. The results indicate that strike action is usually undertaken by a section or group of employees with common representation arrangements and that disputes only rarely spill over to other groups with different representation and negotiating arrangements. Further confirmation of this was obtained when we examined management estimates of the number of employees involved in the most recent strike of one day or longer (Q129c). The median proportion was about one third, with less than 10 per cent of cases involving 90 per cent of the workforce or more.

Where industrial action involved only one section of the workforce, it was more likely to be non-strike action than strike action: one half of managers reported non-strike action by one section, compared with one third reporting strike action of one day or more. In addition, the proportion of the workforce involved in non-strike action was generally lower – the median being about one sixth, compared with one third for strikes. Overtime bans appeared to involve a higher proportion of the workforce than either work-to-rules or blackings.

Again, manual workers were more likely than non-manual workers to take non-strike action, but the difference between the two groups was smaller: 46 per cent compared with 31 per cent. The proportion of cases involving both manual and non-manual workers was similar to that for strike action (about 25 per cent) and again, it was most commonly action involving the whole workforce. Generally, the establishment characteristics associated with the occurrence of a strike (see pp. 217–33) were also associated with a higher proportion of the workforce involved in the stoppage. Thus a greater part of the workforce was involved in the stoppage if the establishment had a predominantly manual workforce, if it was mainly composed of males, if it had few part time employees and if it had full time representatives at the establishment. The proportion of the workforce involved in the strike did not vary with different sizes of establishment. The clearest correlation was with trade union density. In workplaces with 80 per cent or less of (full time) workers belonging to unions, a strike generally involved about one third of the workforce; in those with more than 80 per cent membership density, generally about two-thirds of the workforce went on strike[17]. Given that most strikes concerned only particular sections of the workforce, normally those with common collective bargaining arrangements, this indicates that strikes of one day or more generally received the support of the majority of members of the relevant unions at the establishment.

The same relationships did not hold, however, for non-strike industrial action. The density of trade union membership was moderately correlated with the proportion of the workforce involved in non-strike action, but that was the only workforce characteristic which appeared to have any association with workforce involvement.

Primary worker representatives were asked questions similar to those put to managers, but only in relation to their own section of the workforce (manual or non-manual). This, plus the difficulty of ensuring that different respondents were referring to the same incident, made inter-respondent comparisons of the numbers involved hazardous. A first step was to confine the analysis to cases where a manual worker representative and a manager both reported strike action by manual workers only, and that yielded quite similar average estimates of the numbers involved. The same pattern of greater involvement in strike activity with greater union density existed in the worker representative results as existed in the results for managers. To examine whether there was any general tendency for either type of respondent to overstate or understate the numbers involved requires a complicated form of comparison case by case which has not yet been carried out.

Reasons for industrial action
Replies to our question on the reasons for the most recent industrial action were coded using the same broad categories as the Department of Employment's official records of stoppages of work[18]. Our interest in asking about the reasons for the most recent industrial action experienced, and for using the official classification, was to compare the reasons given for non-strike industrial action with the reasons given for striking. This would widen our understanding of how strikes fit into the more general picture of industrial action. Table IX.14 shows the overall results as reported by managers and the two main types of worker representative (Q131a, b; WQ65a, b).

The predominance of pay issues as the reason for both strikes and other forms of industrial action is readily apparent. Rather fewer non-strike incidents were reported as being over pay issues, but pay was still by far the most common reason given. Action over the duration and pattern of working hours was of secondary importance and seemed equally likely to take the form of strikes or of other action. The latter also applied to all but two of the remaining types of reason in

Table IX.14 **Reasons given for most recent industrial dispute as reported by manager and worker representatives**

Column percentages

	Most recent strike of a day or more			Most recent non-strike action		
	Manager	Manual represen- tative	Non- manual represen- tative	Manager	Manual represen- tative	Non- manual represen- tative
Pay: wage rates and earnings	60[1]	60	63	48	41	57
Pay: extra-wage and fringe benefits	6	9	1	6	5	9
Duration and pattern of working hours	12	19	3	15	18	5
Redundancy questions	4	4	12	6	5	8
Trade union matters	5	5	2	6	5	6
Working con- ditions and supervision	5	2	*	2	5	1
Manning and work allocation	5	5	7	14	20	18
Dismissal and other disciplinary measures	4	6	3	*	1	1
Miscellaneous (including general grievance procedures)	4	6	5	5	7	6
Not answered	9	7	12	6	7	4
Base: establishments where industrial action of the specified type was reported by respondent named in column head						
Unweighted	333	186	71	402	224	208
Weighted	177	94	35	252	121	122

[1] See note E

our classification. The exceptions were manning and work allocation issues, where non-strike action featured more prominently than strikes, and dismissal and disciplinary measures, where non-strike action was hardly used at all. There seems to be an obvious line of explanation to this pattern of results in terms of the 'perishability' of the issues in question. Dismissals and other disciplinary measures, such as transfers or suspensions, presumably require an immediate and quick-acting sanction by the workforce if it is to have any effect, particularly one that remedies a perceived injustice by, for example, reinstatement. On the other hand, disputes over manning and work allocation are unlikely to arise quickly or require immediate resolution. They are more likely to be long-standing issues between management and trade unions, with no externally imposed requirement to settle. For such issues trade unionists appear to consider that a longer lasting and less costly form of pressure is appropriate[19].

With the exceptions of manning and work allocation issues, and discipline and dismissal measures, the issues reported as giving rise to strikes – and indeed to other forms of industrial action – present a broadly similar pattern to that revealed by the official records compiled by the Department of Employment. Exact comparisons are not possible, for several reasons. To begin with, the 12 month period to which our data refer varied from one respondent to another over a four month period, according to when respondents were interviewed. More important, the unit of analysis in our study was the establishment, or in this case, the dispute-affected establishment. For the Department's records the basic unit is the individual strike (or lockout). A further complication is that the official records have a lower cut-off in terms of days and number of workers involved. The data shown in Table IX.14 have a cut-off of one day and exclude small establishments and the primary sector (Orders I and II of the Standard Industrial Classification). For all these reasons precise comparisons between the two sources cannot be made. Nevertheless, the overall picture of the reasons for strikes, as given by the two sources, is consistent.

A further element in the picture is the apparent consistency of the answers given by the different types of respondent. Table IX.14 shows only minor (and readily explainable) differences in the overall distribution between management and worker representatives. This is not to say that there was agreement about the reasons for each particular dispute. Such comparisons can be made on only a very limited sub-sample of the data, mainly because we would need to be sure that different respondents in the same establishment were referring to the same dispute. This has not yet been attempted, but the overall distributions in Table IX.14 encourage the expectation that the degree of agreement between respondents would be high. A reasonable implica-

Table IX.15   Reports (by managers) of most recent industrial action in relaton to duration and whether on consecutive or intermittent days

	Most recent strike of one day or more	Most recent non-strike industrial action
Duration in working days		Column percentages
One	34	8[1]
Two	12	6
Three	7	4
Four	3	2
Five	5	8
6–10	10	19
11–15	14	9
16–20	6	5
21–30	3	11
31–40	1	2
41 or more	3	18
Not answered	2	10
Still in progress	*	1
Action over consecutive or intermittent days		Column percentages
Consecutive	57	91
Intermittent	43	8
Not answered	–	1

Base:[2] establishments with industrial action of type specified in column heads as reported by manager

Unweighted	*333*	*408*
Weighted	*177*	*256*

[1] See note C
[2] In the second half of the table the base changes to establishments where action lasted two or more days

tion of this is that the official records of the reasons given for industrial disputes are not greatly affected by the fact that the sources of information used are rather varied.

Duration and continuity
In asking about the duration of the most recent industrial action, and whether it took place on consecutive working days, we again distinguished between strikes of one day or longer and non-strike action (Q129e, f). As Table IX.15 shows, non-strike action, as expected, was carried on for considerably longer periods than strike action, the typical (median) duration being about two weeks. The typical strike lasted about one day[20]. Quite a high proportion, about one fifth, of incidents

of non-strike action lasted two months or more. When we looked at the main types of non-strike action separately, there was a suggestion that overtime bans may tend to be of longer duration than other types.

According to managers, nearly one third of the most recent strikes of a day or longer involved intermittent stoppages. This figure was without doubt abnormally high because of the industry wide campaign of one and two day stoppages in the engineering industry which began in August 1979. These can be excluded from the results in a rough and ready way by excluding all strikes which respondents reported as beginning in August. This reduces the proportion of strikes that were intermittent to about one sixth. (Eliminating those that started in September reduces the proportion only slightly, to about one eighth.) The intermittent strikes reported were thus not confined to those related to the national engineering stoppage in 1979. A few establishments in various other manufacturing and service sectors reported intermittent strikes, but the numbers affected were too few to permit any further analysis. Surprisingly, some non-strike industrial action was reported by managers as being intermittent: just under 10 per cent of incidents came into this category. Again the industrial distribution of these cases was such that no single widespread dispute could account for it.

Worker representatives were asked similar questions about the duration and continuity of the most recent disputes (WQ63d, e). In aggregate their answers appeared similar to those of managers. Reported differences in duration between strikes and non-strike action were always in the same direction and the proportions reporting intermittent action were comparable.

Locality of action

The proportion of industrial action, both strike and non-strike, that was 'local' (Q130b, c; WQ64b, c), that is, involved only employees at the establishment in question, increased dramatically with size of establishment. As Table IX.16 shows, it also varied by sector, the section of the workforce involved and the type of action. In the private sector, about one quarter of strikes and just over one half of other disputes were local ones. This applied equally whether manual or non-manual workers were involved. By contrast, in the public sector there were large differences between manual and non-manual groups. In about one quarter of the cases involving manual workers strikes and other industrial action were local, whereas they were almost never local so far as non-manual workers were concerned. The very marked difference in the proportion of local disputes involving white collar employees between the public and private sectors (confirmed by worker representatives' responses) is not simply a consequence of choosing a

Table IX.16 Extent to which industrial action was local[1]

Percentages

	All sectors	Private sector	Public sector
Strike – manual workers	25	26	24
Unweighted base	*267*	*208*	*59*
Weighted base	*140*	*99*	*41*
Strike – non-manual workers	15	26	4
Unweighted base	*129*	*70*	*59*
Weighted base	*74*	*37*	*37*
Non-strike action – manual workers	46	60	26
Unweighted base	*289*	*203*	*85*
Weighted base	*167*	*106*	*61*
Non-strike action – non-manual workers	17	53	5
Unweighted base	*173*	*57*	*116*
Weighted base	*132*	*44*	*98*

All bases: establishments where manager reported action involving the section of the workforce specified

[1] Local industrial action was action confined to the sampled establishment and the percentages in the table represent the proportion of establishments where the most recent industrial action of the type specified was local

proportionate measure. The absolute number of local disputes involving non-manual employees was higher in the private sector than in the public, even taking account of the differing numbers of establishments. While national level pay bargaining may account for some of these differences, there must also be other reasons which were beyond the scope of a survey such as this to establish.

Incidence of first time action
In only a minority of establishments did managers report that workers had taken part in industrial action for the first time (Q130a). The overall figures for strike and non-strike action were similar: 30 per cent and 35 per cent respectively. The main difference was that non-manual workers, particularly clerical, secretarial, administrative and managerial employees, were considerably more likely than manual workers to be involved in either type of action for the first time. This was especially so for strike action, where non-manual workers were involved in strikes for the first time in two-fifths of establishments – twice the proportion for manual workers. In general, where any non-manual

groups were taking action for the first time it was much more likely to be non-strike action that they were taking. This could be interpreted as supporting the suggestion that the social inhibitions about taking industrial action among white collar workers are more easily transcended by joining in 'cut price' industrial action than by joining a strike[21].

First time industrial action, of any sort, was much more likely in small establishments. The same pattern was also evident in the responses of worker representatives, who reported similar proportions of first time industrial action (WQ64a). This is consistent with the lower likelihood of small establishments experiencing industrial action, as indicated, for example, by Table IX.4.

Picketing and secondary industrial action

We now turn to an aspect of industrial action that was particularly topical at the time we were planning our survey and one which until that time had been almost totally ignored by industrial relations researchers. A number of industrial disputes from the late 1960s onwards became well known through the use of large scale picketing; disputes at Roberts Arundel, Grunwick, the Saltley coke depot and during the 1974 coalmining dispute were conspicuous examples. In early 1979, the National Health Service stoppage over the next month or so and the national engineering dispute in the autumn were prominent cases. The 1980 Employment Bill, which was being debated in Parliament at the time of our survey, changed the existing law on picketing and restricted lawful picketing to a person's own place of work. Our data refer to the period up to August 1980, before the law was changed, and whilst they can be regarded as a benchmark against which changes in picketing behaviour might be assessed, they cannot be used to estimate the extent of the picketing made unlawful by the Employment Act, 1980[22]. The survey questions on picketing referred to the previous 12 months and therefore excluded the two major stoppages in road haulage and the National Health Service, but they included the engineering stoppages of late 1979 and the steel strike of early 1980.

Both managers and primary worker representatives were asked whether the establishment had been picketed within the last twelve months and, if so, on how many occasions (Q133a; WQ66a). They were then asked a series of questions about the most recent occasion of picketing, including whether it was in connection with a dispute at that establishment, the maximum number of pickets present at any one time, the number of entrances picketed and who organised the picketing. There were also questions on the effects of the picketing and how many of the pickets were employees of the establishment in question.

Reports from the two types of respondent about the occurrence of

Table IX.17 The extent to which establishments were picketed in the previous year (as reported by any respondent)[1]

	All establish- ments	Number employed at establishment			
		25–99	100–499	500–999	1,000 or more
Picketing in previous year	13	8	18	34	54
Base: all establishments					
Unweighted	2040	747	777	249	267
Weighted	2000	1313	553	83	51

[1] The percentages represent those establishments where either the manager or the manual or the non-manual worker representative reported picketing

picketing coincided to a high degree – more so than was the case with the questions about the occurrence of industrial action. However, most of the arguments we adduced for taking combined responses in relation to industrial action also apply here. Table IX.17 therefore shows, for different sizes of establishment, the proportion of cases where any respondent reported picketing in the previous 12 months. Overall, about one eighth of establishments were reported as having been picketed. This proportion of one eighth can be compared with the overall figure of about one quarter of establishments which were reported as having experienced a strike or one third which experienced any form of industrial action.

Incidence of primary picketing and its relationship to strike action
By relating the results from our question on whether the picketing was in connection with a dispute at the establishment ('primary picketing'; Q133b) to the data on industrial action we were able to confirm that primary picketing was almost never connected with non-strike industrial action. The relevant base for examining the proportion of disputes involving picketing was therefore those establishments which had experienced a strike. But 'secondary' picketing had to be excluded. This could be done only approximately, because our question about whether picketing was primary or secondary was asked solely about the last occasion picketing occurred. As with strikes, a single occasion of picketing within the previous year was by far the most common report by both managers and worker representatives. Over 70 per cent of managers gave that answer, and almost the same proportion of primary

Table IX.18   The extent to which strikes were accompanied by primary picketing[1]

Percentages

	Picketing	Unweighted base	Weighted base
All establishments	31	*544*	*318*
Number employed at establishment			
25–99	22	*75*	*124*
100–499	37	*196*	*128*
500–999	31	*105*	*35*
1000 or more	45	*168*	*31*
Overall union density[2]			
Low	(9)[3]	*21*	*15*
Medium	33	*184*	*120*
High	34	*251*	*134*
Closed-shop arrangements (as reported by managers)			
Manual workers			
Comprehensive closed shop	32	*229*	*124*
Partial closed shop	(40)	*45*	*17*
No closed shop	31	*270*	*163*
Non-manual workers			
Comprehensive closed shop	(20)	*36*	*27*
Partial closed shop	42	*79*	*27*
No closed shop	32	*429*	*250*

Base: establishments where any respondent reported a strike or lock-out in the previous 12 months

---

[1] The percentages represent those establishments where any respondent reported the last occasion of picketing as primary as a proportion of those where any respondent had reported a strike or lock-out

[2] See note H

[3] See note B

worker representatives. This is sufficiently common to justify taking the most recent case of picketing as characteristic of picketing throughout the year. If we do this the overall proportion of establishments affected by primary picketing is six per cent.

About one third of strikes involved primary picketing (see Table IX.18). Primary picketing appeared to be less common in small establishments (those with fewer than 100 employees) but above this size the chances of a strike involving primary picketing appeared to be independent of the size of establishment. In addition, strikes appeared to involve primary picketing less often when union membership density

Table IX.19 The extent to which strikes of one day or more were accompanied by primary picketing in relation to the characteristics of the strike[1]

Percentages

	Picketing	Unweighted base	Weighted base
All establishments	41	333[2]	177
Strike lasted one to three days	37	159	93
Strike lasted four or more days	46	160	80
Proportion of workforce taking part			
1 to 29 per cent	36	145	70
30 to 69 per cent	42	84	45
70 to 100 per cent	49	73	49
First time workers involved had taken action	38	93	53
Not first time workers involved had taken action	44	225	116
Strike involved only this establishment	50	124	46
Strike involved other establishments	37	209	131
Manual and non-manual workers involved	57	63	37
Manual workers involved	40	205	104
Non-manual workers involved	36	66	37

Base: establishments with a strike of one day or more as reported by manager

[1] The percentages represent those establishments where the last occasion of picketing was primary (as reported by any respondent) as a proportion of those where the manager had reported a strike of one day or more
[2] See note G

was low, but there was little, if any, difference between establishments with medium and high union density. However, establishments which had a partial closed shop were rather more likely to have a strike picketed than were establishments with either a comprehensive closed shop or no closed shop. It also appeared that strikes were more likely to involve picketing the longer the strike went on and the greater the proportion of the workforce involved in the strike (Table IX.19). Strikes in which all sections of the workforce took part (according to management) involved picketing in the majority of cases. Widespread strikes were less often primary picketed than 'local' strikes. Employees striking for the first time appeared less likely to set pickets than 'experienced' strikers.

The general picture which emerged from these results is that picketing is aimed at fulfilling at least three functions. First, the association

Table IX.20   The characteristics of the most recent primary picketing

	Manager	Manual worker representative	Non-manual worker representative
Maximum number of pickets			Column percentages[1]
1 to 6	43	44	36
7 to 20	38	33	34
21 to 100	18	20	13
101 or more	2	1	8
Not answered	1	3	9
Number of gates picketed			Column percentages[1]
One	72	53	48
Two	16	30	33
Three or more	12	18	18
Organiser of the picket			Column percentages[2]
Shop stewards at this establishment	71	83	78
Local full-time official of trade union	20	11	16
Shop stewards of other establishment of same employer	3	–	4
Shop stewards of another employer	*	–	–
Other union official	2	1	2
Employees themselves	6	5	2
Not answered	2	*	5
Base: establishments where respondents at column head reported primary picketing in previous year			
Unweighted	*124*	*109*	*94*
Weighted	*66*	*55*	*35*

[1] See note C
[2] See note E

with strike duration and the apparently greater reluctance of first time strikers to picket suggests that picketing is seen as a means of reinforcing the willingness of strikers to continue the strike. Secondly, the association between the incidence of picketing and strikes concerning all sections of the workforce suggests that picketing is viewed as a means to an effective withdrawal of labour. Thirdly, given that widespread strikes were picketed in a substantial minority of cases, it appears that picketing may be regarded as a means of trying to bring maximum pressure on employers by attempting to ensure that a high proportion of establishments are affected by strike action.

Characteristics of primary picketing
Still referring to primary picketing (and the last occasion if there was more than one), we asked about the maximum number of pickets present, how many of them were establishment employees, over how many entrances they were spread and who organised the picketing (Q133c, d, e, f; WQ66c, d, e, f). According to managers, the maximum number of pickets present at any one time was about seventeen on average, although the typical (median) figure was ten. Table IX.20 shows the distribution. Mass primary picketing was rare, but not insignificant. Naturally, larger establishments often had several entrances and thus had greater numbers of pickets. When we took only those cases where a single entrance was picketed, the maximum number of pickets in the typical (median) case was six: in 44 per cent of cases the maximum number was between one and five; in 47 per cent of cases it was seven or more, with one per cent of these being over 50[23]. The difference between the median for all establishments and the median for those with a single picketed entrance shows that the large numbers of pickets overall are at least partly explained by the presence of multiple entrances.

There was some disagreement between management and worker representatives about the extent to which pickets were employees of the establishment. Managers reported that a minority of pickets were not members of the workforce, whereas, according to worker representatives, almost everyone involved in the picketing was an employee of the establishment. Some of the differences between respondents may have been the result of differences in knowledge, while others may have occurred because different incidents were being reported: we did not attempt in our analysis to match respondents case by case. A third source of difference may, however, have been the greater tendency of managers to report that local union officials had been involved in the picketing, at least in the sense of organising it, but also possibly in the sense of taking part. There was, however, close agreement between

Table IX.21 **Effects of most recent primary picketing**

Percentages

People, goods or services affected	Manager	Manual worker representative	Non-manual worker representative
Establishment or contractors' employees	35[1]	40	38
Establishment employees	22	23	30⁻
Contractors' employees	18	31	23
Goods or services being received or sent out	54	50	64
Goods or services being received	44	43	57
Goods or services being sent out	35	41	37
Any effect	**61**	**65**	**64**
Not answered	*	*	4
Base: establishments where respondents at column head reported primary picketing in previous year			
Unweighted	*124*	*109*	*94*
Weighted	*66*	*55*	*35*

[1] See note F

managers and worker representatives about the most common organisers of picketing. Establishment based shop stewards and local officials were most frequently mentioned (Table IX.20). It appeared that only rarely did employees organise picketing without the help of local representatives, based either at their own establishment or at a nearby establishment of the same employer.

Effects of primary picketing

We asked respondents (Q133g; WQ66g) whether, on the last occasion, picketing prevented any of the following from entering or leaving the premises:

employees of the establishment;
contractors' employees working at the establishment;
goods or services being received;
goods or services being sent out.

In general, respondents agreed that in about 60 per cent of cases picketing had had the effect of preventing goods or services entering or leaving the establishment or of preventing some of the establishment's employees or those of others from entering. It was clear from results that the most common effect of primary picketing was the prevention of goods and services from entering the establishment (see Table IX.21). It also commonly prevented the dispatch of goods or services. One or other of these effects was mentioned by over one half of our management respondents. Effects upon the movement of people were less widespread, and were mentioned by about one third of managers. It seemed that picketing was almost as likely to prevent contractors' employees entering an establishment (and not all establishments would have had them) as it was to prevent employees of the establishment itself. Roughly speaking, primary picketing stopped at least some employees of the establishment reporting for work in about one quarter of cases. It had a widespread impact on the establishment – preventing employees from going to work and the receipt of, and dispatch of, goods or services – in only one in eight cases, according to management respondents. There may well have been other effects of picketing, particularly on the strikers and on management, that we made no attempt to measure[24].

Secondary picketing
We defined secondary picketing as picketing which was 'not in connection with a dispute at this establishment'. Approximately one twelfth of establishments (8 per cent) were reported to have experienced secondary picketing. This figure is based upon reports by any of the three main respondents and refers only to the most recent occasion within the previous 12 months (Q133b; WQ66b). Thus, in overall terms, secondary picketing as we define it was rather more common than primary picketing in 1979–80, although again it affected quite a small minority of establishments. Establishments which experienced secondary picketing were widely spread throughout the economy: in our sample, almost every Order of the Standard Industrial Classification had at least one case of this kind of picketing. It is unlikely that this would be so if, for example, the major stoppages in the steel and engineering industries had been the only ones to prompt the secondary action. Secondary action must surely have arisen from a wide variety of disputes. It was also most commonly experienced by the kinds of establishment which had experienced primary picketing: larger establishments, and those with predominantly male and full time employees. It rarely occurred at establishments with no recognised trade unions or with no trade union members.

External secondary picketing
Broadly speaking, our results showed that establishments which experienced secondary picketing were the kind that experienced any sort of industrial action or, more particularly, strikes. This is as we would expect if the secondary picketing was always carried out by

employees of the establishment, but there were also instances where secondary pickets were not establishment employees picketing their own establishment about a dispute elsewhere.

We use the term 'external secondary picketing' to cover cases where none of the pickets was an employee of the establishment being picketed and the picketing was not in connection with a dispute at the picketed establishment. The remaining cases of secondary picketing may or may not have involved non-establishment employees, but we have no way of categorising these cases reliably. 'External secondary picketing' accounted for about one half of all cases of secondary picketing. Thus, according to both managers and worker representatives, about three per cent of all establishments had experienced this kind of picketing. About one third of these cases were in the metal manufacturing and mechanical engineering sectors, reflecting the widespread stoppages in those sectors during the period. There were also significant numbers in the distribution sector. Instances had taken place, however, in nearly all of the main industrial sectors, the exceptions being business and financial services and miscellaneous services, which had no instances of external secondary picketing.

The likelihood of an establishment's being affected by external secondary picketing increased if it was larger and if it had substantial trade union membership amongst its employees, although some establishments with no trade union members at all (according to management) were affected, and some affected were in the smallest size category (25 to 49 employees). The latter results suggest, first, that external secondary picketing was not confined to establishments where the pickets might reasonably have expected a sympathetic response from fellow trade unionists and, secondly, that this sort of picketing is also subject to some of the organisational influences that affect industrial action in general, particularly the organisational 'economies of scale'. The reasons, however, are presumably rather different. External secondary picketing is perhaps more common at larger establishments and at those with many trade union members because such establishments are more visible and more strategically important for the dispute giving rise to the secondary picketing. Unfortunately, it is not practical to take this line of analysis much further because of the small number of establishments involved.

Apart from the clear cases of external secondary picketing discussed above, the remaining cases involved some pickets from the establishment's workforce and possibly others from elsewhere. We cannot distinguish the identity of pickets from our relatively simple survey questions any more than we have done already. Table IX.22 shows the comparison between primary picketing and the two sorts of secondary picketing for the number of pickets, the identity of picket organisers

Table IX.22 **Comparison of primary and secondary picketing characteristics as reported by managers**

	Primary picketing	External secondary picketing[1]	Other secondary picketing
Maximum number of pickets			
Median	10	7	6
Average	17	11	12
Organiser of picketing		Column percentages	
Worker representatives of this establishment	71	–	69
Local union official	20	43	14
Others	11	33	12
Not known	2	21	3
Picketing affected		Percentages	
Employees leaving or entering work	35	21	34
Goods or services	54	55	42
Base: establishments where manager reported picketing of the type specified in column heads in the previous year			
Unweighted	*124*	*79*	*72*
Weighted	*66*	*59*	*42*

[1] External secondary picketing was defined as picketing where none of the pickets was an employee of the establishment and the picketing was not in connection with a dispute at the picketed establishment

and the reported effects, if any. A noteworthy feature of the results is the lower likelihood of external secondary picketing preventing employees entering the establishment to work.

Secondary blacking
We first asked respondents if, during the previous 12 months, goods or services had been blacked by trade union members at the establishment in connection with a dispute elsewhere. Secondly, in establishments where there had been industrial action in the previous year, we asked about blacking of the organisation's customers' or suppliers' goods or services in connection with a dispute at the respondent's establishment (Q134; Q135; WQ67; WQ68). These two questions, looking at opposite sides of the same coin, yielded similar results: about four per cent of all establishments were affected by secondary blacking or, to put it another way, about one sixth of those involved in industrial action of

any kind. These results are based upon managers' responses, but worker representatives provided a very similar picture.

The small number of establishments involved permits only limited analysis of establishment characteristics in relation to secondary blacking. In general, the limited analysis carried out revealed that secondary blacking appeared to have affected quite a wide variety of establishments, as often in the public as in the private sector, although the proportions of establishments affected were small. Distribution appeared to have experienced secondary blacking more than other sectors, which may be because establishments in distribution are commercially related to a wider range of other establishment than is usual[25], or because their dependence on transport may make them particularly susceptible. Establishments with full time worker representatives were more commonly affected and union membership density was also positively associated with the occurrence of secondary blacking, although the association was more obvious from worker representative responses than from those of managers. There was a weak association with establishment size. If we take the union affiliation of our primary respondents as an indicator of the main manual or non-manual union at the establishment, certain types of union appeared to be involved in secondary blacking more frequently than others. Among manual trade unions it was the traditional craft unions, notably in engineering and printing, that appeared to be disproportionately involved. Among non-manual unions, those that organise professional workers were less involved.

Notes

1. J. Kelly and N. Nicholson, 'Strikes and other forms of industrial action', *Industrial Relations Journal*, November–December 1980, pp. 20–31; William Brown, Ed., *The Changing Contours of British Industrial Relations* (Basil Blackwell, Oxford, 1981).
2. E. Batstone *et al*, *The Social Organisation of Strikes* (Basil Blackwell, Oxford, 1978).
3. G. Kalton and H.J. Schuman, 'The Effect of the Question on Survey Responses: A Review', *Journal of the Royal Statistical Society*, 1982, Serial A, Part I, pp. 42–73.
4. The annualised average number of workers involved in stoppages for the survey period was 2.1 million, compared with an average of 1.5 million for the period 1966–81 (Department of Employment *Gazettes*).
5. The arguments are summarised in P.K. Edwards, 'The Strike-proneness of British Manufacturing Establishments', *British Journal of Industrial Relations*, July 1981, pp. 135–148.
6. In fact, the measure used is the number of full time manual workers who were union members divided by the number of manual workers. Managers were not asked about union membership among part time employees.
7. William Brown, Ed., *op. cit.*
8. P.K. Edwards, *op. cit.*
9. Earlier evidence for large manufacturing establishments was given in W.W. Daniel, *Wage Determination in Industry* (Political and Economic Planning No. 563, London, 1976). A recent exception is the work of P.K. Edwards (*op. cit.*). He found

no clear connection between a plant's strike record and whether 'a significant group of manual workers were paid by results'. But the dependent variable was not defined in relation to manual workers.

10. See, for example, Robert Taylor, *The Fifth Estate* (Pan Books, London, 1978).

11. Penelope A. Lloyd, *Incentive Payment Schemes* (British Institute of Management, London, 1976).

12. J. Storey, 'An inter-industry analysis of strike frequency', *Economica*, Vol. 43, 1976, pp. 349–65.

13. C.T.B. Smith *et al*, *Strikes in Britain* (HMSO, London, 1978); Department of Employment *Gazette*, monthly.

14. William Brown, Ed., *op cit*; P.K. Edwards, *op cit*.

15. See page xii for the criteria adopted for the minimum number of observations in tables.

16. This was done by excluding establishments where the most recent strike of one day or more was reported by the manager as having begun in August or September 1979. Some of these strikes will not have been related to the engineering dispute and the exclusions therefore err in the direction of severity.

17. The figures used here are the median proportion involved in the strike, as estimated by management.

18. See 'Stoppages of work due to industrial disputes: revised classification for cause', Department of Employment *Gazette*, February 1973, p. 117. The nine main categories ('sections') of the classification were used, but unlike official records, which use further subdivisions to cater for multiple or complex 'causes', our coding system allowed multiple coding among the nine categories.

19. E. Batstone *et al*, *op cit*, pp. 41–2.

20. The median figure for strikes of one day or more, shown in Table IX.15, is three days. If strikes of less than one day are included, the median figure becomes one day.

21. E. Batstone *et al*, *op. cit*.

22. The survey questions were framed in a general way because the precise changes in the law could not be predicted, but also because it is inappropriate to incorporate precise and complicated legal distinctions into survey questions.

23. The Department of Employment's *Code of Practice* (HMSO, London, 1980), published after the period covered by the survey, said that 'pickets and their organisers should ensure that in general the number of pickets does not exceed six at any entrance to a workplace; frequently a smaller number will be appropriate'.

24. Some of the indirect effects of picketing have been noted in Arthur Marsh and James Gillies, 'The Incidence of Picketing in 1979', *Personnel Review*, Vol. 10, No. 2, 1981.

25. In manufacturing, the typical establishment sold about one quarter of its output to three customers. It seems most unlikely that the output of establishments in distribution is as concentrated as this.

X Some Outcomes Associated with Labour Relations Arrangements

In the bulk of our report we have described and analysed the distribution of different industrial relations practices, procedures and institutions. In this chapter we raise the question of whether different arrangements were associated with different outcomes that might be regarded as desirable by managers, employees, unions or the community generally. Of course, our study was not established or designed to measure the effects of industrial relations institutions as much as to describe those institutions and offer some suggestions that might explain variations in their distribution. At the same time, our schedules did include some measures of outcomes and it is worth looking at the results while making it clear that the measures were not as comprehensive or as precise as they would have been had our main purpose been to measure effects. The measures that we did have were of two main types. The first category included the evaluations of managers and employee representatives of different aspects of industrial relations such as the general climate, the value of shop steward training, the working of formal procedures and, from managers only, the financial performance of the establishment. The second category included what might be regarded as harder information about outcomes such as the incidence of strikes and other forms of industrial action, levels of pay for different categories of employee, redundancies, dismissals for reasons other than redundancy and disciplinary fines. We have looked at many of these measures in earlier chapters. Here we focus upon three measures that have not received attention. They are, first, managers' and employee representatives' assessments of the general climate of industrial relations at their establishments; secondly, managers' accounts of financial performance; and thirdly, managers' reports of levels of pay.

General evaluations of industrial relations

Management assessments of the state of industrial relations in their workplaces[1] often stand in contrast to opinion poll data about the problems of industrial relations in this country[2]. In the present study our management respondents once again gave a generally favourable overall assessment of relationships in their establishments (Q146). Nearly half (47 per cent) gave them the highest possible rating, 'First

Table X.1 General evaluations of industrial relations by management and union respondents

	Management respondent	Non-manual representative	Manual representative
All establishments where specified interviews were held		Column percentages	
First rate	48	36	37
Good	34	21	19
Fairly good	15	22	24
Not bad	1	9	9
Fairly poor or worse	2	12	11
Mean score[1]	5.3	4.5	4.5
Base: all respondents in column headings			
Unweighted	*2040*	*1016*	*1040*
Weighted	*2000*	*722*	*779*
Strictly comparable establishments		Column percentages	
First rate	37	35	35
Good	35	21	20
Fairly good	24	23	22
Not bad	2	9	9
Fairly poor or worse	2	12	12
Mean score	5.0	4.5	4.5
Base: establishments where all three respondents were interviewed			
Unweighted	*724*	*724*	*724*
Weighted	*428*	*428*	*428*

[1] The five point scale shown in the table is a compression of the full scale according to which answers were coded. The mean score was calculated by attaching arbitrary values of from +6 to +1 to the top six points in the full scale. The percentage distributions have been recalculated using those who gave a rating as the base

class', or 'Excellent' or 'Couldn't be better'. Ninety-five per cent thought that their industrial relations were at least fairly good, while only two per cent thought that they were poor or worse (Table X.1). Worker representatives, both manual and non-manual, gave slightly less favourable ratings (WQ74) than managers about the state of industrial relations at their places of work[3], but even among worker representatives, 80 per cent of the manual category thought that relationships were at least fairly good, while 76 per cent of non-manual representatives took a similar view. Such evaluations, however, become most useful when they are related to the different characteristics and circumstances of workplaces. We have seen at different points in the report that assessments of the general climate of industrial relations were less favourable where little information on the financial circumstances of

Table X.2   General evaluations of industrial relations in relation to the incidence of strikes and other industrial action

	Union not recognised	Union recognised		
		No action	Action but not strike	Strike action
Management respondent				
First rate (per cent)	55	44	30	31
Mean score[1]	5.3	5.3	4.7	4.8
Manual union representative				
First rate (per cent)	n.a.[2]	41	20	22
Mean score	n.a.	4.7	3.5	4.2
Non-manual union representative				
First rate (per cent)	n.a.	35	24	30
Mean score	n.a.	4.5	4.2	4.3

Bases: in each case the base is establishments where the specified respondents were interviewed

[1] See note 1 to Table X.1
[2] Not applicable

Table X.3   General evaluations of industrial relations by managers in relation to industrial sector

	All establishments		No industrial action in previous year		Some industrial action in previous year	
	First rate (per cent)	Mean score	First rate (per cent)	Mean score	First rate (per cent)	Mean score
Miscellaneous services	60	5.5	63	5.5	§[1]	§
Textiles and clothing	60	5.4	63	5.5	§	§
Distribution	52	5.4	50	5.4	§	§
Financial services	52	5.3	(53)[2]	(5.3)	§	§
Professional services	52	5.3	53	5.4	§	§
Food, drink and tobacco/chemicals	48	5.2	50	5.3	(33)	(4.9)
Mechanical and electrical engineering	47	5.2	58	5.3	31	4.8
Vehicle manufacture	41	5.0	§	§	(37)	(4.6)

Base: all establishments in selected sectors

[1] See note A
[2] See note B

Table X.4 **Management evaluations of industrial relations in relation to union density**

Mean scores

	No manual trade union members	Proportion of manual workers who were trade union members				
		1–24	25–49	50–89	90–99	100
Mean score[1]	5.5	5.1	5.2	5.2	5.3	5.4
Base: establishments with manual workers but no industrial action by manual workers in previous year						
Unweighted	249	82	68	137	125	171
Weighted	399	90	78	130	90	174

[1] See note 1 to Table X.1

the establishment was provided to employee representatives (see Chapter VI), where formal procedures were unsatisfactory and where disciplinary fines had been imposed (see Chapter VII). Apart from such sources of variation the strongest influence upon managers' judgements about the state of industrial relations seemed to be whether there had been any industrial action in the previous 12 months and essentially whether there had been any industrial action by manual workers (see Table X.2). Indeed, when variations in relation to whether there had been any industrial action at the establishment were taken into account, it was difficult to find other systematic sources of variation among the characteristics of workplaces that have generally accounted for major differences in industrial relations practices and procedures in this report, such as size, ownership and sector. For instance, there were marked differences overall in relation to industrial sector, and these were consistent with popular stereotypes of the state of industrial peace in different sectors (see Table X.3). But when we analysed workplaces where there had been industrial action separately from those where there had been none, the differences in relation to industrial sector largely disappeared.

A similar pattern emerged when we examined other apparent sources of variation. One important source of variation that did survive analysis independently of whether or not there had been a strike was the level of union membership among manual workers at the establishment. That variation is shown in Table X.4. It is clear that managers gave the most favourable assessments of their industrial relations where there were no manual trade union members. Where there were *any* manual unionists, however, then managers rated their industrial relations more highly the more fully unionised was the workforce. In consequence, evaluations

Table X.5 Accounts of financial performance and investment in relation to pattern of union recognition

	Neither manual nor non-manual recognised	Non-manual recognised not manual	Manual recognised not non-manual	Both manual and non-manual recognised
Financial performance				
Mean score[1]	1.0	(0.7)[2]	0.8	0.7
Above average (per cent)	53	(38)	45	43
Trend in investment				
Mean score	1.1	(1.4)	0.9	1.0
Investment increasing (per cent)	58	(69)	58	58
Base: private sector				
Unweighted	*548*	*38*	*278*	*548*
Weighted	*317*	*49*	*307*	*317*

[1] With regard to both financial performance and trend in investment, answers were coded on three point scale. The mean scores were calculated by attaching arbitrary values of $+2$ to productive response; -2 to a negative response and zero to an intermediate response

tended to be as favourable in circumstances where all manual workers were unionised as they were where there was no membership.

As was the case with managers, a very strong influence upon manual worker representatives' views of industrial relations was also whether or not there had been a strike. Indeed, there was a very strong correlation between management assessments and those of the corresponding union representatives. It is noteworthy, however, that, as already mentioned, employee representatives did rate the industrial relations climate less highly than managers, and non-manual representatives gave lower ratings than manual counterparts.

Financial performance and trend in investment

We asked managers in trading organisations, first, how they felt that the financial performance of their establishment compared with that of other establishments and firms in the industry (Q10a) and, secondly, whether capital investment in the establishment had been rising, falling or stable over the previous two or three years (Q10b). Analysis of their answers was less fruitful than we hoped it would be. First, in relation to financial performance, 48 per cent of those managers who made a judgement assessed the performance of their establishment as above average while only six per cent felt that it was below average. Secondly,

Table X.6 Financial performance and trend in investment in relation to industrial action among manual workers

	Manual union not recognised	Manual union recognised		
		No action	Non-strike action	Strike
Financial performance				
Mean score[1]	0.9	0.8	1.0	0.5
Above average (per cent)	53	44	58	38
Trend in investment				
Mean score	1.1	1.0	1.0	0.9
Investment increasing (per cent)	58	56	65	59
Base: private sector				
Unweighted	*341*	*464*	*79*	*270*
Weighted	*519*	*440*	*46*	*132*

[1] See note 1 to Table X.5

the biggest contrast in answers to both questions was between the nationalised industries and the private sector. Managers in the nationalised industries were markedly more likely to feel that they could answer neither of the questions. Where they did make a judgement, they were much more likely to feel that their financial performance was average and their investment stable. In consequence, nationalised industries achieved substantially lower overall scores on both counts. As nationalised industries were concentrated in particular sectors and strongly associated with particular industrial relations practices, it was appropriate to exclude them from further analysis in relation to other possible sources of variation. Thirdly, when nationalised industries were excluded, the league table which emerged after analysis in relation to industrial sector showed some surprising results, with vehicle manufacture and textiles being near the top for both measures. We did ask managers to compare the performance of their establishment with that of others in the same industry and it appeared that that focus limited the scope for analysing answers across industries. Nevertheless, it was still of interest to relate managers' accounts of financial performance and investment to different measures of unionisation. The indications were, however, that where trade unions were recognised managers did tend to rate their financial performance less favourably than in circumstances where there was no recognition (see Table X.5). There was, however, no indication that accounts of trend in investment were associated with patterns of trade union recognition. Table X.6 shows reports of financial performance and investment, in relation to the position of the establishment regarding strikes of manual workers in the previous twelve months. There was no clear cut pattern. Where there had been strikes, management rated financial performance less favourably than average, but where there had been non-strike action, management rated performance more favourably than average.

Levels of earnings

One of the main outputs of economic enterprises to which labour relations institutions and practices are relevant is the earnings of people who work in those enterprises. It is, however, difficult to measure the earnings of different groups at an establishment through asking just a few questions in a sample survey such as ours. The pay of group members may vary both among the members and from week to week or period to period depending upon hours or outputs or shifts. The total remuneration of different groups may be very different even though their cash earnings are the same. Similarly, rates per hour may vary substantially while gross weekly pay remains the same. In our present study, we simply asked managers what was the gross pay of the typical[4] worker in the following four broad categories: semi-skilled manual workers; skilled manual workers; clerical workers and middle managers (Q111). They were asked to identify into which of a number of broad bands (generally £10 per week wide) the earnings of different groups fell. Clearly, that approach represented a crude method of measuring earnings. The chief limitation in our method was that we included no measure of hours worked and could not calculate hourly rates as opposed to gross weekly earnings. In particular, as we did not specify *full time* employees in our earnings question, we had to take into account the possibility that some of the earnings figures provided reflected part time earnings. We did not think that would have been very likely or common, for two reasons. First, we asked for the earnings of a typical employee, and it would be rare for part time workers to be typical. Secondly, we judged that managers generally think in terms of full time earnings, with part time pay being a proportion of such earnings, and would tend to respond in terms of full time pay. But we still had to cater for the possibility that part time earnings were reflected in some of our pay figures. Accordingly, we carried out an analysis of variations in pay in relation to the proportion of part time workers employed at establishments and we checked that all the associations reported in this chapter remained when establishments with similar proportions of part time employees were compared. It was certainly the case that the pay reported for manual workers was strongly associated with the proportion of part time workers employed. But there were strong reasons for expecting that full time rates would be lower where a high proportion of part time workers were employed. Principally, the level of part time working was very strongly associated with the proportion of women employed, and we also found that earnings tended to be lower the higher the proportion of women in the workforce. Table X.11, presented later in the chapter, shows that the association between pay and proportion of part time workers was indeed partly an incidental consequence of the proportion of women employed. But the analysis also shows that there remained an association between the level of part time working and reported pay for manual workers that was independent of the proportion of women employed. Again, it was possible and credible that full time rates were lower when a high proportion of part time workers were employed, for reasons that were independent of the proportion of women employed. But we could not establish that that was the case and the association we found between the proportion of part time workers and levels of pay confirmed that we had to ensure that in our analysis any associations reported were independent of the proportion of part time workers. Two further points arising from that analysis warrant mention at this stage. First, in cases where there was a high proportion of part time workers, many managers felt unable to give an earnings figure, suggesting that the question did cause them some difficulty in such circumstances. For instance, where over 40 per cent of the workforce were part time, 18 per cent of managers did not provide an answer to the question on the weekly pay of a typical semi-skilled worker, compared with only four per cent of counterparts where five per cent or fewer were part time. Secondly, it was chiefly in relation to those establishments with very substantial levels of part time working (over 40 per cent) that the generally strong associations that we report in the remainder of this chapter became less strong.

Apart from the detailed internal analysis to which we subjected our findings on pay, we also sought to check them against other sources of information. When we compared differences in our survey data with data from the New Earnings Survey (NES), in so far as it was possible[5], we found that the rank orders for pay in relation to industrial sector and region were very similar according to the two sources. Overall, we judged that while our data may have had severe weaknesses as measures of the *actual earnings* of different categories, they could still indicate whether establishments paid more or less to different categories and hence provide a sound basis for exploring patterns of *variations* as between different types of establishment and category of employee.

On the other hand, the analysis we present here has to be regarded as preliminary. Apart from any limitations that there might have been in our data, the variations in the earnings of particular categories (without taking into account differences in the patterns as between different

Table X.7   Level of earnings in relation to demand for products and level of financial performance

Pounds per week[2]

	Demand in previous year			Financial performance in previous year		
	Rising	Stable	Falling	Above average	About average	Below average
Semi-skilled	75	77	79	77	76	79
Skilled	96	103	100	100	99	104
Clerical	71	72	73	71	72	75
Middle managers	120	120	120	120	119	119

	Change in size of workforce							
	In previous year					In previous five years		
	Major[1] increase	Minor increase	Stable	Minor decrease	Major decrease	Substantial increase	Stable	Substantial decrease
Semi-skilled	72	76	74	71	78	74	73	76
Skilled	101	96	96	92	98	99	95	97
Clerical	69	76	76	68	70	72	73	69
Middle managers	120	124	124	118	117	122	123	117

Bases:[3] establishments that gave pay figures

[1] See note 4 at the end of the chapter for an account of how weekly pay figures were calculated
[2] In the previous year a major change was a change of 20 per cent or more and a minor change was a change of between 5 and 20 per cent. In the previous five years, a substantial change was a change of 20 per cent or more
[3] For pay figures bases are establishments that employed people in the specified occupational categories and where managers provided pay data for those categories. In consequence the base varied from group to group and specifying a base for each cell in the table would obscure the pattern so we do not include base numbers in our tables on pay. But we do follow our normal practice of not quoting a percentage if the unweighted base is fewer than 20 and of putting the percentage in brackets if the base is 20 or more but fewer than 50

categories) were so complex that it was difficult to unravel them using our method. At the same time, the results of our preliminary analysis were so striking that they warrant presentation here. Our preliminary focus was very much on the pay of manual workers and, to a lesser extent, on the manual/non-manual differential. While presenting the analysis, we accept that our information on pay represents one area which deserves substantial further analysis from different perspectives and using different methods.

As already mentioned, the distribution of earnings revealed by our findings showed so many major and systematic sources of variation that we had some problem in presenting them in a form other than that of a long list. We deal with that difficulty by considering, first, the extent to which levels of earnings were associated with the financial and market circumstances of establishments and, secondly, the relationship between pay levels and the other main characteristics of workplaces. Thirdly, having established the general framework, we examine any connections between earnings and labour relations institutions and practices.

Financial circumstances and pay levels

As we have mentioned earlier in the report, in cases where establishments were part of trading businesses we designed a number of measures of their product markets, their labour markets and financial performance. These measures included how the demand for the establishment's products had been moving in the previous twelve months; what changes had occurred in the size of the establishment's workforce in the previous twelve months and the previous five years; how far the pattern of capital investment in the workplace had changed in the previous year; and how the financial performance of the establishment compared with others in similar circumstances.

When we analysed the earnings of different groups by the answers of managers to these questions the pattern revealed was remarkable (see Table X.7). It is clear that there was no association between any of the four measures and the pay of any group. People were paid as much where the demand for products was falling as they were where it was rising. Their earnings were as high in workplaces which were judged to be below average performers as they were in establishments where managers judged economic performance to be above average. It made no difference to earnings whether the size of the workforce had decreased substantially over the previous twelve months or over the previous five years. Of course, it is true that so far as our measures of product market circumstances and financial performance were concerned, our analysis was based upon all trading organisations, including nationalised industries. So far as the measures of changes in the size of the workforce were concerned, our analysis was based upon all types of employer, including local and national government. It is common in public discussion of pay determination for commentators to talk of the market and the non-market sectors and to imply that pay in the private sector is constrained by market or financial circumstances while in the public sector there is no such constraint[6]. Accordingly, it was possible

Table X.8   Levels of earnings in relation to product demand and change in size of workforce

Pounds per week

	Demand for products			Changes in workforce over previous five years		
	Rising	Stable	Falling	Sub-stantial[1] increase	Stable	Sub-stantial decrease
Semi-skilled manual workers						
Private sector (not head office)	74	78	79	76	77	76
Nationalised industries (not head office)	86	87	93	83[2]		90
Central or local government	n.a.	n.a.	n.a.	66	64	72
Skilled manual workers						
Private sector (not head office)	95	103	100	101	99	98
Nationalised industries (not head office)	107	112	114	106[2]		111
Central or local government	n.a.	n.a.	n.a.	79	83	84

Base:[1] establishments that gave pay figures

[1] See footnotes to Table X.7
[2] As the number of nationalised industry establishments where the workforce had increased substantially was not a sufficiently large base on its own, it is combined with those where the workforce had been stable

that our findings were distorted by the inclusion of nationalised industries and public administration and if we isolated the private sector we would find variations in pay levels that were related to financial and market circumstances. Table X.8 shows the result. So far as trend in the demand for products was concerned, it was clear that in the private sector there was no consistent association with the pay of manual workers. In nationalised industries there was, if anything, a tendency for people to be more highly paid where product demand was falling.

A similar pattern was apparent in relation to changes in the size of the workforce. Pay levels for both semi-skilled and skilled workers in the private sector were very similar whatever had happened to movements in the size of the workforce over the previous year or the previous five years. Among nationalised industry establishments there was a slight tendency for people to be paid more where the workforce was being run down. In public services establishments there was no association in either direction between changes in workforce size and levels of pay.

Generally, there was so little connection between pay levels and our measures of market circumstances that one would have had severe reservations about the adequacy of one or both of the two sets of measures, were it not for the fact that both proved satisfactory in other analyses. Our measures of pay levels showed that they varied substantially and systematically in relation to a whole range of structural and organisational variables. As we have already explained, our findings were consistent with known sources of difference in pay levels, such as industrial sector and region. In cases where there was no external check on the differences revealed, those variations were readily explained in a plausible way. Similarly, while, as we outlined earlier in the chapter, we had reservations about our measure of financial performance, our measures of product demand and change in the size of the workforce over different periods varied in expected ways in relation to each other and other characteristics of establishments.

Accordingly, the indications from our findings were that the level of money earnings received by different groups employed in trading establishments owed little to the financial performance and market circumstances of those establishments. They certainly owed very much more to the structural and organisational characteristics of establishments that we discuss in the remaining part of this chapter[7]. Now it may be that the pattern we uncovered in the present survey was partly a consequence of the fact that at the time we carried out our interviewing Britain was moving into the deepest recession it had known since the war. It may be that in those circumstances the general economic climate has more impact upon pay levels than do variations in financial circumstances between individual plants[8]. Only a time series analysis will resolve that issue.

The main sources of variation in pay levels

While pay levels were not associated with our measures of the market circumstances and performance of establishments, they were very strongly related to a range of structural and other characteristics. The two strongest and simplest of these were the size of establishments and the workforce composition, as reflected in the proportion of women employed and the proportion of part time workers employed. First, the association between pay levels and the number of people employed was very strong and consistent (see Table X.9). The more people employed on site, the higher were the mean earnings of all four occupational groups. It was also the case that both the lowest decile and the highest decile tended to increase systematically with establishment size.

The association between pay levels and establishment size persisted independent of workforce composition in terms of either women or part

Table X.9 Weekly earnings of different job levels

Pounds per week[1]

	All establishments		Number employed at establishment					
	under 50	25–49	50–99	100–199	200–499	500–999	1000–1999	2000 or more
Semi-skilled manual workers								
Lower decile	under 50	under 50	under 50	51	54	63	62	67
Mean	74	67	76	75	80	83	85	88
Upper decile	100	91	105	100	109	105	110	122
Skilled manual workers								
Lower decile	59	57	67	66	76	77	84	85
Mean	96	90	97	95	103	104	107	110
Upper decile	125	118	128	124	134	135	138	140
Clerical workers								
Lower decile	51	under 50	52	55	57	57	59	66
Mean	72	69	72	73	75	75	75	84
Upper decile	93	89	95	94	95	92	96	104
Middle management								
Lower decile	89	83	90	90	94	103	105	114
Mean	121	117	121	121	125	132	135	143
Upper decile	160 or more	160 or more	160 or more	160 or more	160 or more	160 or more	160 or more	160 or more

Base:[1] establishments that gave pay figures

[1] See notes to Table X.7

time workers. While it is not at all unexpected that pay levels should increase systematically with establishment size, the explanation of that association is less immediately apparent. One possibility would be simply that larger organisations have more resources and can afford to pay more. That explanation was not at all consistent with our analysis. First, we found that, while there was the tendency for pay levels to increase with *establishment* size, there was no such tendency for levels to increase with *enterprise* size when the size of workplaces was held constant. That is to say, there was no tendency for very large enterprises to pay more than small ones. The number of people employed at a particular location was the crucial variable, not the total number of people employed. Secondly, when we examined the position of different occupational levels we found, for instance, that the number of *manual* workers employed on site was the crucial source of variation in the pay of manual workers, rather than the total number of employees who were employed on site. For both semi-skilled and skilled manual workers there was a strong tendency for pay levels to increase the more manual workers were employed. When workplaces with similar numbers of manual employees were compared, however, there was no tendency for earnings to increase the larger was the size of total workforce at the establishment. Accordingly, the overall association between total establishment size and the pay levels of manual workers was an incidental consequence of the fact that, generally, larger establishments tended to employ larger numbers of manual workers. Thus, on two measures of size (the number of people employed by the total organisation and the total complement at the establishment) there was no independent association between the pay levels of manual workers and size. That pattern is certainly not consistent with any suggestion that the strong association between the pay levels of manual workers and the number of manual workers employed on site was a consequence of greater corporate resources.

A second possible explanation of the size effect was that it simply reflected sectoral differences. That is to say, those sectors of employment that have traditionally been high payers, such as some parts of manufacturing, also tend to operate relatively larger establishments, while the low paying sector, such as miscellaneous services, tend to operate smaller workplaces. Our findings certainly showed that there were major sources of variation as between different sectors along broadly familiar lines. At the same time, sector and establishment size remained independent sources of variation. Sectoral differences persisted within each main size band. Similarly, within each sector there remained a tendency for earnings to be higher in larger establishments. Ownership, as measured by a simple contrast between public and private ownership, did little to explain variations in pay levels. There

Table X.10   Earnings of different groups in relation to proportion of manual workforce who were women

Pounds per week[1]

	Proportion of manual workers who were women (per cent)						
	No women	1–20	21–40	41–60	61–80	81–99	All women
Semi-skilled	82	88	75	67	64	59	54
Skilled	103	107	97	89	88	75	62
Clerical	74	77	73	69	69	64	66
Middle management	126	123	119	114	115	114	118

Base:[1] establishments that employed manual workers and gave pay figures

[1] See notes to Table X.7

was more variation within both the private and the public sectors than there was between the two sectors. For instance, average pay for manual workers in local or central government tended to be relatively low and similar to the pay of those in private services, while manual workers in nationalised industries tended to receive relatively high average earnings similar to those in the higher paying parts of manufacturing.

Linked to sector but again partly independent of sector was the second major source of variation in the pay of manual workers that we highlighted at the beginning of the section. That source was as important as it was striking. It was the composition of the workforce as reflected in the proportions of manual workers who were women (see Table X.10). The higher was the female proportion of the manual workforce the lower was the level of pay for semi-skilled and skilled workers. The trend was marked and consistent. In cases where all manual workers were women, pay levels were only just over one half of those in cases where hardly any or no manual workers were women. The earnings of clerical and managerial workers did not follow the same marked and consistent trend. Accordingly, the managerial differential relative to manual workers was much larger in establishments where a high proportion of the workforce were women. As we explained in the introduction to this section on earnings, the association between the pay of manual workers and the proportion of the workforce who were women raised in its most acute form the issue of whether our pay figures reflected part time earnings to any extent. Table X.11 analyses the relationship between pay and the gender composition of the workforce in establishments with differing levels of part time working. The

Table X.11 A: levels of pay of semi-skilled manual workers in relation to proportion of women employed and proportion of part time workers

Pounds per week[1]

Proportion of employees who were part-time	Proportion of manual workers who were women		
	1–39 per cent	40–69 per cent	70–100 per cent
5 per cent or less	89	70	63
Over 5 to 40 per cent	80	68	60
Over 40 per cent	§[2]	59	57

B: levels of pay of skilled manual workers in relation to proportion of women employed and proportion of part time workers

5 per cent or less	106	96	97
Over 5 to 40 per cent	103	89	76
Over 40 per cent	§	83	74

Base:[1] establishments that employed manual workers and gave pay figures

[1] See notes to Table X.7
[2] See note A

analysis shows that the proportion of the workforce who were women and the proportion of the workforce who were part time were both associated with the pay of manual workers in an independent way. Equally, when we analysed the pay of manual workers in relation to the composition of the workforce within establishments of differing sizes, there remained a strong tendency for earnings to be lower the higher the proportion of women employed.

The low earnings of women relative to men have long been chronicled, as has the tendency for the differential to be explained partly by the fact that women are much less likely to gain access to skilled manual and professional or managerial jobs[9]. Equal pay, equal opportunities and maternity rights legislation have been introduced to help correct inequalities. Our present findings, however, confirm a very important dimension to the pattern of female inequality. As the pay of women tends to be low not only because women are concentrated in particular types of occupational grade but also because they are concentrated in low paying establishments, the effectiveness of the measures taken so far to correct inequalities must be limited. For instance, that pattern very substantially limits the scope that there is for reducing inequalities as between the sexes by increasing the opportunities for advancement at people's places of work or by reducing differentials in pay between men and women at their places of work. Clearly, inequality that is institutionalised in different segments of the economy presents problems of a quite different order[10].

As we have already indicated, however, the strong association between the proportion of women employed at an establishment and levels of pay did not explain the relationship between size and pay levels. Again, they were both strong independent sources of variation. Remaining possible explanations of the strong tendency for larger establishments to pay more were, first, the possibility that larger workplaces have to provide higher financial rewards to attract people in view of the lower intrinsic rewards that they furnish, owing to greater specialisation and bureaucratisation. Secondly, there may be an inherent organisational tendency within larger workplaces to push pay levels upwards because the larger the number of people employed at a workplace the larger the number of comparisons that can be made between individuals and groups within the workplace as a basis for claiming pay increases on the grounds of comparability. In short, the larger the workplace the longer may be the leap-frog chain. Thirdly, we have consistently seen that trade union representation and organisation tended to increase with increase in the size of establishments. It may be that the tendency for larger workplaces to pay more was an incidental consequence of the tendency for unionisation to be higher in such workplaces.

We have no means of establishing from our present study how far the level of pay furnished by larger workplaces represented compensation for any deprivations involved in working at a larger establishment. There was, however, one feature of larger workplaces that was linked to worker motivation and also to levels of earnings. That was systems of payment-by-results. We saw in Chapter VIII that manual workers were more likely to be paid by results the greater the number of people employed at the establishment. It was also the case that in workplaces where a majority of some group of manual workers were paid by results manual workers also tended to be paid substantially more. Perhaps, though, the most striking and persuasive feature of our analysis was the way that non-manual earnings were essentially the same whether or not manual workers were paid by results. Accordingly, the contrast between manual workers in the different circumstances did not simply reflect incidental differences between generally high paying and generally low paying establishments. The differential between manual and non-manual employees was clearly much more narrow in circumstances where manual workers were paid by results. Again, however, PBR did not wholly explain the variations in relation to establishment size. It remained the case that larger establishments paid more even when we confined analysis to those establishments that did operate PBR or to those who did not. A further characteristic of larger establishments that could be associated with the tendency for such workplaces to pay more was clearly the level of trade union organisation. We consider that possibility in the next section.

Pay levels and trade union organisation

It is commonly supposed that one purpose of trade unions is to increase the money wage of union members. In fact, it is more consistent with evidence to regard trade unions as protective institutions rather than as maximising organisations. People are more likely to give as their reason for belonging to a trade union the security or protection they are thereby afforded than that they hope or expect that the union will achieve higher earnings for them[11]. In practice, it is possible to see that trade unions operate more to insulate members from the consequences of being exposed to market forces or of a weak or unfavourable market position than to maximise their benefit in favourable market or financial circumstances[12]. At the same time, there remains the question of whether people do achieve higher rates of money earnings as a result of being in a trade union[13] and, an even more difficult question, whether they do achieve a higher proportion of the total product of the enterprise as a result of trade union membership and activity.

It is not possible for us to consider the second of these two questions here, but, on the face of it, our present findings provided a very positive answer to the first. That is to say, our findings showed that the higher the level of trade union membership, organisation and activity at a workplace the more trade union members tended to earn compared with counterparts elsewhere. There appeared to be clear evidence of direct benefit from trade union membership and activity in relation to money earnings. While the association between our measures of unionisation and levels of pay were very strong, however, we had to treat them with some caution, initially, in view of the other very strong correlates with pay levels. We have seen that numbers of manual workers employed on site and the proportion of women employed and the proportion of part time workers employed were all very strongly associated with the pay levels of manual workers. It was also the case that those same characteristics were strongly related to levels of trade union membership and organisation. Before we accepted that unionisation was associated with pay levels independently of size and workforce composition we needed to examine the extent of the association when establishments of different sizes were compared and when establishments with different proportions of women among the workforce were compared. Accordingly, in the rest of this chapter, we look, first,

Table X.12   Levels of earnings among manual workers in relation to trade unic density and establishment size

Pounds per weel

	All establishments	Proportion of manual workers who were trac union members (per cent)					
		None	1–24	25–49	50–89	90–99	All
Semi-skilled workers							
All establishments	74	64	68	71	75	84	85
25–99 employed	71	64	66	71	73	(76)	82
100–499 employed	77	65	72	70	74	86	89
500–999 employed	83	§[2]	§	(75)[3]	78	89	93
1000 or more employed	86	§	§	(71)	72	93	91
Skilled workers							
All establishments	96	87	90	92	95	105	106
25–99 employed	93	87	88	92	92	(98)	103
100–499 employed	98	90	95	90	96	106	107
500–999 employed	104	§	§	(102)	99	110	113
1000 or more employed	108	§	§	(101)	102	114	116
Clerical workers							
All establishments	72	69	70	66	71	76	77
Middle management							
All establishments	121	113	116	118	116	126	126

Base:[1] establishments that gave pay figures

[1] See notes to Table X.7
[2] See note A
[3] See note B

at the overall association between unionisation and pay levels. Secondly, we explore the extent to which differences persisted when we compared establishments of similar size. Thirdly, we examine how far unionisation was still associated with higher earnings when we compared workplaces with similar proportions of women and similar proportions of part time workers.

First and perhaps most importantly, Table X.12 shows that the higher the proportion of manual workers who were trade union members the more manual workers tended to earn, whether they were skilled or semi-skilled. That strong and consistent tendency remained even when differences in establishment size were taken into account. Indeed, Table X.12 shows that the level of manual worker trade union

Table X.13 Levels of earnings in relation to patterns of manual and non-manual trade union recognition

Pounds per week[1]

	Both recognised	Manual union recognised/ non-manual not recognised	Non-manual union recognised/manual not recognised	Neither recognised
All establishments				
Semi-skilled	76	83	61	68
Skilled	96	103	79	92
Clerical	73	71	72	70
Middle management	123	117	130	116
Establishment size 25–99				
Semi-skilled	69	84	59	67
Skilled	88	103	78	91
Clerical	70	71	72	69
Middle management	119	117	133	114
Establishments size 100–499				
Semi-skilled	80	81	(63)[2]	70
Skilled	99	102	(81)	94
Clerical	74	71	(73)	76
Middle management	124	114	(121)	122

Base:[1] establishments that gave pay figures

See notes to Table X.7
See note B

membership and the size of establishments were both major sources of variation in the pay of manual workers, but suggests that the level of trade union membership was more strongly associated with levels of pay. The pattern of non-manual earnings in the same establishments did not follow a similar pattern.

Perhaps, though, the association between pay and trade unionism is shown in a more interesting way by Table. X.13. The most striking contrast in that analysis lies between establishments where manual trade unions were recognised but non-manual were not and those where non-manual unions were recognised but manual unions were not. The manual/non-manual differential was dramatically different in these two different circumstances. In circumstances where manual unions were recognised but non-manual unions were not, the differential was relatively narrow. In circumstances where non-manual unions were recognised but manual unions were not the differential was relatively very broad. That pattern also persisted when differences in establishment size were taken into account.

Beyond the patterns that we have already described, we had further indications, first, that in circumstances where unions were recognised, earnings were higher than in cases where they were not, independently of the level of trade union membership in the two contexts; secondly, where there was a closed shop for some group of manual workers, then earnings for manual workers tended to be higher, independently of the general level of trade union membership; and, thirdly, the more immediate was the most important level of bargaining for manual workers, the better did they fare. That third tendency was very strong overall, but as we explain later, it appeared to be largely a consequence of the fact that the different bargaining levels were strongly associated with the proportion of women employed.

A final aspect of the interrelationship between levels of earnings and labour relations institutions which was worthy of note was the association between pay levels for manual workers and the number of different unions and bargaining groups that represented manual workers. When the effect of differences in the size of workplaces was taken into account there was little variation in the pay of either semi-skilled or skilled manual workers in relation to the number of manual unions. There was, however, some indication of a tendency for manual workers to earn more when separate bargaining was practised than when negotiations were conducted through one bargaining unit, even when differences in relation to size and number of manual unions were taken into account. That tendency was more marked for skilled manual workers.

The inter-relationship between different influences upon levels of pay

We have shown in this chapter that there were four main characteristics of establishments that were associated with our measures of the pay levels of different groups and especially the pay of manual workers and the differential between manual and non-manual employees. We checked that establishment size, proportion of women employed and proportion of part time workers were each an independent source of variation. We have also checked and confirmed as we have gone along that establishment size and unionisation were associated with pay levels in an independent way. We needed to check, too, that the association we found between pay levels and trade union organisation was not simply an incidental consequence of the association between manual trade union organisation and the proportion of women employed or the proportion of part time workers employed. That process showed that the associations between manual pay levels and unionisation more fully survived analysis within categories of establishment that employed different proportions of part time workers than it did analysis which controlled for the proportion of women employed. Accordingly, to simplify the exposition we confine the account in the rest of the chapter to the qualifications that needed to be made to our earlier analysis in the light of comparisons made between establishments that employed similar proportions of women. Such comparisons showed first, that it remained true that manual workers were paid substantially more where they were represented by recognised unions and non-manual workers were not. The manual/non-manual differential remained much narrower under such circumstances than it was where non-manual unions were recognised and manual unions were not. It remained true, too, that in circumstances where a majority of some groups of manual workers were paid by results, manual grades earned more and the differential between manual and non-manual workers was less.

Other associations between pay levels and arrangements for industrial relations were, however, modified when we took into account the proportion of women among the manual workforce. It remained true that manual workers in places where trade union membership was high earned substantially more than manual workers where no manual workers were union members, but the clear and continuous relationship between pay and level of trade union membership did not persist. Similarly, where comparisons were possible, it appeared to remain true that manual workers in places that had closed shops earned more than counterparts elsewhere, even when differences in levels of trade union membership and the gender mix in the workforce were taken into account. But the association became patchy. The association between pay levels and the most important level of bargaining over rates of pay virtually disintegrated when the sexual composition of the workforce was taken into account. There was, however, still some tendency for skilled manual workers to receive more the nearer to the establishment was the most important level of bargaining. The finding that was most strongly confirmed by this further analysis was the strong independent influence exercised on the pay of manual workers by the number of women among the manual workforce. The analysis also suggests, however, that the very strong overall association between pay levels and different measures of trade union organisation was partly a consequence of the tendency for manual trade union organisation to be lower in circumstances where a higher proportion of women were employed.

Notes

1. For instance, the original workplace industrial relations survey (Government Social Survey, *Workplace Industrial Relations* (HMSO, London, 1968)) developed an index of managers' satisfaction with the industrial relations system in their establishments based on attitudes to four key features, and found that 79 per cent were satisfied with all four while 95 per cent were satisfied with three or more.
2. See the review of opinion poll data on industrial relations and trade unions in Robert Taylor, *Workers and the New Depression* (Macmillan, London, 1982).

3. Indeed, managers in workplaces where employee representatives were also interviewed were less enthusiastic than managers in places where no representative was interviewed but they remained very favourable and much more positive than union representatives (see second half of Table X.1).

4. Interviewers were briefed to ask supplementary questions to identify the modal category if the description *typical* created difficulties. As managers were asked to report into which of a range of earnings bands the typical figure fell the question caused less difficulty than it would have if we had asked for an actual figure. The sums shown in the tables of weekly pay were derived from the calculation of a mean of the mid-points of the earnings bands identified by managers. Accordingly the figures may be regarded as an approximation to a mean of modal earnings.

5. It was impossible to make strict comparisons between our pay data and the results of the New Earnings Survey. Our figures were means calculated from modal earnings for establishments. The NES figures are mean pay for groups of individuals across different establishments. At the manual level our figures referred to skilled manual workers and simi-skilled manual workers. The only NES figures with which we were able to compare our data were those for full time manual men and full time manual women, respectively.

6. F.T. Blackaby, *The Future of Pay Bargaining* (Heinemann, London, 1980).

7. Our present findings on the lack of association between the financial and market circumstances of establishments and *levels of pay* were consistent with the earlier PSI study of wage determination (W.W. Daniel, *Wage Determination in Industry* (Political and Economic Planning No. 563, London, 1976)). That study showed that there was little association between the financial and market circumstances of manufacturing plants and the level of the periodic *increase* in rates of pay agreed between managers and trade union representatives. Of course, the size of increases in pay are a different issue from levels of pay at any particular point in time and may be expected to react more sensitively to market pressures, but both sets of findings concern the relationship between pay and the market circumstances of employers.

8. Similarly, it may have been that results of the PSI study of wage determination (see note 7) were partly a consequence of the fact that it was carried out when inflation was accelerating faster than at any other time in Britain. At that time the general increase in the cost of living may have swamped all other influences.

9. Michael Fogarty, Isobel Allen, Patricia Walters, *Women in Top Jobs, 1968–79* (Heinemann Educational Books, London, 1981).

10. Differences in levels of pay associated with the segmentation of employment opportunities, notably between high and low paying firms in the same specific industry, have been documented elsewhere. See, for example, C. Craig *et al*, *Labour Market Structure, Industrial Organisation and Low Pay* (Cambridge University Press, Cambridge, 1982).

11. For instance, among the advantages of union membership listed by union members in the original survey of workplace industrial relations (see note 1), items concerned with protection in one form or another far outnumbered all others.

12. W.W. Daniel, 'Influences on the Level of Wage Settlements in Manufacturing Industry', in F.T. Blackaby, Ed., *The Future of Pay Bargaining* (Heinemann Educational Books, London, 1980).

13. This question has received much attention in the United States, where suitable data sets are available for analysis. In Britain attention has largely been focused on the differences between workers 'covered' by collective agreements and those not covered, using data from the 1973 and 1978 New Earnings Surveys. See, for example, M.B. Gregory and A.W.J. Thomson, 'The Coverage Mark-up, Bargaining Structure and Earnings in Britain, 1973 and 1978', *British Journal of Industrial Relations*, March 1981, pp. 26–37. A different approach, using trade union membership data, has recently been reported by M.B. Stewart, *Relative Earnings and Individual Union Membership in the U.K.* (University of Warwick, mimeo, May 1981).

XI   Conclusions

Our analysis has confirmed our view that the comprehensiveness of the present survey was its main strength compared with previous studies of its kind. The coverage of nationalised industries, public services and private services as well as private manufacturing industry enabled us to explore the diversity in the British system of industrial relations, to correct impressons that are developed from focusing upon just one sector and to highlight the way that differences in ownership are very strongly associated with key features of industrial relations. The inclusion of smaller establishments than have previously been covered enabled us to carry out more satisfactory analysis of variations in relation to size and to demonstrate that institutional industrial relations have substantial relevance for small establishments. The comprehensive questioning on non-manual as well as manual workers enabled us to make comparisons throughout and, for instance, to identify the way in which concentration of employment appeared to have quite different implications for white collar than for blue collar union density and recognition. Interviewing employee representatives as well as managers provided valuable extra information. In addition, for instance, we judged that the combination of the accounts of managers and employee representatives of industrial action provided us with a substantially more sound measure of the extent of strikes and other sanctions than would have been possible with either account on its own. The design of the sample enabled us to give results in terms of the population of establishments that operated different practices as well as the population of employees who were covered by those practices. Those characteristics make the survey a uniquely rich source of data on workplace industrial relations in Britain. As we said in our introduction, we have been able to give only a very general account of the main findings in this book and one of the prime purposes of the book is to encourage others to use those data for further analysis.

While we are confident about the strengths of our study, we are also aware of its limitations for purposes of analysing industrial relations as a whole. We concentrated upon factual information and did not include much attitudinal or evaluative data. Our primary focus was the establishment and we have had little to say about other important levels and contexts of decision making in industrial relations. We have necessarily had much more to say about institutions and structures than about processes. By design, our survey had a large number of different

purposes rather than a single purpose. That is to say, we set out to
provide good information on a wide range of industrial relations practices, procedures and institutions rather than to design an instrument
that would enable us to analyse one issue or set of issues in great detail
and depth. As we covered such a wide range of topics and issues,
we have inevitably been very selective in our references to previous
research and in the use of our findings and analysis to amplify, modify
or question the results of previous research. Equally, any summary of
the findings from our survey must also be selective. We hope that our
selection of the main findings and conclusions to be drawn from the
study will encourage readers to test our analysis against the information
in the body of the report and, indeed, the raw data in the original
survey.

Trade union recognition and growth

In a later section of these conclusions we show that there has been a
substantial growth in Britain of joint consultative committees that deal
with matters of substance. The growth, we suggest, is slightly at odds
with the traditional view of the British system of industrial relations.
That view has been that one of the main distinguishing characteristics
of the British system compared with that of some other parts of Western
Europe is the high level of trade union organisation at the workplace
and the representation of workers' views and interests through shop
stewards, as union representatives, rather than works councils[1]. While
the results of our present survey do show that there has been substantial
growth in the number and coverage of joint consultative committees,
they do not suggest that this has been at the expense of union recognition and organisation. Indeed, there has been a parallel growth in
trade union densities and representation at the workplace. Trade union
membership grew very substantially during the 1970s and reached a
peak at about the time of our survey. We found that over one half of all
our establishments recognised unions for manual workers. The greater
the number of manual workers employed, the more likely unions were
to be recognised. In consequence, the large majority of manual workers
worked in places where unions were recognised. In the private sector
there was a marked tendency for the recognition of non-manual unions
to be less common, but, overall, levels of recognition and union density
were not very far behind those for manual workers.

Where manual unions were recognised and fifty or more manual
workers were employed, the large majority of establishments had shop
stewards and the majority had convenors or senior stewards. Where 500
or more manual workers were employed, full time convenors were very
common, and where 1,000 or more manual workers were employed,
nearly three-quarters of establishments had full time convenors. As we

highlight in other parts of these conclusions, there appeared to have been substantial growth in the number of full time convenors in the period following the mid-1970s. Again, when we compared the incidence of non-manual and manual stewards and convenors in circumstances where there was union recognition, non-manual stewards and convenors were only slightly less common.

It was clear that trade union representation of workers within workplaces was normal for manual workforces throughout British industry. For non-manual workers it was normal in the public sector and common in the private sector. It was also clear that workplace union representatives were engaged in the joint regulation with managers of a wide range of issues not directly related to pay. In over one half or more of the cases where manual unions were recognised, manual representatives negotiated over physical working conditions, redeployment of staff within the establishment, manning levels, redundancy, changes in production methods and recruitment. Non-manual workplace representatives also engaged in bargaining over a wide range of issues.

The inclusion of nationalised industries, public services and private services in our survey as well as private manufacturing industry very substantially enriched our analysis of sources of variation in trade union recognition and union densities. The comprehensiveness of the survey forced into prominence the importance of ownership as a major source of variation in key features of institutional industrial relations. When analysis of trade union recognition was confined to manufacturing industry, it appeared that the structural or organisational characteristics of workplaces, such as the number of people employed at the establishment or the size and complexity of the total organisation of which it was part, were the characteristics of workplaces most strongly associated with union recognition and densities. When, however, the public sector was included in the analysis, the picture changed radically. Recognition was much more common and was not related to size in anything like the way it was in the private sector. Overall, ownership was the main source of variation in the extent of recognition. In the nationalised industries recognition was almost universal and union densities were very high. In public administration, recognition was also very widespread, but densities were lower. In the private sector, recognition was lower, but densities were higher relative to levels of recognition compared with public administration.

Although when analysis was confined to the private sector establishment and organisation size emerged as the largest sources of variation, there were important riders to that conclusion. First, there were important variations in relation to type of owner within the private sector. Independent establishments (which might presumably be regarded as small firms in comparison with large corporations) were substantially less likely to recognise unions than were establishments that were part of larger organisations. That difference was independent of the number of people employed by the establishment or the organisation. Secondly, so far as manual unions were concerned, the higher the proportion of women employed the less likely unions were to be recognised, independently of the other sources of variation.

Generally the sources of variation in union recognition and density were similar for manual and non-manual grades. But there were also differences, some of which, we have argued in the text, were relevant to ideas about the growth of non-manual unions. First, the contrast between the public and the private sectors was even more marked for non-manual groups than for manual workers. Secondly, it appeared that organisation size and the contrast between independent establishments and those that were parts of groups were both more strongly associated with non-manual than with manual recognition. Thirdly, as far as manual workers were concerned, the important aspect of establishment size in relation to recognition was *the number of manual workers employed*, as might be expected. For non-manual groups, in contrast, the *total number of people employed* at the establishment was more strongly associated with recognition than the number of non-manual employees. We argued in the text that the second two points represented important qualifications to the idea of employment concentration as an influence upon white collar union growth.

We have stressed in this section the importance of ownership as a source of variation in union recognition. While public sector establishments were more likely to recognise unions, it was not, however, the case that union activity was more common in the public sector when establishments that recognised unions were compared. Indeed, where unions were recognised, public sector establishments, for instance, were less likely to have stewards and convenors and local bargaining was less common.

The closed shop

Our findings confirm that there has been very substantial growth over the past 20 years in the requirement that people should be members of trade unions in order to obtain or retain their jobs. They also confirm that there has been an even more substantial change in the form of such closed shop arrangements. In the early 1960s McCarthy estimated that three and three-quarters million people were members of closed shops[2]. That number represented 16 per cent of the workforce at the time. In 1978 Gennard concluded that at least 5.2 million people were closed shop members and they represented 23 per cent of the workforce[3]. We found that 27 per cent of the people employed by establishments included in our survey were covered by closed shops.

It remained the case that the closed shop was very much more characteristic of the organisation of manual than that of non-manual workers, but there has also been some tendency for the arrangement to become more common among non-manual groups. The estimate for the early 1960s was four per cent. Gennard's analysis suggested 11 per cent. Our survey indicated that nine per cent of non-manual employees were required to be union members. By contrast we found that 44 per cent of manual workers were covered by closed shops.

Our analysis combined with that of Gennard to suggest that the bulk of the growth in the closed shop has taken the post-entry form. We found that 82 per cent of closed shop members were required to join a union as a condition of employment while only 18 per cent had to have the appropriate union card before they could become candidates for jobs. The comparable figures in Gennard's study were 84 per cent and 16 per cent. While McCarthy estimated that four-fifths of closed shop members belonged to the post-entry form in the early 1960s, the 1966 workplace industrial relations survey for the Donovan Commission implied that the pre-entry form was nearly as common as the post-entry form in manufacturing and construction[4].

Our analysis of the closed shop differed from that of earlier studies, first, in the importance attached to different sources of variation in its distribution and, secondly, in our assessment of the form taken by the institution. Following the example of McCarthy, Gennard carried out most of his analysis in relation to industrial sector. McCarthy clearly saw the closed shop as being imposed upon managements by unions in response to the labour market conditions and bargaining requirements that were characteristic of particular industries. He was struck by the way in which the institution was concentrated in particular industries, especially mining, metal manufacture, engineering, shipbuilding and paper, printing and publishing. Gennard plotted the way in which there has been a decline in the number of closed shop members in those traditional sectors as a result of the fall in the total number of people employed by those industries. He showed that the decline in traditional sectors has been more than compensated for by the growth of the closed shop in sectors which McCarthy found to be largely open, such as food, drink and tobacco, clothing and footwear, public utilities and transport and communications. But industrial sector remained the basis of his analysis. We found that the ownership of establishments, their size and the size of the organisations of which they were part were substantially stronger sources of variation than industrial sector. In relation to ownership, nationalised industries were much more likely to operate closed shops than any other type of employer independently of size and sector. Outside public employment, there was a strong and consistent tendency for the closed shop to be more common the larger was the number of people employed on site. Independent of establishment size, there was also a strong tendency for the closed shop to be more common the larger was the size of the total organisation of which the establishment was part. Here it was especially noticeable, as we stressed in our introduction to these conclusions, that the largest contrast lay between the single establishment enterprise and larger multi-establishment enterprises. This comparison underlined the importance of different types of private ownership in addition to the significance of public as compared with private ownership.

Overall, our analysis of sources of variation in the closed shop suggested that the institution represented one end of a general union density continuum. The sources of variation in the distribution of the closed shop mirrored those associated with trade union density and recognition. Analysis in relation to union density, with the closed shop and full membership at one extreme, generally showed a steady and consistent trend rather than a dichotomy between open and closed shop establishments. In short, McCarthy tended to conceive of the closed shop as a specific institutional form that was distinct from, if not independent of, union density or the general level of union organisation. He saw it as being imposed by unions in response to the requirements of union organisation in particular sectors. The Warwick survey results suggested that, at least in manufacturing industry, the growth of the closed shop, particularly since the mid-1970s, could be explained as much by management policies concerning the comprehensiveness of representation and bargaining arrangements as it could by trade union pressure[5]. Weekes and his colleagues had earlier highlighted managerial preferences and the advantages the closed shop gave them in their relationships with trade unions. Dunn has more recently suggested that the growth of the closed shop had depended more on management aquiescence than upon positive encouragement[6]. There are two pieces of evidence from our data which bear upon the contention that management policies are associated with the growth of the closed shop. First, there was the way in which ownership was a major source of variation in the extent of the closed shop. Secondly, there was the very high proportion of cases where closed shops among manual workers covered all the manual workers in an establishment and were not confined to particular occupational groups.

The second point at which our analysis differed, in emphasis at least, from that of Gennard was in the extent to which the closed shop has matured. Gennard argued that in the early 1960s only one fifth of closed shop arrangements were embodied in any formal agreement[7]. Even where there was a formal arrangement it characteristically consisted of only one sentence specifying that a category of employees should 'become and remain members of the union'. Since, then, he argued, closed shop arrangements have become increasingly subject to more and more refined and lengthy union membership agreements which frequently specify arrangements for joining the union, grounds for claiming exemption from joining the union and procedures for dealing with any dispute over union membership. He suggested that 'on a conservative estimate well over half' the closed shop population was covered by formal closed shop agreements. An analysis of a sample of such agreements showed, for instance, that there were grounds for exemption in the large majority of cases and, where there were such grounds, there was normally more than one exemption.

Our findings were not wholly consistent with that picture. We found, it is true, that in three-quarters of establishments where managers reported that they had closed shops they also reported that they had written agreements concerning the institution. But we also found that in only one half of establishments with closed shops did managers report any exemption[8]. Of particular interest was the way in which, contrary to all the other trends for arrangements to become more formalised in larger establishments, there was a marked tendency for grounds for exemption to be less common in larger workplaces. Moreover, in cases where there were exemptions, the average number reported was one and a half, whereas according to Gennard's analysis it was substantially more.

Similarly, Gennard listed a series of seven safeguards to protect the interests of individuals that were included in his union membership agreements, of which the most common was the inclusion of a 'special procedure to handle union membership agreement appeals and problems' (52 per cent). We found that in only one quarter of establishments with closed shops was there reported any special procedure for dealing with disputes over the closed shop. Our findings suggest that Gennard's two stage operation (which involved, first, estimating what proportion of the closed shop population was covered by formal agreements and, secondly, analysing the contents of a number of sophisticated union membership agreements) gave an exaggerated impression of the extent to which the closed shop has become controlled by formal agreements that provide for exemptions and safeguards.

The issue of the check-off is frequently linked with the closed shop and here our research produced clear findings. It is frequently argued that the introduction of a closed shop operates as a powerful incentive to managements to operate a check-off in order to avoid the possibility of the problems arising from lapsed membership. We found, first, that there has been a very substantial growth in the extent of the check-off. The 1966 workplace industrial relations survey for the Donovan Commission showed that only ten per cent of all plants that recognised trade unions deducted trade union subscriptions from their work people's pay packets. Since that time the practice has spread to the large majority of workplaces that recognised unions. It was universal in our nationalised industry establishments, operated by four out of five establishments that were parts of groups and, indeed, was found in three-quarters of all establishments that recognised unions. Secondly, however, the check-off in its contemporary form appeared to have very little direct association with the closed shop. It was much more widespread than the closed shop. The practice was more common the higher was the proportion of the workforce who were union members but was independent of whether a closed shop existed. That is to say, the check-off was as common in establishments with a high level of union membership but no closed shop as it was in establishments with a similar level of membership reinforced by a closed shop.

Trade union organisation

In Chapter IV we filled in more details of the picture of trade union organisation at the workplace and extended it to the context of the wider union. In many ways the overall picture was similar to that described by the workplace industrial relations survey for the Donovan Commission for the six manual trade unions it covered[9] and later described by Brown and his colleagues for the GMWU[10]. Our picture was, however, much more extensive in terms of the unions covered and, in relation to the Donovan survey, richer, in that it was able to relate elements of union organisation to other characteristics of the workplace, its industry and so on. Some of our findings will be relevant to debates about trade union democracy.

We found important differences between trade union branches whose members were drawn from a single workplace and branches encompassing members from several workplaces or employers. Branches based at the workplace were smaller, and meetings were attended by a higher proportion of members. In all types of branch, but especially geographically based ones, shop stewards were much more frequent in their attendance than were other branch members. Stewards also commonly held positions on their branch committee.

As the Donovan survey showed for 1966, the appointment of manual union shop stewards was most commonly made by a show of hands at a meeting of union members. This remained the case in 1980 and was also evident for non-manual stewards. However, although a minority practice, ballots for shop steward appointments were held in almost all the major trade unions. Some method of periodic reappointment was reported in most cases, normally once per year, but in about half the cases there had been no alternative candidate. In larger workplaces with many stewards it was common for senior shop stewards to be elected by their fellow stewards rather than by ordinary members.

Contact with local full time union officials by shop stewards appeared to arise from a variety of problems and be more frequent with larger constituencies. Where the meetings also involved management, there was a suggestion that the problems were serious – establishments involved in such meetings were more likely to have experienced industrial action during the same period.

Joint shop stewards' meetings were reported in only a minority of establishments with two or more manual, or two or more non-manual, unions. They were more likely where the unions negotiated on pay on a joint basis, in larger establishments and where there was a full time convenor. However, the weak association with establishment level pay bargaining suggests that the meetings were involved with other issues besides pay. Further analysis in relation to the scope of bargaining could throw more light on their functions and complement more intensive studies of these meetings[11].

Our findings extend in several ways the picture of shop steward combine committees given in previous research, mainly in the engineering industry. Stewards in multi-establishment organisations reported meeting stewards from other workplaces in nearly one half of cases and more often in larger enterprises and in establishments with strong trade union organisation. For these meetings, the association with pay bargaining arrangements was clear and the most commonly given reason for starting them was to exchange information and ideas. The sector in which the most recently established meetings were reported was the health services, a sector which experienced increasing difficulties in pay settlements in the period up to 1980.

The position of personnel and industrial relations managers

In many ways, as we reported in Chapter V, our findings about the role and characteristics of personnel managers were disappointing, compared with our original design. We had had in mind that the survey would enable us to carry out an analysis of a professional or occupational group in its institutional setting. That design was based on the assumption that our respondents would principally be personnel or industrial relations managers in some sense of the term. The assumption was not unreasonable in view of the apparent indications of previous research. In practice, it proved not to be justified. Only around one half of our respondents reported that they spent a major part of their time on personnel matters. Only around one half of those people who spent a major part of their time on personnel matters had job titles which identified them as personnel managers of some type. In consequence, only about one quarter of our respondents were specialists as we termed them. Moreover, one half of our personnel specialists had no formal qualifications for personnel work. Where they had any qualification, by far the most common type was membership of an occupational association. Overall, we developed the impression from our initial findings and analysis that the bulk of personnel work was done by people who were not specialists. Where the work was done by specialists, the most common type of preparation for personnel management was *on the job* experience and training in the establishment or organisation where people were employed. Formal educational or professional qualifications played little part. That impression was reinforced when we found that the more recent recruits to personnel work were less likely than our respondents to have formal educational qualifications for the job.

While our findings on the number and characteristics of personnel managers did not provide us with the type of analysis for which we had been hoping when we designed our schedule, they did provide us with a clear picture of the management function. That picture was moderated by the fact that the chief source of variation in the incidence of specialist personnel managers was establishment size. The larger the number of people employed, the more likely establishments were to have specialist personnel managers and the more likely those managers were to have formal qualifications. Consequently, the proportion of employees covered by personnel specialists was substantially larger than the proportion of establishments covered. Nevertheless, the picture painted by our findings did appear to contrast sharply with the Warwick study which was clearly impressed by how widespread specialist personnel management had become in the previous 10 or 20 years and how much emphasis was given to personnel management[12]. There were two main reasons for the contrast. First, Warwick studied larger establishments than we did and adopted a looser definition of *personnel specialist*. Secondly, however, Warwick did show that there had been growth in the number of personnel specialists. It focused attention on the growth. We focused more attention on the proportion of establishments that lacked personnel specialists, despite the changes that have occurred, and the proportion of personnel specialists that lacked formal qualifications.

Our results were much more in accord with Warwick on the matter of the representation of the personnel function on the governing bodies of organisations (or *board representation* in the private sector). When we compared findings from the appropriate sub-sample of our establishments with the Warwick figures, they were very similar. There also emerged a similar pattern of variation, and the variations were important. Both studies found that there was some representation of the personnel function on governing bodies in about two-thirds of cases and that there was specialist representation in about one third. The main general source of variation was the total size of the organisation. In addition, however, there were marked and consistent differences in relation to bargaining levels. Where the company was the most important level of bargaining over the pay of manual workers, then specialist representation on the board was very much more common. When establishment or plant bargaining was most important, then it was much less common. It appeared that the representation of personnel or industrial relations management upon the governing bodies of organisations was strongly associated with the centralisation of pay bargaining.

Joint consultation and participation

As we mentioned in an earlier section on union recognition, a traditional distinction between the British system of industrial relations and some continental European systems has been that British workers have tended to be represented at their places of work by trade union shop stewards, while continental counterparts have tended to be represented by workers councils. We showed in that earlier section that, if anything, shop steward representation in Britain increased in the period leading up to our survey. At the same time, our findings in Chapter VI showed that that traditional form of representation was accompanied by a growth in works committees or joint consultative committees with labels of that kind. We found that 37 per cent of our workplaces had consultative committees. There was clear confirmation of substantial growth[13]. One fifth of the committees had been established within the previous three years and two fifths within the previous five. There was very little sign, over that period, of any attrition of committees in places that had them previously. Committees were more common in the public sector than in the private. They were also substantially more common in larger workplaces and those belonging to larger organisations. In consequence, the proportion of employees covered by formal consultation arrangements very considerably exceeded the proportion of workplaces that had them, and committees were more common in circumstances where unions were also highly organised. Indeed, we found that over one half of the employees represented by our establishments were in workplaces that had both a joint consultative committee and trade union recognition. That pattern contrasts markedly with the traditional view of the British industrial relations system.

Historically, there have been, in Britain, attempts to develop and promote joint consultative machinery in parallel to collective bargaining arrangements with unions. The idea was that joint consultation provided a basis for an exchange of views over matters of common interest while collective bargaining provided a basis for resolving differences relating to areas of conflict [14]. Collective bargaining machinery was seen as the channel of representation which dealt with the more important matters and which included the representatives with power. The development of productivity bargaining during the 1960s extended the range of issues that were dealt with under collective bargaining to include manning levels, working practices and overtime and 'contributed to the recognition of the authority of shop stewards and to the formalisation of plant bargaining'[15]. In the face of such developments, starved of substance and influence, joint consultative committees tended to wither and die[16]. The more recent growth of consultative committees in workplaces with established trade union representation represents a reversal of that trend.

The main general issue raised by the growth of joint consultative committees during the later half of the 1970s was whether they developed as an adjunct to, or as an alternative to, trade union representation and collective bargaining. There was little doubt from the overall pattern of our findings that, in general, contemporary joint consultation in Britain took place within the framework of an integrated system of representation based upon trade union recognition. First, as we have already mentioned, formal joint consultative committees tended to be most common in the types of workplace where trade union organisation was also most highly developed. Secondly, unions played a major part in appointments to consultative committees. Unions and staff associations appointed all representatives for 45 per cent of committees. They chose some of the representatives in a further 11 per cent of cases. Moreover, it was, again, the larger workplaces where unions were more likely to have influence. Thirdly, and perhaps most importantly, matters of substance were most likely to be discussed in consultative committees where those matters were also the subject of negotiations at the workplace. For instance, when people were asked the most important issues that had been discussed in committees over the recent period, the three items mentioned most frequently were levels of manpower, productivity and issues relating to pay. We analysed answers in relation to the answers to our other questions asking whether those matters or matters relating to them were negotiated at the establishment, at a higher level, or not at all. We found that, for instance, the more likely levels of manning were to be subject to local joint regulation, the more likely they were to appear, too, on the agenda of the most important matters that were the subject of joint consultation. It was clear that there was a considerable overlap in matters that were subject to consultation and negotiation and no general tendency for managers to avoid negotiations over matters of substance on the grounds that they were appropriate to joint consultation.

In contrast with the main pattern, however, there was also evidence that, in a minority of workplaces, joint consultation was being established in the absence of, or perhaps as an alternative to, trade union representation and collective bargaining. First, in a very small minority of establishments the existence of some form of non-union committee for employee representation coincided with some evidence of resistance to trade unions. Such establishments tended to be small private sector workplaces. Secondly, there were indications that the more recently established joint consultative committees were more likely to provide representation for sections of the workforce that did not have union representatives than to extend representation for those who did.

Overall, our findings gave the impression that there have been substantial developments in Britain on a voluntary basis to promote worker involvement, in the absence of any general legislative framework to promote worker involvement in decision making, such as that which exists in many other European countries. In addition to our evidence on the growth of joint consultative committees, one quarter of managers and a similar proportion of union representatives reported that there had been some attempt during the previous three years to increase worker involvement at the establishment. In some cases the answers did not provide clear evidence of any of the conventionally accepted methods of promoting worker involvement, but one quarter of establishments having been involved in some initiative did represent a high figure.

Three further points relevant to employee involvement warrant passing reference. First, there were strong indications that the Health and Safety at Work Act, 1974 did provide a boost to the spread of joint health and safety committees. One half of our establishments had such committees and two-thirds of these were introduced after the legislation. Secondly, the enabling legislation of 1978 relating to share option schemes did appear to have encouraged their spread, though they were still rare and heavily concentrated in particular sectors, like financial services and distribution. Thirdly, however, despite evidence of different kinds of initiative in relation to worker involvement, many managers provided workers or their representatives with little or no information on the financial position of the establishment or business and there were also indications that failure to provide such information was associated with a generally poorer industrial relations climate. As noted in Chapter VI, substantial use was made of statutory provisions on disclosure of information as the basis for requests for information in a substantial minority of cases.

Procedures

The survey has provided important evidence of the growth and formalisation of industrial relations procedures since the late 1960s. We saw in Chapter VII that the growth of disciplinary procedures was particularly marked, although there was still a substantial minority of small establishments in the private sector, notably small firms, where managers did not report the existence of a formal disciplinary procedure. Judging from the dates when written disciplinary procedures were introduced, the various legislative initiatives of the 1970s were an important stimulus. However, it remained the case that establishments with trade union representation were those most likely to have the more formalised, written procedures. Indeed, in such establishments disciplinary procedures were usually agreed with the trade unions and set out in a document signed by both management and unions. This was by no means common in 1969 when comparable survey evidence was collected[17].

Procedures for disciplinary matters and for dealing with pay disputes commonly had some provision for calling in a third party when issues could not be resolved locally. Such a provision was even more common where the procedure was the subject of a written agreement, signed by unions and management. A variety of third parties was specified in procedures and a similar variety was exhibited in relation to their actual use in disputes. However, trade union officials were brought in to help settle disputes much more commonly than they were mentioned in the formal, written procedures, an indication of the flexibility with which procedures were treated.

Both management and worker representative respondents reported that most disputes were dealt with under the formal procedures that they had. Worker representatives reported substantially lower levels of satisfaction with their establishments' procedures than did managers. The length and complexity of the procedure was the prime source of dissatisfaction, the view that the procedure favoured management being of secondary importance. Dissatisfaction with the working of disciplinary procedures was strongly associated with a less favourable assessment of the establishment's general state of industrial relations.

Pay related issues

We have drawn substantially upon the themes and topics included in Chapter VIII in other parts of these conclusions. Accordingly, our intention here it to highlight only those points that are not covered elsewhere. As far as levels of collective bargaining were concerned, the chief strength of our present findings relative to previous studies[18] was that it revealed fully the diversity of systems of pay determination in Britain. For instance, the Warwick study concluded, 'single employer agreements have largely replaced multi-employer agreements as the major influence upon the pay of manual workers'. Our present findings confirmed that that important conclusion was true for manufacturing industry, and pay determination in manufacturing industry is of major importance, but our results also demonstrated that for other important sectors such as construction, private services and local government there was a very different pattern. When practice in the non-unionised sectors and the nationalised industries and national government was added to the pattern, then the full diversity of the British system of pay determination was exposed. Also revealed were the formidable obstacles to the regulation of that system that are simply built into the structures involved and are independent of the distribution of power and preferences.

As we have repeatedly noted throughout the report, the striking feature of the pattern for non-manual workers is that it was so close to that for manual workers. In the private sector, non-manual groups were, of course, less likely to have their pay regulated by collective bargaining, as we have shown in our section on recognition and union densities. But even in the private sector white collar pay was widely regulated through collective bargaining. And where there were negotiations over pay, then levels of bargaining for non-manual workers were very similar to those for manual groups. The only difference was that bargaining for non-manual groups was just slightly more likely to be centralised.

The second feature of Chapter VIII that warrants comment in this concluding section is the evidence of the persistence of major differences in the systems of control and remuneration applied to workers of different levels on the basis of a crude distinction between manual and non-manual grades. In large parts of manufacturing industry, all manual workers were required to clock on in the morning and clock off in the evening, while no such system of control was applied to non-manual workers. Similarly, it was normal for white collar workers to receive full pay when absent through sickness but it was not so for their blue collar counterparts. Differences were not so marked in the public sector or in smaller workplaces. It was in large, private sector establishments that the different treatment of blue and white collar groups was so marked.

Industrial action
The incidence of strikes has been a major focus of industrial relations research. Our analysis in Chapter IX builds upon and extends that tradition. In particular, our survey provided, for the first time, information on picketing and more substantial analysis than has previously been available of industrial action other than strikes.

Overall, our analysis confirmed, first, that the incidence of both strikes and other industrial action was strongly associated with workforce size, the preponderance of male, full time employees, the level of unionisation and with the establishment being the main locus of collective bargaining[19]. There was little support for any strong connection between the occurrence of disputes and such matters as the presence of agreed procedures, joint consultative machinery, manufacturing technology and multi-unionism. Trade union density was the characteristic most strongly related to the proportion of the workforce involved in a stoppage. Intermittent recurrent strikes were more widespread than the national engineering stoppage in 1979 which brought them to public notice. Industrial action other than strikes was a feature of non-manual employment in particular and was particularly common among non-manual employees taking industrial action for the first time.

In view of the growing proportion of non-manual workers in the national labour force, the results suggest that the incidence of strikes is no longer an adequate measure of the level of overt industrial conflict. Indeed, broadly speaking, less than one half of the establishments affected by any type of industrial action were affected by a strike which would have come within the definition used for the official records. Our findings show that that definition provides a particularly inadequate measure of industrial conflict in local and national government and, to a lesser extent, in food and chemicals, textiles and clothing, miscellaneous manufacturing and the health and education services.

The association between all types of industrial action and systems of payment-by-results provided a second striking feature of the analysis. That association was revealed in the present survey by the way that strikes were substantially more common in workplaces where PBR operates and by earlier evidence[20] of the extent to which disputes over rates for the job under PBR were cited as the trigger events for industrial action, at least in manufacturing. All the indications are that there has been a long-term tendency for payment systems to come under reform, but it appears that such reform has not been sufficient to stop payment systems remaining a major source of industrial disputes. Ironically, it also appears that, in the face of the long-term trends, different phases of national incomes policy have tended to give a cyclical boost to forms of PBR[21]. Our analysis suggests that, given the positive association between PBR and industrial conflict, it is possible that one effect of some stages of incomes policy may have been to encourage changes prone to generate conflict[22].

Thirdly, our survey included, for the first time, information on the extent and impact of picketing. Previously, this information was not available on even a limited scale. Overall, the impression created by our findings was, first, that picketing and, especially, secondary picketing as we defined it in Chapter IX, was common, albeit at a time of widespread strike activity, but did not always have any direct effects. Pickets tended to be set up in about one third of the cases where strikes occurred, which meant that in the previous year about six per cent of workplaces were subject to picketing. Picketing associated with a dispute at another workplace was slightly more common and occurred in eight per cent of cases. Both management and union respondents agreed that pickets had no direct effect in about one third of cases: they prevented the movement through the picket line of neither goods and services nor employees. Where pickets did have an effect they tended more frequently to interrupt the movement of goods and services (which occurred in just over one half of cases) than of people (which occurred in just over one third of cases). Generally, secondary picketing tended to occur at the same kinds of establishment, principally larger workplaces, as did primary picketing, presumably reflecting the 'economies of scale' to trade unions. According to worker representatives, almost everyone involved in cases of primary picketing was an employee of the establishment, and managers reported that people other than employees were involved in only a small minority of cases. Even according to management accounts, primary picketing was organised by local shop stewards (71 per cent) or local full time officers (20 per cent) in 91 per cent of cases. In other cases it was organised by shop stewards from other establishments in the same organisation, other union officials or the employees themselves.

Levels of pay

As we explained in the body of the report, our study was not explicitly designed to measure the effects or consequences of different industrial relations practices. At the same time, we did incidentally include a number of measures of what might be regarded as outcomes of the industrial relations system. Among these were the pay levels of different occupational groups, and our findings in relation to pay were of major interest and importance. Our measurement of pay levels and differentials was necessarily crude. We asked into which of a range of wage bands fell the typical weekly pay of four broad occupational levels. We would not pretend, that, as measures of actual earnings, the answers to such a question would come anywhere near the precision and accuracy of the New Earnings Survey (NES). In particular, we accept that our failure to include any measure of hours of work against which we could relate weekly pay does limit the scope for analysis and require some caution in the expression of our conclusions. On the other hand, our results did appear robust as measures of which establishments tended to pay more and which tended to pay less for different occupational levels. The variations in pay revealed did appear to be consistent with those shown by the NES in so far as comparisons were possible. The variations to which we attached importance persisted when we excluded establishments with substantial numbers of part time workers. In short, we judged that our results provided a sound measure of variations in pay levels and the great advantage of our survey was that it enabled us to relate those *variations* in pay levels and differentials to a very wide range of structural, organisational and labour relations characteristics of workplaces in a way that has not been possible with information that provides more precise details of pay. The results of our analysis were very striking.

Focusing upon the pay of manual workers, where the pattern was in many ways more interesting, we were unable, first, to establish any consistent relationship between levels of pay and any of the measures of the financial or market circumstances of establishments that we built into the schedule. People earned as much where the demand for products was falling as they did where demand was rising. Similarly, in workplaces where the size of the workforce had been reduced in the previous year or the previous five years, workers earned similar amounts to those in establishments where the complement had been increasing. We have more reservations about our measures of the financial performance of establishments and trends in capital investment than about our information on product demand and changes in the size of the workforce. But it was also the case that managers' assessments of financial performance and investment were not associated with pay levels. The findings remained unaltered whether we based our analysis upon all relevant establishments or confined it to the private sector, and when we took other sources of variation into account. It would not, of course, be possible to conclude from this 1980 cross-sectional data that pay levels had not reacted over time to financial and product market forces.

Secondly, there were very strong and consistent relationships between pay levels and other characteristics of workplaces. The two strongest were the number of people employed and the proportion of women employed. The larger the establishment, the higher people were paid. The higher the proportion of women employed, the less people were paid. The two sources of variation were not only especially strong, they were also of intrinsic interest. We were readily able to show that variations in relation to size were not simply a consequence of larger organisations having more resources which enabled them to pay more. The critical influence on pay was the number of people of a particular level who were employed on site. When that influence was held constant, there was no tendency for pay levels to increase the larger was the total number of people employed on site. Nor was there any tendency for pay levels to be higher the larger was the total organisation of which the establishment was part. Our findings relating to women were, of course, especially subject to the limitation concerning information on hours of work. But the association between female density and pay levels for manual workers was remarkably strong, was independent of the proportion of part time workers and underlined an important dimension of inequality at work as between the sexes. The main measures that have been taken to promote equality at work have been directed at achieving equal pay and equal pay within establishments. The implication of our present findings is that women could have full equality of opportunity in relation to the men with whom they work and they could have full equality of pay relative to their male colleagues, but women would still be paid less than men overall because a large part of the difference lies between establishments that employ a lot of women as compared with those that employ a lot of men, rather than within such establishments.

Thirdly, in view of the strong association between levels of pay and both the number of the relevant job level employed on site and the proportion of the relevant group who were female, it was inevitable that pay levels would be strongly associated with levels of trade union organisation. Union organisation was itself, of course, strongly associated with the number employed on site and the gender mix. However, even when we held constant the size of the workforce and its composition, there remained some tendency for earnings to be higher in places where the level of union organisation was high.

With all the recognised limitations of our information about pay levels, the indications of our analysis were clear. There appeared to be no association between the pay levels of manual workers and the market and financial circumstances of establishments in so far as we were able to measure them. There appeared to be strong associations between pay levels and the structural and organisational characteristics of workplaces, especially size, gender mix and trade union organisation.

Change and formalisation
Finally, it is worth bringing together a number of results from our survey which bear upon changes in the character of British industrial relations at workplace level and, in particular, highlight the growth of formal institutions and practices. As we made clear in the Introduction, we did not design the survey with the measurement of change as our principal aim. That would have resulted in a survey with a very different design, and major weaknesses for our descriptive and analytical purposes. Nevertheless, we have throughout the report attempted to compare our results with previous survey findings, despite some severe methodological difficulties. Nearly all of those comparisons have

shown a growth in the formality of workplace industrial relations, either in terms of the presence of institutions such as committees or the presence and use of formal procedures and processes. There are likely to be many reasons for such developments and the reasons are as difficult to identify from cross-sectional evidence as the changes themselves. Nevertheless, it would be surprising if the changes made in the legal and administrative frameworks of industrial relations had not had some effect, in addition to the policies and initiatives of employers, managers and trade unionists both at the workplace level and at higher levels of employing organisations and trade unions. A further likely source of change is the changing characteristics of workplaces. Again the lack of earlier information collected on a strictly comparable basis prevents us from drawing firm conclusions. But the size of workplaces and their controlling enterprises, the ownership of the workplaces, the composition of the workforce and, to a lesser extent, industrial sector have been so frequently associated in our analysis with the presence of formal industrial relations practices that it would be very surprising if, for example, changes in the size of workplaces had not brought about some of the growth in formality. These two themes – the changes in the legislative context and the changes in the mixture of different types of workplace as possible influences upon industrial relations practices – are illustrated in the following paragraphs. We return to them at the end of the chapter when briefly reviewing developments since the survey was conducted.

Perhaps the clearest illustrations from our evidence of the increasing formalisation in institutional terms were the growth of joint consultative committees and joint health and safety committees. Our evidence on the timing of the introduction of health and safety committees makes it very difficult to avoid the conclusion that the legislation made a major impact. The growth of formal consultative machinery, however, had no direct legislative encouragement and arose for reasons which were beyond the scope of our survey to explore.

The formalisation of procedures was most firmly established in the case of disciplinary procedures, where earlier comparable evidence was available. The impact of the various legislative initiatives of the 1970s was apparent in this development and it is possible that the effects may have spilled over into other types of procedure such as general grievance procedures and negotiating procedures. The increasing coverage of formal closed shop arrangements that include written agreements with specified exemptions and procedures for dealing with disputed cases, can also be seen as partially arising from the legislation of the mid-1970s. Formal arrangements for shop stewards to have time off work for trade union business were used with a frequency which suggested that the introduction of legal rights supporting such arrangements provided an impetus to formalisation.

Our present findings confirm that there is a strong association between formalisation and the specialisation of managerial roles[23] and so it is not surprising that we found a parallel growth in specialist personnel and industrial relations management. Indeed, it may be that the growth of specialist industrial relations management was associated with the formalisation encouraged by the legislation of the 1970s rather than being a direct consequence of that legislation. Moreover, our findings also confirm that both formalisation and specialisation are strongly related to size[24]. That association makes it likely that the growth of employment in larger establishments and larger enterprises would lead to greater formality in industrial relations practices and more specialised staff.

On the other hand, the trends towards larger establishments and larger enterprises have not continued into the early 1980s. Employment has fallen especially sharply in the largest establishments and manufacturing industry. In association with that pattern, total trade union membership has dropped for the first time since the 1930s. Economic conditions have generally become more difficult since the beginning of the decade and both these and other important changes in the environment where employers operate have already made an impact upon British industrial relations. Our picture of workplace industrial relations has been based on the results of a survey carried out in mid-1980. That time may prove to have been a turning point for British industrial relations. Whether the subsequent changes are short term ones or are part of a longer term trend it is as yet too early to say. Our present analysis of the relationships beween the characteristics of workplaces and industrial relations practices will provide an indication of the likely implications of present trends. Future surveys will provide evidence as to whether or not those indications are confirmed.

Notes

1. William Brown, Ed., *The Changing Contours of British Industrial Relations* (Basil Blackwell, Oxford, 1981).
2. W.E.J. McCarthy, *The Closed Shop in Britain* (Basil Blackwell, Oxford, 1964).
3. J. Gennard, S. Dunn and M. Wright, 'The extent of Closed Shop Arrangements in British Industry', Department of Employment *Gazette*, January, 1980.
4. Government Social Survey, *Workplace Industrial Relations* (HMSO, London, 1968).
5. William Brown, Ed., *op. cit.*
6. B. Weekes, M. Mellish, L. Dickens and J. Lloyd, *Industrial Relations and the Limits of Law* (Basil Blackwell, London, 1975); S. Dunn, 'The Growth of the Post-entry Closed Shop in Britain since the 1960s: Some Theoretical Considerations', *British Journal of Industrial Relations*, November 1981, pp. 275–96.
7. J. Gennard, S. Dunn and M. Wright, 'The Content of British Closed Shop Agreements', Department of Employment *Gazette*, November 1979.
8. It is not necessarily the case that there was a marked difference in Gennard's

findings compared with ours, as opposed to a difference in the presentation of those findings. For instance, Gennard carried out a two stage operation. He first estimated what proportion of the closed shop population was covered by formal agreements. He then took a sample of formal agreements and expressed the number that specified grounds for exemption as a *proportion of agreements*. Our 50 per cent of all establishments with closed shops which had agreements specifying grounds for exemption represented 68 per cent of establishments with written agreements, a proportion that was closer to Gennard's figure. Our judgement, however, would be that our 50 per cent more fairly represented the general availability of grounds exemption from closed shops than did Gennard's two stage operation with its changing base for percentages.

9. W.E.J. McCarthy and S.R. Parker, *Shop Stewards and Workshop Relations*, Research Paper No. 10, Royal Commission on Trade Unions and Employers' Associations (HMSO, London, 1968).

10. W. Brown, R. Ebsworth and M. Terry, 'Factors Shaping Shop Steward Organisation in Britain', *British Journal of Industrial Relations*, July 1978, pp. 139–59.

11. Notable examples are Shirley Lerner and John Bescoby, 'Shop Steward Combine Committees in the British Engineering Industry', *British Journal of Industrial Relations*, July 1966 and E.V. Batstone, I. Boraston and S. Frenkel, *Shop Stewards in Action* (Basil Blackwell, Oxford, 1977).

12. William Brown, Ed., *op. cit.*

13. W.R. Hawes and C.C.P. Brookes, 'Joint Consultation in British Industry', Department of Employment *Gazette*, April 1980, pp. 353–61; William Brown, Ed., *op. cit.*; Peter Cressey, John Eldridge, John MacInnes and Geoff Norris, 'Participation Prospects: Some Scottish evidence', Department of Employment *Gazette*, March 1981, pp. 117–24.

14. H.A. Clegg, *A New Approach to Industrial Democracy* (Basil Blackwell, Oxford, 1960).

15. H.A. Clegg, *The Changing System of Industrial Relations in Great Britain* (Basil Blackwell, Oxford, 1979).

16. W.E.J. McCarthy, *The Role of Shop Stewards in British Industrial Relations*, Research Paper No. 1, Royal Commission on Trade Unions and Employers' Associations (HMSO, London, 1966).

17. Government Social Survey, *Disciplinary and Dismissal Practices and Procedures* (1969, unpublished).

18. See William Brown, Ed., *op. cit.* and W.W. Daniel, *Wage Determination in Industry* (Political and Economic Planning No. 563, London, 1976).

19. P.K. Edwards, 'The Strike-proneness of British Manufacturing Establishments', *British Journal of Industrial Relations*, July 1981, pp. 135–148.

20. W.W. Daniel, 1976, *op. cit.*

21. Michael White, *Payment Systems in Britain* (Gower, in association with the Policy Studies Institute, 1981).

22. Certain stages of incomes policies have included exceptions for increased productivity which have encouraged the introduction of PBR, as we showed in Chapter VIII. As the forms of PBR encouraged by incomes policy have, however, most frequently been of a collective nature, they are not necessarily the forms most frequently associated with industrial action. Our information in this study was not sufficiently detailed to explore that possibility.

23. D.S. Pugh and C.R. Hinings, *Organisational Structure: Extensions and Replications* (Saxon House, Farnborough, 1976).

24. D.S. Pugh and C.R. Hinings, *op. cit.*

Appendix A Questions and definitions

This appendix contains details of the questions used in the survey interviews which have been referred to in the main text and, in a later section, of how the responses to some of those questions have been used to define variables shown in the tables. The prefix Q indicates a question number on the main management interview schedule; the prefix WQ refers to questions on the two primary worker representative questionnaires. Questions put to secondary respondents were a selection of those put to primary respondents and have not been separately indicated. The absence of a worker representative question reference number in brackets below a management question number does not necessarily mean that no equivalent question was asked, only that the results have not been used in preparation of the text[1].

The report discusses the results of the overwhelming majority of questions asked in the survey interviews. The only substantial section of the questionnaires not covered in the report has been subjected to separate analysis[2].

Questions referred to in the text
Chapter II

Page	Question	
20, 46	Q23	(a) How many unions are there that have members among the MANUAL employees of this establishment?
		(c) How many full-time MANUAL employees are members of these unions?
20	Q24	(a) Are any of these unions RECOGNISED by management for negotiating pay and conditions for any sector or sections of the manual workforce in this establishment?
		INTERVIEWER: IF AGREEMENTS ARE NEGOTIATED AT A HIGHER LEVEL BUT UNIONS ARE RECOGNISED BY MANAGEMENT TO DISCUSS THE APPLICATION OF AGREEMENTS AT THIS ESTABLISHMENT, COUNT THE UNIONS AS RECOGNISED HERE. IF 'YES' ASK
		(b) Which ones? RECORD ANSWERS IN GRID BELOW. PROBE 'Any others?' UNTIL 'No', THEN CHECK THROUGH LIST WITH RESPONDENT.
46	Q25	IF ONE UNION ONLY RECOGNISED AT Q24b ENTER IN GRID BELOW AND CONTINUE. IF NO UNIONS RECOGNISED AT Q24a SKIP TO Q46. OTHERWISE CONTINUE WITH Q25.
		(c) Which is the largest of these (negotiating) groups? Which the second largest?
33	Q28	(a) Are there, at this establishment, any stewards or representatives from the manual unions acting as SENIOR STEWARDS, OR CONVENORS?
		NOTE: IF THERE IS ONLY ONE STEWARD OR REPRESENTATIVE HE SHOULD BE CONSIDERED AS SENIOR.

Page	Question	
		(b) Are they acknowledged by management as such?
		IF YES TO (a) OR (b) ASK (c)
		(c) How many such representatives are there?
37	Q29	(b) How many such representatives (i.e. senior stewards or convenors who in practice spend all or nearly all of their working time on trade union affairs concerning this establishment) are there?
37	Q30 (WQ32)	(a) Have ANY manual stewards in this establishment whether senior or not received courses of training or instruction for their jobs as stewards during the last year?
		IF YES ASK (b)–(d).
		(b) How many stewards have had such training? WRITE IN NO.
		(c) Were any of the courses . . . READ OUT ALTERNATIVES: Held at the initiative of the management; Or of the unions; Decided, in terms of *content*, by the management
		(d) How far, in your opinion, does such training help stewards in their jobs as worker representatives? READ OUT: A great deal; A fair extent; Not very much; Not at all.
29	Q38	REFER TO Q25. ASK Q38–Q42 IN RESPECT OF THE LARGEST NEGOTIATING GROUP OF MANUAL UNIONS.
		Now I would like to ask you about one of the negotiating groups of manual workers at this establishment. WRITE IN AND STATE NAME OF THIS NEGOTIATING GROUP.
		(a) Are there any written agreements in which this negotiating group is recognised for negotiating pay and conditions? IF YES, 'How many?'
		IF 'No' SKIP TO Q39.
		ASK (b)–(c) ABOUT THE MOST IMPORTANT (I.E. COVERING THE LARGEST NUMBER OF EMPLOYEES) AGREEMENT IF MORE THAN ONE.
30		(b) When was this agreement originally signed?
		IF IN LAST FIVE YEARS ASK
		(c) How was recognition brought about? PROBE FULLY.
33	Q43	REFER TO Q25c. ASK Q43–44 IN RESPECT OF THE SECOND LARGEST NEGOTIATING GROUP OF MANUAL UNIONS, IF APPROPRIATE (SEE INSTRUCTIONS).
		Now I would like to ask you some questions about another negotiating group of manual workers.
		WRITE IN AND STATE NAME OF NEGOTIATING GROUP.
		(a) Are there any written agreements in which this negotiating group is recognised for negotiating pay and conditions? IF 'Yes', 'How many?'
48	Q45 (WQ17)	REFER TO Q24 and Q25.
		IF ONLY ONE UNION RECOGNISED, SKIP TO INSTRUCTIONS AFTER Q50. IF MORE THAN ONE UNION RECOGNISED, ASK Q45a. IF MORE THAN ONE *NEGOTIATING GROUP* ASK Q45c.
		(a) Representatives of all the recognised manual unions negotiate jointly with management about pay and conditions of workers here. Do you prefer joint negotiations or would you prefer different sections of the manual workforce to negotiate separately?
49		(b) Why do you say that? PROBE FULLY FOR DETAILS.
		(c) Some of the representatives of the recognised manual unions negotiate separately with management about pay and conditions of workers here. Do you prefer separate negotiations or would you prefer *all* sections of the manual workforce to negotiate jointly?
		(d) Why do you say that? PROBE FULLY FOR DETAILS.
20	Q52	(c) Which of the Unions/staff associations has the largest non-manual membership? RECORD ANSWER IN GRID BELOW.
20	Q53	(a) Are ANY of these unions or staff associations RECOGNISED by

management for negotiating pay and conditions for any section or sections of the non-manual workforce in this establishment?

INTERVIEWER: IF AGREEMENTS ARE NEGOTIATED AT A HIGHER LEVEL BUT UNIONS ARE RECOGNISED BY MANAGEMENT TO DISCUSS THE APPLICATION OF THE AGREEMENTS AT THIS ESTABLISHMENT, COUNT THE UNIONS AS RECOGNISED HERE. IF 'Yes' ASK

(b) Which ones? RECORD ANSWERS IN GRID BELOW. PROBE 'Any others?' UNTIL 'No', THEN CHECK THROUGH LIST WITH RESPONDENT.

38   WQ20   (a) There are provisions in the Employment Protection Act by which time off can be claimed for union duties and activities. Have you used these provisions to obtain time off for stewards or members of your group or union? IF YES ASK
(b) How has the time been used? READ OUT ALTERNATIVES: Training for stewards; Stewards' duties concerning this establishment; Activities of union members (SPECIFY); Others (SPECIFY).

37   WQ32   (c) Were any of the courses . . . READ OUT ALTERNATIVES: (i) held in working hours? or outside working hours? (ii) held in this establishment? held by TUC or union training college? or at a jointly agreed educational establishment? or elsewhere (please specify).

Chapter III

Page	Question	
60	Q31 (WQ34)	(a) DO the manual workers at this establishment normally have to be members of a union in order to have or to keep their jobs? IF YES ASK 'All or some?' IF 'NO' AT Q31a, SKIP TO Q37b.

IF 'YES, ALL', AT Q31a, ASK (b).

IF 'YES, SOME' AT Q31a, SKIP TO Q32.

(b) Do recruits for any of the jobs covered by this closed shop arrangement have to be union members BEFORE starting work?

IF YES, ASK 'For ALL of the jobs covered by the closed shop arrangement or just for SOME?'

IF 'NO' AT Q31b, SKIP TO Q31j.

IF 'YES, ALL' AT Q31b, SKIP TO Q33

IF 'YES, SOME' AT Q31b, CONTINUE WITH (c)–(h).

(c) For these jobs where union membership is required BEFORE starting work, how many workers are involved?

(d) Which groups of manual workers does this arrangement cover? READ OUT LIST. Skilled manual workers; Semi-skilled manual workers; Unskilled manual workers.

FOR EACH 'YES' ASK

(e) All of the ———— workers, or just some?

(f) For these jobs where union membership is not required until STARTING WORK OR AFTERWARDS, how many workers are involved?

(g) Which occupation or groups of manual workers does this arrangement cover? READ OUT LIST. FOR EACH 'YES' ASK

(h) All of the ———— workers or just some?

ASK IF 'NO' AT Q31b.

(j) How long after starting work are the new recruits allowed before they have to join a union?

60   Q32 (WQ35)   (a) Do recruits for any of the jobs covered by this closed shop arrangement have to be union members BEFORE starting work? IF YES ASK 'For ALL of the jobs covered by the closed shop arrangement or just for some? IF 'NO' ASK Q32(e)–(h).

Page	Question	
		IF 'YES, ALL' ASK Q32(b)–(d).

IF 'YES, SOME' ASK Q32(b)–(h).

(b) For those jobs where union membership is required BEFORE starting work, how many workers are involved?

(c) Which occupations or groups of workers does this arrangement cover? READ OUT LIST. Skilled manual workers; semi-skilled manual workers; Unskilled manual workers.

FOR EACH 'YES' ASK

(d) All of the ———— workers, or just some?

IF 'ALL' AT Q32a SKIP TO Q33.

IF SOME AT Q32a CONTINUE WITH (e)–(h).

(e) For those jobs where union membership is not required until STARTING WORK OR AFTERWARDS how many workers are involved?

(f) Which occupations or groups of workers does this arrangement cover? READ OUT LIST. FOR EACH 'YES' ASK (g).

(g) All of the ———— workers or just some?

(h) How long after starting work are the new recruits allowed before they have to join a union?

77 Q33 (a) Is there a single closed shop arrangement at this establishment or are there different arrangements for different groups of manual workers?

IF DIFFERENT ASK

(b) Is the most recent closed shop arrangement the one that covers the largest group of manual workers?

IF 'NO' ASK

(c) Which group of manual workers has most recently established a closed shop arrangement?

62 Q34 IF THERE IS MORE THAN ONE CLOSED SHOP ARRANGEMENT AT Q33 ASK Q34–36 ABOUT THE ARRANGEMENT COVERING THE LARGEST GROUP OF WORKERS.

(a) Is this (closed shop) practice supported by an arrangement or agreement with management? IF YES ASK 'A written or an oral agreement?'

IF 'YES' ASK

(b) How long has this arrangement or agreement been in operation (regardless of when it was formally agreed)?

62 Q35 (a) Are there agreed exemptions from this closed shop practice? IF YES ASK

(b) What are they? Key/specialist post held; Long service; Religious belief; Conscience; Reasonable grounds; Part time/temporary; Apprenticeship; Not member of union when agreement made; Already member of union not party to the agreement; Other (SPECIFY). PROBE FULLY UNTIL 'Nothing else'.

77 Q36 (a) Is there an agreed procedure for considering cases in which the requirement to be a union member is in dispute?

IF 'YES' ASK

(b) Is this the normal grievance procedure or a specific procedure relating to closed shop disputes?

63 Q37 (a) Have the closed shop arrangements given rise to any issues here in the past 3
(WQ41 years? IF YES, 'What issues?' PROBE FULLY UNTIL 'Nothing else'.
WQ42a) (b) Do you have here a system for deducting manual employees' trade union dues from their pay?

60 Q62 Do ALL the non-manual workers at this establishment normally have to be
WQ34 members of a union or associaton in order to have or keep their jobs?

IF 'NO' ASK 'Do ANY of the non-manual . . .'

IF 'NO' AT Q62a, SKIP TO Q68b.

IF 'YES, ALL' AT Q62a, ASK (b).

IF 'YES, SOME' AT Q62a, SKIP TO Q63.

(b) Do recruits for any of the jobs covered by this closed shop arrangement have to be union/association members BEFORE starting work?

Page	Question	
		IF 'YES' ASK 'For ALL of the jobs covered by the closed shop arrangement or just for SOME?'

IF 'YES' ASK 'For ALL of the jobs covered by the closed shop arrangement or just for SOME?'
IF 'NO' AT Q62b, SKIP TO Q62j.
IF 'YES, ALL' AT Q62b, SKIP TO Q64.
IF 'YES, SOME' AT Q62b, CONTINUE WITH (c)- h).
(c) For these jobs where union/association membership is required BEFORE starting work, how many workers are involved?

60 Q63   (a) Do recruits for any of the jobs covered by this closed shop arrangement have
    (WQ35) to be union/association members BEFORE starting work? IF YES ASK 'For ALL of the jobs covered by the closed shop arrangement or just for some? IF 'NO' ASK Q63(e)–(h).
IF 'Yes, ALL' ASK Q63(b)–(d).
IF 'YES, SOME' ASK Q63(b)–(h).
(b) For those jobs where union/association membership is required BEFORE starting work, how many workers are involved?
(c) Which occupations or groups of workers does this arrangement cover? READ OUT LIST AND RECORD ANSWERS IN GRID BELOW: Clerical/ Admin/Secretaries; Foremen/Supervisors; Junior technical/Professional. FOR EACH 'YES' ASK
(d) All of the ———— workers, most or just some?
IF 'ALL' AT Q63a SKIP TO Q64.
IF 'SOME' AT Q63a, CONTINUE WITH (e)–(h).
(e) for those jobs where union/association membership is not required until STARTING WORK OR AFTERWARDS, how many workers are involved?
(h) How long after starting work are the new recruits allowed before they have to join a union/association?

77 Q64   (a) Is there a single closed shop arrangement at this establishment or are there different arrangements for different groups of non-manual workers?
IF SINGLE SKIP TO Q65.
IF DIFFERENT ASK
(b) Is the most recent closed shop arrangement the one that covers the largest group of non-manual workers?

77 Q65   IF THERE IS MORE THAN ONE CLOSED SHOP ARRANGEMENT AT Q64 ASK Q65 ABOUT THE ARRANGEMENT COVERING THE LARGEST GROUP OF WORKERS.
(a) Is this closed shop practice supported by an arrangement or agreement with management? IF YES ASK 'A written or an oral agreement?'
IF YES ASK
(b) How long has this arrangement or agreement been in operation (regardless of when it was formally agreed)?

77 Q66   (a) Are there agreed exemptions from this closed shop practice?
IF YES ASK
(b) WHAT ARE THEY? (READ OUT) Key specialist post held; Long service; Religious belief: Conscience; Reasonable grounds; Part time/temporary; Apprenticeship; Not member of union when agreement made; Already member of union not party to the agreement; Other (SPECIFY). PROBE FULLY UNTIL 'Nothing else'.

77 Q67   (a) Is there an agreed procedure for considering cases in which the requirement to be a union/association member is in dispute?
IF YES ASK
(b) Is this the normal grievance procedure a specific procedure relating to closed shop disputes?

74 Q68   (a) Have the closed shop arrangements given rise to any issues here in the past 3
    (WQ41   years? IF YES, 'What issues?' PROBE FULLY UNTIL 'Nothing else'.
    WQ42a) (b) Do you have here a system for deducting non-manual employees' union or association dues or subscriptions from their pay?

Chapter IV

Page Question

86   WQ1   First of all, I would like to ask you about the SENIOR STEWARDS OR CONVENORS in *your union* at this establishment.
INTERVIEWER: IF ONE STEWARD ONLY FROM UNION, TREAT AS A *SENIOR* STEWARD. ASK WQ1, WQ2, THEN WQ5.
(a) Who elects the SENIOR STEWARDS OR CONVENORS in your union? READ OUT ALTERNATIVES: Your own union members; All unions (including other unions); Your own union stewards; All stewards (including stewards from other unions); Other answer.
(b) How are they elected? READ OUT ALTERNATIVES: Show of hands; Postal ballot; Non-postal ballot; Other method (SPECIFY).
(c) Do senior stewards or convenors IN PRACTICE have to stand for re-election?
IF 'YES' ASK
(d) How often?
(e) In the last year have there been elections for senior stewards in your union?
IF 'YES' ASK
(f) Did TWO OR MORE candidates stand for the same post on any occasion in the last year? READ OUT ALTERNATIVES: On all occasions; On most occasions; On some occasions; Very few occasions; Never.
(g) Do senior stewards or convenors TECHNICALLY have to stand for re-election?

86   WQ3   Can we now talk about stewards in your UNION at this establishment OTHER THAN SENIOR STEWARDS?
(a) How are stewards *OTHER THAN SENIOR* elected in your Union? READ OUT ALTERNATIVES: Show of hands; Postal ballot; Non-postal ballot; Other method (SPECIFY).
(b) IN PRACTICE, do stewards in your union have to stand for re-election? IF 'YES' ASK (c)–(e), IF 'NO' SKIP TO (d).
(c) How often?
(d) In the last year have there been elections for stewards in your union?
IF 'YES' ASK
(e) Did TWO OR MORE candidates stand for the same post on any occasion in the last year?
(f) Do stewards in your union TECHNICALLY have to stand for re-election?

91   WQ5   Thinking now of ALL stewards, whether senior or not:
(a) In the last year have any stewards here in your union (including yourself) held any *other* positions in the union?
IF 'YES' ASK
(b) Which? PROBE 'Any others?' UNTIL 'No'.

82   WQ6   Can we now talk about the relationship between the members of your union in this establishment and the branch to which they belong.
(a) What does the branch consist of? Please choose the most appropriate description from this card (SHOW CARD Z): Members of this establishment only: Members of this establishment and other establishments – same employer; Members of this establishment and other establishments – other employer; Members of this establishment, other establishments of same employer, and other establishments of a different employer.
(d How many members in total are there in the branch?
(e) During the last year, how many members attended branch meetings, generally?
(f) During the last year how many times did your branch meet?
(g) Do you personally attend branch meetings? IF 'YES' How often have you attended in the past year?

Page	Question	
92	WQ18	Still thinking about the negotiating group you represent . . .

(a) During the last year, did you meet with a FULL-TIME OFFICIAL of your union to discuss matters affecting the workers you represent? IF 'YES' ASK 'How often?'

(b) During the last year, did you and the local full-time official of your union meet with management to discuss matters affecting the workers you represent? IF YES ASK 'How often?'

| 92 | WQ19 | (a) During the last year, have you contacted your NATIONAL OFFICIAL or your union head office about matters affecting the workers you represent? |
| 97 | WQ27 | REFER TO WQ7b. IF MORE THAN ONE UNION IS LISTED ASK WQ27 AND WQ28. IF ONLY ONE UNION, SKIP TO WQ29. |

Can we talk about stewards meetings where there are no other participants present?

(a) Do you have a committee of manual stewards which includes some representatives from your own union and some from other manual unions? IF NO SKIP TO WQ28. IF YES ASK (b)–(e)

(b) How frequently does this committee meet?

(c) Are these meetings held in working hours? IF YES ASK 'Always or only sometimes?'

(d) Does this committee have (READ OUT): A written constitution; Standing orders; A Minute Book

(e) Which unions are represented on the present committee? PROBE 'Any others?' UNTIL 'No'.

| 100 | WQ28 | (a) Apart from this committee, do you have meetings of stewards from your union and stewards from other unions in this establishment? IF NO SKIP TO WQ29. IF YES CONTINUE WITH (b) and (d). |

(b) How frequently do meetings of this sort occur?

(c) Are these meetings held in working hours? IF YES ASK 'Always or only sometimes?'

(d) Are minutes taken at these meetings? IF YES ASK 'How frequently'? READ OUT ALTERNATIVES: Very frequently; Quite frequently; Not at all frequently; No, not at all.

| 96 | WQ29 | ASK ALL |

(a) Are there meetings of stewards from your own union only, apart from branch meetings? IF YES ASK (b) and (d). IF NO SKIP TO INSTRUCTIONS BEFORE WQ30.

(b) How frequently are these meetings held?

(c) Are these meetings held in working hours? IF YES ASK 'Always or only sometimes?'

(d) Are minutes taken at these meetings? IF YES ASK 'How frequently'? READ OUT ALTERNATIVES: Very frequently; Quite frequently; Not at all frequently; No, not at all.

| 100 | WQ30 | ASK WQ30 ONLY IF ESTABLISHMENT IS PART OF A MULTI-ESTABLISHMENT ORGANISATION (Q3 MANAGEMENT QUESTIONNAIRE) OTHERWISE GO TO WQ31. |

(a) Do you have meetings between the manual stewards here and the manual stewards in other establishments of this organisation (excluding branch meetings)? IF NO SKIP TO Q31. IF YES CONTINUE With (b)–(h).

(b) How often are these meetings held?

(c) Do you go to these meetings?

(d) For how long have these meetings been taking place?

(e) Why was it decided to start these meetings? PROBE FOR DETAILS.

Page Question (f) Have you found any difficulties in organising these meetings? PROBE FOR DETAILS.

(g) Has management (at this establishment) given any financial help towards setting up and running these meetings?

IF YES ASK

(h) What form did this help take? PROBE 'Anything else?'

103   WQ31   *ASK ALL*

(a) Are there meetings between stewards of manual unions in this establishment and those in other organisations (i.e. working for other *employers*)?

IF YES CONTINUE WITH (b)–(h).

IF NO SKIP TO WQ32.

(b) How often are these meetings held?

(c) Do you go to these meetings?

(d) For how long have these meetings been taking place?

(e) Why was it decided to start these meetings? PROBE FOR DETAILS.

(f) Have you found any difficulties in organising these meetings? PROBE FOR DETAILS.

(g) Has management (at this establishment) given any financial help towards setting up and running these meetings?

IF YES ASK

(h) What form did this help take? PROBE 'Anything else?'

Chapter V

Page Question
107   Q11   (a) Please could you tell me what the title of your job here is?
109   Q13   (a) Please look at this card. SHOW CARD B. I am going to read out a list of different work responsibilities and activities. Can you tell me, for each, whether it forms a part of your job? READ OUT (i) Determining or negotiating terms of employment; (ii) Setting up industrial relations procedures; (iii) Recruitment and selection of employees; (iv) Training of employees; (v) Overall responsibility for systems of payment; (vi) Job evaluation schemes or job grading; (vii) Dealing with disciplinary cases.

IF YES TO ANY AT (a) ask;

(b) Do you spend a major part of your time on these and other personnel or industrial relations matter?

112   Q16   (a) Do you have formal qualifications in personnel management or a closely related subject? IF YES ASK (b)

(b) What qualifications?

(c) Do you have two years or more experience in personnel or industrial relations management? IF YES ASK

(d) Was most of this experience gained – In this establishment? In another establishment of the same organisation? With another employer?

(e) Have you had within the last two years, formal training of one day or more on personnel matters or industrial relations? IF YES, ASK

(f) What sort of course was it? Please choose a phrase from this card: Course run by own organisation; Educational establishment; Commercial training or consultancy organisation; Professional organisation; Other.

Q16(a) was repeated for the respondent's most recent recruit in personnel or industrial relations.

123   Q18   I would now like to ask you about the top governing body (in the UK) of the organisation.

(a) What is that body?

(b) Is there someone on that body who has responsibility for industrial relations? for personnel matters? IF YES TO BOTH ASK

Page	Question	
		(c) Is that the same person or different people?
123	Q19	Is that/either of these the MAIN JOB?
118	Q20	(a) Thinking now of industrial or employee relations, have any matters during the last 12 months caused management here to seek advice from a person or organisation outside this establishment? IF YES, ASK (b) and (c).
		(b) From any person in an organisation on this card: ACAS? Management consultant? CBI? Other employers' organisation/association? Full-time officer of a trade union? Solicitor? Barrister? Accountant? Other (SPECIFY). IF MORE THAN ONE CODED ASK
		(c) From whom have you sought advice most often?
120	Q21	(a) Is this establishment – AND, IF PART OF A MULTI-ESTABLISH-MENT ORGANISATION, either directly or indirectly or through the parent organisation – a member of an Employers' Association that negotiates on behalf of its members with unions or staff associations to regulate pay or terms of employment?

Chapter VI

Page	Question	
140	Q41	I am going to read out a number of other issues besides pay that affect this negotiating group.
		READ OUT: (i) Holiday entitlement; (ii) Length of working week; (iii) Pensions; (iv) Physical working conditions; (v) Recruitment, i.e. the total number of employees taken on; (vi) Redeployment within this establishment; (vii) Redundancy; (viii) Manning levels; (ix) Major changes in production methods; (x) Capital investment.
		Please choose a phrase from this card (SHOW CARD F) to indicate how these issues are dealt with here: 'Negotiated at establishment'; 'Negotiated not at establishment'; 'Not negotiated'; 'Other answer' (SPECIFY).
147	Q46	(a) Are there manual union representatives who meet management to discuss matters affecting the workforce or sections of it? IF 'YES', How many? IF NO, ASK
		(b) Are there manual union representatives who meet management to discuss matters relating to individual manual workers? IF YES, How many?
141	Q47	(a) Is there a committee of manual worker representatives which discusses with management matters affecting the workers – whether in respect of individuals, sections of the workforce, or the whole workforce?
		IF YES ASK
		(b) What is the name of this committee?
		(c) When did this committee first meet?
		(d) How frequently does senior management attend meetings of this committee?
		(e) What is the name and job title of the senior representative of the non-manual workers of this committee?
147	Q48	(a) Apart from committees, are there any individual non-union manual worker representatives who discuss with management matters affecting the workforce – whether in respect of individuals, sections of the workforce, or the whole workforce? IF YES, ASK
		(b) How many such representatives are there?
140	Q72	I am going to read out a number of other issues besides pay that affect this negotiating group.
		READ OUT: (i) Holiday entitlement; (ii) Length of working week; (iii) Pensions; (iv) Physical working conditions; (v) Recruitment, i.e. the total number of employees taken on; (vi) Redeployment within this establishment; (vii) Redundancy; (viii) Manning levels; (ix) Major changes in production methods; (x) Capital investment.
		Please choose a phrase from this card (SHOW CARD F) to indicate how these

Page	Question	

Page Question issues are dealt with here: 'Negotiated at establishment'; 'Negotiated not at establishment'; 'Not negotiated'; 'Other answer' (SPECIFY).

147 Q77 (a) Are there non-manual union/association representatives who meet manage-
(WQ43) ment to discuss matters affecting the workforce or sections of it? IF YES, How many? IF NO, ASK
(b) Are there non-manual union/association representatives who meet management to discuss matters relating to individual non-manual workers? IF YES, How many?

141 Q78 (a) Is there a committee of non-manual worker representatives which discusses with management matters affecting the workers – whether in respect of individuals, sections of the workforce, or the whole workforce?
IF YES ASK
(b) What is the name of this committee?
(c) When did this committee first meet?
(d) How frequently does senior management attend meetings of this committee?
(e) What is the name and job title of the senior representative of the non-manual workers of this committee?

147 Q79 (a) Apart from committees, are there any individual non-union non-manual
(WQ45) worker representatives who discuss with management matters affecting the workforce – whether in respect of individuals, sections of the workforce, or the whole workforce? IF YES, ASK
(b) How many such representatives are there?

146 Q118 (a) Are any employees here covered by a job evaluation scheme?
IF YES ASK
(b) How many schemes are there at this establishment?
IF ONE ONLY COMPLETE (c)–(k) ABOUT THIS SCHEME. IF MORE THAN ONE, IDENTIFY THE MOST RECENTLY SET UP SCHEME AND ASK (c)–(k) ABOUT THIS SCHEME.
(c) When was the scheme introduced?
(d) how many employees are currently filling jobs covered by the scheme?
OBTAIN FIGURES FOR MEN AND WOMEN SEPARATELY
(e) What job (or occupation) was ranked HIGHEST in the scheme?
(f) What job (or occupation) was ranked LOWEST in the scheme?
(g) Is there a committee which reviews the scheme and decides upon the grading of new or changed jobs?
IF YES ASK (h), OTHERWISE SKIP TO (j).
(h) Are there employee representatives on the committee?
IF YES ASK
(i) Are these representatives chosen through trade unions or staff associations?
(j) On what basis does the scheme operate?
IF ESTABLISHMENT IS PART OF MULTI-ESTABLISHMENT ORGANISATION (Q3) ASK
(k) Are employees of your organisation in any other establishment besides this one covered by the same job evaluation scheme?

129 Q120 INTERVIEWER: EXCLUDE FROM THIS QUESTION COMMITTEES
(WQ55) THAT DEAL WITH ONE SPECIFIC ISSUE, E.G. CANTEEN, RECREATION, SOCIAL, WELFARE.
Now I should like to ask you about the arrangements within this establishment for CONSULTATION between managers and employees.
(a) Apart from Health and Safety Committees, do you have any joint committees of managers and employees primarily concerned with CONSULTATION rather than negotiation?
IF YES SKIP TO (e).
IF NO ASK (b)–(d), THEN SKIP TO Q124.
(b) Have you ever had such a committee in this establishment?
(c) When did it last meet?

Page Question (d) Why does it no longer meet?
IF YES TO Q120(a) ask
(e) How many such committees are there?
(f) What are their names? RECORD ANSWER BELOW FOR THE TWO
MAJOR COMMITTEES IF MORE THAN TWO.
FOR EACH:
(g) Is the worker representation manual only, non-manual only or both?

Page	Question	
132	Q121 (WQ56)	ASK Q121 FOR EACH COMMITTEE NAMED AT Q120(c). (a) How often do(es) the committee(s) meet? (b) What proportion of these meetings are attended by *senior* management? (c) When were these committee(s) introduced? ASK IF ANY UNION MEMBERS (MANUAL OR NON-MANUAL). (d) Are any of the employee representatives chosen by trade unions or staff associations? IF YES: 'All of the employee representatives or just some?'
135	Q122 (WQ58)	Is the discussion at this committee communicated to others in management? IF YES ASK 'How?'
139	Q123 (WQ59)	What would you say was the most important matter discussed by this committee in the last 12 months? PROBE FOR DETAILS.
148	Q124 (WQ60a)	In practice, how much information about the establishment would you say management here gives the worker representatives including shop stewards and representatives of staff associations? READ OUT LIST BELOW. About . . . (i) Pay and conditions of service; (ii) Manpower requirements; (iii) Financial position of this establishment.
148	WQ60b	How useful would you say the manual unions have found this information in discussions or negotiations?
142	Q125	Have you had any requests from union representatives for information under the provision of the EMPLOYMENT PROTECTION ACT on disclosure of information?
148	WQ61	Have you requested information from management under the provision of the EMPLOYMENT PROTECTION ACT on disclosure of information?
142	Q126	(a) How are Health and Safety matters dealt with in this establishment? Please choose a phrase from this card. SHOW CARD M. Joint committee specifically Health and Safety; Joint committee Health and Safety and other matters; Workforce representatives; Management alone (i.e. no Health and Safety consultation); Other (SPECIFY). IF JOINT COMMITTEE SPECIFICALLY FOR HEALTH AND SAFETY ASK (b) How long has this committee been established?
154	Q143 (WQ71)	(a) Has the management made any major change in the last 3 years with the aim of increasing employees' involvement in the operation of the establishment? IF YES ASK (b) Please describe the changes.
152	Q146 (WQ74)	Finally may I ask you your opinion of the general state of relations between management and workers at this establishment? PROBE FULLY.

Chapter VII

Page	Question	
159	Q83	Now I would like to ask you about any FORMAL industrial relations procedures you may have here, either for manual or non-manual employees. Are there here formal procedures for dealing with . . . READ OUT: (a) DISPUTES OVER PAY AND CONDITIONS of any group of employees; (b) DISCIPLINE AND DISMISSALS OTHER THAN REDUNDANCY; (c) INDIVIDUAL GRIEVANCES.
168	Q84	In the past year has a body or person outside this establishment been brought in to help settle a dispute about —————?

Page Question IF NO SKIP (b)–(e). AFTER COMPLETING BOTH COLUMNS, GO TO
Q105.
(b) On how many occasions?
IF MORE THAN ONCE ASK (c)–(e) ABOUT LAST OCCASION.
(c) What body or person? PROBE: Any others?
(d) Did this outside intervention help to settle the dispute?
IF YES ASK: Greatly or somewhat?
IF ACAS AT (c) ASK
(e): What form of help did ACAS provide? Mediation/conciliation; Arbitration;
Other (SPECIFY).

172   Q85   I would now like to ask you about the formal procedures for dealing with
disputes over pay and conditions. Are these procedures substantially the same
for all the workers concerned or are they different for different groups?

172   Q86   Ask Q86–Q92 ABOUT THE FORMAL PROCEDURE. IF MORE THAN
ONE SET OF FORMAL PROCEDURES INDICATED IN Q85 ASK
ABOUT THE PROCEDURE THAT APPLIES FOR THE LARGEST
OCCUPATIONAL GROUP, HAVING DESCRIBED THAT GROUP
BELOW.
(a) Is the procedure set out in a written document or only agreed orally?
IF WRITTEN DOCUMENT ASK
(b) How long has the procedure been set out in a written document?

173   Q87   Does this procedure apply to . . . READ OUT ALTERNATIVES:
The whole of your industry; Several different employers within the industry;
Elsewhere in your organisation; This establishment only; Other answer
(SPECIFY).

174   Q88   (a) Still thinking of the procedure for settling disputes over pay and conditions,
is this group of workers represented by unions or staff associations?
IF YES ASK (b)–(d)
(b) Was the procedure agreed between management and union/staff associations?
IF YES ASK (c) and (d).
(c) Is this procedure the subject of a written document signed by both parties?
(d) Was the agreement made here or at a higher level in the organisation?

174   Q89   (a) In the event of a failure to agree at the establishment, is there a provision
within the procedure for a body or person outside the establishment to be
brought in to arbitrate or conciliate?
IF YES ASK
(b) Which outside bodies are involved in the final stage of the procedure?
PROBE: Any others?
IF ACAS ASK (c) THEN Q90. IF NOT ACAS SKIP TO Q90.
(c) According to the formal procedure does this involve conciliation, arbitration
or both?

174   Q90   (a) In the past year has a body or person outside this establishment been brought
in to help settle a dispute at this establishment about pay and conditions?
IF NO SKIP (b)–(e) AND GO TO Q91.
(b) On how many occasions?
IF MORE THAN ONCE ASK (c)–(e) ABOUT LAST OCCASION.
(c) What body or person? PROBE: Any others?
(d) Did this outside intervention help to settle the dispute? IF YES ASK,
Greatly or somewhat?
IF ACAS AT (c) ASK
(e) What form of help did ACAS provide? Mediation/conciliation; Arbitration;
Other (SPECIFY).

175   Q91   In practice, are most disputes over pay and conditions dealt with under the
procedure we have been discussing?

175   Q92   (a) In general, how satisfied are you with the working of the procedure for

Page	Question	
		dealing with disputes over pay and conditions? READ OUT: Very satisfied; Quite satisfied; Not very satisfied; Not at all satisfied. IF NOT VERY OR NOT AT ALL SATISFIED, ASK (b) Why is that? PROBE FULLY.
162	Q93	I would now like to ask you about the formal procedures for dealing with DISCIPLINE AND DISMISSALS. Are these procedures substantially the same for all the workers concerned or are they different for different groups?
163	Q94	ASK Q94–Q104 ABOUT THE FORMAL PROCEDURE. IF MORE THAN ONE SET OF FORMAL PROCEDURES INDICATED IN Q93 ASK ABOUT THE PROCEDURE THAT APPLIES FOR THE LARGEST OCCUPATIONAL GROUP, HAVING DESCRIBED THAT GROUP BELOW. (a) Is the procedure set out in a written document or only agreed orally? IF WRITTEN DOCUMENT ASK (b) How long has the procedure been set out in a written document?
165	Q95	Does this procedure apply to . . . READ OUT ALTERNATIVES: The whole of your industry; Several different employers within the industry; Elsewhere in your organisation; This establishment only; Other answer (SPECIFY).
167	Q96	(a) Still thinking of the procedure for settling disputes over discipline and dismissals, is this group of workers represented by unions or staff associations? IF YES ASK (b)–(d) (b) Was the procedure agreed between management and union/staff associations? IF YES ASK (c) and (d). (c) Is this procedure the subject of a written document signed by both parties? (d) Was the agreement made here or at a higher level in the organisation?
167	Q97	(a) In the event of a failure to agree at the establishment, is there a provision within the procedure for a body or person outside the establishment to be brought in to arbitrate or conciliate? IF YES ASK (b) Which outside bodies are involved in the final stage of the procedure? PROBE: Any others? IF ACAS ASK (c) THEN Q98. IF NOT ACAS SKIP TO Q98. (c) According to the formal procedure does this involve conciliation, arbitration or both?
168	Q98	(a) In the past year has a body or person outside this establishment been brought in to help settle a dispute at this establishment about discipline and dismissals? IF NO SKIP (b)–(e) AND GO TO Q99. (b) On how many occasions? IF MORE THAN ONCE ASK (c)–(e) ABOUT LAST OCCASION. (c) What body or person? PROBE: Any others? (d) Did this outside intervention help to settle the dispute? IF YES, ASK, Greatly or somewhat? IF ACAS AT (c), ASK (e) What form of help did ACAS provide?
170	Q102	In practice, are most matters in respect of disputes dealt with under the procedure we have been discussing?
170	Q103 (WQ52)	(a) In general, how satisfied are you with the working of the procedure for dealing with disputes over discipline and dismissals? READ OUT: Very satisfied; Quite satisfied; Not very satisfied; Not at all satisfied. IF NOT VERY OR NOT AT ALL SATISFIED ASK (b) Why is that? PROBE FULLY.
159	Q104	Is the procedure for discipline and dismissals separate and different from the general grievance procedure or the same?

Chapter VIII

Page   Question   which *either* form the basis for subsequent negotiations *or* directly result in pay increases for this group of manual workers? National/industrywide/more than one employer; Region/district/more than one employer; This employer/organisation/*all* establishments; This employer/organisation/*some* establishments; This establishment/plant; Statutory Wages Council; No negotiations/employer decides; Other (SPECIFY). PROBE 'Any others?' UNTIL 'No'. RECORD ANSWER BELOW. CODE ALL THAT APPLY.

(b) On the LAST OCCASION of a pay increase for this group of manual workers, which level would you say was the most important?

195   Q49   On the last occasion on which rates of pay for MANUAL workers at this establishment were increased, was the increase determined by a Statutory Wages Council or was it decided by some other method?
IF OTHER METHOD ASK
(b) How was it determined? PROBE FOR DETAILS.

178   Q70   (a) I am going to show you a card on which are listed various levels at which pay negotiations can take place.
At which of the levels shown on this card are there negotiations with the unions which *either* form the basis for subsequent negotiations *or* directly result in pay increases for this group of non-manual workers? National/industrywide/more than one employer; Region/district/more than one employer; This employer/organisation/*all* establishments; This employer/organisation/*some* establishments; This establishment/plant; Statutory Wages Council; No negotiations/employer decides; Other (SPECIFY).

191   Q71   REFER TO ANSWERS TO Q39b.
IF ON OCCASION OF LAST INCREASE THE MOST IMPORTANT LEVEL OF NEGOTIATIONS WAS OUTSIDE THE ESTABLISHMENT (CODES 1–4 OR 6) ASK Q40a.
IF ON OCCASION OF LAST INCREASE THE MOST IMPORTANT LEVEL OF NEGOTIATIONS WAS WITHIN THE ESTABLISHMENT *AND* THE ESTABLISHMENT IS PART OF A LARGER ORGANISATION (REFER TO Q3) ASK Q40b.
OTHERWISE SKIP to Q41
(a) Were there consultations between management here and management negotiators outside the establishment before final agreement on the last increase for this group of non-manual workers was reached?
(b) Were there consultations with management at higher levels in the organisation before the final agreement on this increase was reached?

197   Q72   I am going to read out a number of other issues besides pay that affect this negotiating group.
READ OUT: (i) Holiday entitlement; (ii) Length of working week; (iii) Pensions; (iv) Physical working conditions; (v) Recruitment, i.e. the total number of employees taken on; (vi) Redeployment within this establishment; (vii) Redundancy; (viii) Manning levels; (ix) Major changes in production methods; (x) Capital investment.
Please choose a phrase from this card (SHOW CARD F) to indicate how these issues are dealt with here: 'Negotiated at establishment'; 'Negotiated not at establishment'; 'Not negotiated'; 'Other answer' (SPECIFY).

183   Q75   (a) I am going to show you a card on which are listed various levels at which pay negotiations can take place.
At which of the levels shown on this card are there negotiations with the unions which *either* form the basis for subsequent negotiations *or* directly result in pay increases for this group of non-manual workers? National/industrywide/more than one employer; Region/district/more than one employer; This employer/organisation/*ALL* establishments; This employer/organisation/ *SOME* establishments; This establishment/plant; Statutory Wages Council; No negotiations/employer decides; other (SPECIFY).

314   *Workplace Industrial Relations in Britain*

Page	Question	
		PROBE 'Any others?' UNTIL 'No'.
		RECORD ANSWER BELOW. CODE ALL THAT APPLY.
		(b) On the LAST OCCASION of a pay increase for this group of non-manual workers, which level would you say was the MOST IMPORTANT?
195	Q80	On the last occasion on which rates of pay for NON-MANUAL workers at this establishment were increased, was the increase determined by a Statutory Wages Council or was it decided by some other method?
		IF OTHER METHOD ASK
		(b) How was it determined? PROBE FOR DETAILS.
191	WQ15	(a) Before the final agreement on this last increase was reached, were there consultations with the members or stewards or representatives in your negotiating group? Yes, members including stewards; Yes, stewards or representatives only; No consultations; Other answer.
		IF YES ASK
		(b) What form did these consultations take? READ OUT: Postal ballot; Ballot/non-postal; Show of hands; Other answer (SPECIFY).
200	Q108	*ASK ALL*
		Now, I'd like to ask you about methods of payment that exist in this establishment.
		For each of the following groups of employees, could you say whether the MAJORITY of them are PAID BY RESULTS – that is, does their pay vary according to the amount of work done or its value (rather than just the number of hours worked)? READ OUT LIST AND CODE ANSWERS BELOW.
		(i) Unskilled/semi-skilled male manual workers; (ii) Unskilled/semi-skilled female manual workers; (iii) Skilled workers (male and female); (iv) Clerical/Admin./Secretarial staff; (v) Foremen/supervisory staff; (vi) Technical/Professional staff; (vii) Middle and senior management.
		IF YES TO ANY ASK (b) OF EACH.
		(b) Was WORK STUDY used in determining the rates to be paid?
		IF YES TO ANY ASK
		(c) Compared with three years ago, are there more employees, fewer employees, or about the same number of employees who are being paid by results?
208	Q109	(c) Can you tell me, firstly for manual workers at this establishment, and then for non-manual workers, methods of recording starting and finishing times? (SHOW CARD H. INDICATE WHETHER 'ALL', 'MOST', 'SOME' OR NONE' OF EACH GROUP USE EACH METHOD): Clocking in; Being checked in; Signing a book; None of these.
210	Q110	Do any employees when they are off SICK (not including chronic illness and permanent disability) receive less than full pay? IF YES, SHOW CARD H AND CONTINUE.
		Please choose a phrase from this card for manual and non-manual employees: All; Most; Some; None; Other answers.
210	Q112	ASK INDUSTRIAL AND COMMERCIAL ESTABLISHMENTS ONLY.
		(a) Does the company that owns this establishment operate a share ownership scheme for any of its employees?
		IF YES ASK (b)–(d).
		(b) When was the scheme introduced?
		(c) How many employees of this establishment are ELIGIBLE for the scheme?
		(d) How many employees of this establishment are PARTICIPATING in the scheme?
200	Q118	(a) Are any employees here covered by a job evaluation scheme? IF YES ASK
		(b) How many schemes are there at this establishment?
		IF ONE ONLY COMPLETE (c)–(k) ABOUT THIS SCHEME. IF MORE THAN ONE, IDENTIFY THE MOST RECENTLY SET UP SCHEME AND ASK (c)–(k) ABOUT THIS SCHEME.
		(c) When was the scheme introduced?

Page   Question   (d) How many employees are currently filling jobs covered by the scheme? OBTAIN FIGURES FOR MEN AND WOMEN SEPARATELY.
(e) What job (or occupation) was ranked HIGHEST in the scheme?
(f) What job (or occupation) was ranked LOWEST in the scheme?
(g) Is there a committee which reviews the scheme and decides upon the grading of new or changed jobs?
IF YES ASK (h), OTHERWISE SKIP TO (j).
(h) Are there employee representatives on the committee?
IF YES ASK
(i) Are these representatives chosen through trade unions or staff associations?
(j) On what basis does the scheme operate?
IF ESTABLISHMENT IS PART OF MULTI-ESTABLISHMENT ORGANISATION (Q3) ASK
(k) Are employees of your organisation in any other establishment besides this one covered by the same job evaluation scheme?

Chapter IX
Page   Question

214   Q127   Now I would like to ask you about different forms of industrial action there may
      (WQ62)   have been here.
              REFER TO WORKFORCE DATA SHEET. IF MANUAL WORKERS PRESENT ASK (a) SHOW CARD N.
              (a) Could you please tell me if any of the forms of industrial action on this card have taken place among the manual workers in this establishment during the last 12 months? Strikes of less than one day/whole shift; Strikes of one day/shift or more; Ban or restriction on overtime; Work to rule; Lock out; Go slow; Blacking of work; Work in/sit in; Other industrial action (SPECIFY).
              IF YES ASK 'Which?' PROBE: 'Any others?' UNTIL 'No'. RECORD ANSWERS BELOW. FOR EACH ASK
              (b) On how many occasions in the last 12 months? WRITE IN BELOW.
              REFER TO WORKFORCE DATA SHEET. IF NON-MANUAL WORKERS PRESENT ASK Q128a.
214   Q128   (a) Now among the non-manual workers? PROBE: 'Any others?' UNTIL 'No'. RECORD ANSWERS BELOW.
              (b) On how many occasions in the last 12 months? WRITE IN BELOW.
              IF NO INDUSTRIAL ACTION IN THE LAST 12 MONTHS OR 'STRIKE OF LESS THAN ONE DAY/WHOLE SHIFT' ONLY (CODE A) SKIP TO Q132d
              IF STRIKE OF ONE DAY OR MORE (CODE B) ASK Q129 IN RESPECT OF THE MOST *RECENT* STRIKE.
              IF OTHER INDUSTRIAL ACTION REPEAT Q129 IN RESPECT OF THE MOST *RECENT* OCCURRENCE.
235   Q129   Now I would like to ask you about the most recent ———— at this establish-
      (WQ63)   ment.
              (a) What was this action? Strike; Overtime ban; Work to rule; Lock out; Go slow; Blacking; Work in/Sit in; Other (SPECIFY).
              (b) Was it among manual or non-manual employees or both?
              (c) How many employees took part?
              (d) When did it begin?
              (e) How many working days did it last?
              (f) Were these days consecutive working days or intermittent?
              (g) Apart from senior management, how many sections of the workforce of this establishment were involved in this industrial action – all, some or just one?

Page	Question	
		IF SOME SECTIONS OR JUST ONE SECTION AT (g) ASK
		(h) Which sections? Manual; Manual semi-skilled; Manual un-skilled; Non-manual clerical/admin; non-manual foremen/supervisor; Non-manual junior technical/professional; non-manual senior technical/professional; Other (SPECIFY).
240	Q130 (WQ64)	(a) Was this the *first* time that this/these sections of the workforce had taken industrial action?
		(b) On this occasion were employees at any other establishment involved in similar industrial action?
		IF YES AT (b) ASK
		(c) Establishments within this organisation, outside this organisation or both?
236	Q131 (WQ65)	What would you say was the reason for the action?
		PROBE FULLY.
		(a) Most recent strike?
		(b) Most recent other dispute?
242	Q133 (WQ66)	(a) Has this establishment been PICKETED during the last 12 months? IF YES, ASK 'On how many occasions?'
		IF NONE SKIP TO Q134, OTHERWISE CONTINUE WITH (b). IF MORE THAN ONE OCCASION ASK ABOUT LAST OCCASION.
		(b) On the last occasion of picketing was it in connection with a dispute at this establishment?
		(c) What was the maximum number of people participating in the picketing at any one time?
		(d) Over how many gates/entrances were those pickets spread?
		(e) How many of the pickets were employees of this establishment?
		(f) Who organised the picketing? Shop stewards in this establishment; Full-time local area official; Other (SPECIFY).
		(g) Did the picketing prevent any of the following (READ OUT) from entering or leaving the premises? Employees of this establishment; Contractors' employees working at this establishment; Goods or services being received; Goods or services being sent out.
251	Q134 (WQ67)	During the last 12 months has there been any blacking of goods or services here by trade unionists in connection with an industrial dispute somewhere else?
		IF ANY INDUSTRIAL ACTION (CODE 'YES' AT Q127a OR Q128a) ASK Q135.
251	Q135 (WQ68)	During the last 12 months has there been any blacking of this organisation's customers or suppliers goods or services by trades unionists in connection with an industrial dispute at this establishment?

Chapter X

Page	Question	
257	Q10	(a) In the recent past, say the last 2–3 years, has capital investment in this establishment been: (READ OUT) Rising; Falling; Neither; Other answer.
		IF 'NEITHER' OR 'OTHER ANSWER' PROBE FOR FURTHER INFORMATION.
		(b) How would you assess the financial performance of this establishment, compared with other establishments and firms in the same industry?
260	Q111	(a) Over the last month what has been the gross pay of the typical employee in each of these groups I am going to read out? Please choose a letter from this card. SHOW CARD J AND READ OUT (i)–(iv).
		(i) Semi-skilled manual workers; (ii) skilled manual workers; (iii) Clerical workers; (iv) Middle management.
		(b) Have any employees had deductions from their pay in the last 12 months for any of the following reasons? READ OUT LIST AND RECORD ANSWER

Page   Question   BELOW: Bad work; Loss or damage to the employers' property; Other disciplinary offence.
IF YES TO ANY ASK
(c) How many employees had such deductions?
254   Q146   Finally may I ask you your opinion of the general state of relations between
(WQ74)   management and workers at this establishment? PROBE FULLY.

Notes on breakdown (independent) variables

The questions listed so far in this appendix have been those that we used in the book as substantive dependent variables. For example, when we reported findings on the incidence and details of different forms of industrial action we referred to the relevant questions in the interview schedule and have listed those questions in the appendix. In addition, however, we have occasionally used answers to questions on industrial action as an independent variable to analyse variations in other industrial relations practices and procedures in relation to establishments' experiences of industrial action.

Generally, in the report, it will be clear from what question or questions we have derived breakdown variables and those questions will have been quoted in earlier sections of the appendix. Here we describe the main independent variables used in the report where the questions on which they were based have not already been quoted, and provide some notes on variables whose derivation needs some explanation.

Number employed at establishment

Workforce Data Sheet
1   (a)   How many full-time employees do you have on the payroll at this establishment?
2   (b)   How many part-time employees do you have?

Number of manual workers at establishment

Workforce Data Sheet
3   (a)   Taking both full-time and part-time together, how many manual employees do you have?

Number of non-manual workers at establishment

Workforce Data Sheet
4   (a)   Again taking both full-time and part-time together how many non-manual employees do you have?

Number employed by organisation

Q4   (d)   What is the total number of employees, in the UK, of that organisation?

Demand for products in previous year

Q9   Over the past 12 months would you say that demand for the main products or services of this establishment has been rising? falling? neither?

Capital investment and financial performance

Q10   (a)   In the recent past, say the last 2–3 years, has capital investment in this establishment been increasing? falling? stable?
       (b)   How would you assess the financial performance of this establishment compared with other establishments and firms in the same industry? – Better than average? About average? Below average?

Ownership (type of employer)
Q2   (a)   What is the formal status of this establishment (or the organisation of which it is part)? Please choose a phrase from this card
  Coding   1. Limited company (private or public)
      2. Partnership/Self proprietorship
      3. Trust/Company limited by guarantee
      4. Co-operative
      5. Public Corporation (Trading)/Nationalised industry
      6. Other Public Corporation
      7. Quango
      8. Local/Central Government (including NHS and Local Education Authorities

  Labels   Private sector: Codes 1 to 4
      Public sector: Codes 5 to 8
      Nationalised industries: Code 5
      Public services or
      public administration: Codes 6 to 8
Q3   Is this establishment a SINGLE INDEPENDENT establishment or one of several belonging to the same organisation or group within the UK?
Q5   Is this establishment UK owned or owned by an organisation outside the UK?

Industry (industrial sector)
Q1   (a)   What is the main activity of this establishment? PROBE: Is there any other main activity?
  Coding Standard Industrial Classification, 1968

Labels	SIC Orders
Food/Chemicals	III, IV, V
Metals/Mechanical engineering	VI, VII, XII
Electrical engineering	VIII, IX
Vehicles	X, XI
Textiles/Clothing	XIII, XIV, XV
Miscellaneous manufacturing	XVI, XVII, XVIII, XIX
Construction*	XX, II
Utilities/Transport/Communication	XXI, XXII
Distribution	XXIII
Financial services	XXIV
Professional/scientific services	XXV
Miscellaneous services	XXVI
Public administration	XXVII

  Amalgamations
  Manufacturing   III to XIX
  Services   XXI to XXVII

*Includes a small number of establishments from Order II. See Appendix B for details.

Industrial relations climate
Q146   See page 309
(WQ74)

Full coding	Condensed coding
Very good	First rate
Good	Good
Quite good	Fairly good
Neither good nor bad	Not bad
Quite bad	
Bad	Fairly poor or worse
Very bad	

Manual union density

Q22   You say there are ……….. (SPECIFY NUMBER) MANUAL employees here. Are any of them members of unions?

Q23 (c) How many full-time MANUAL employees are members of these unions?

Numerator	Number of full-time manual trade union members	
Denominator	Number of manual workers (Workforce Data Sheet, 3.)	
Bands	Low	Less than 30 per cent
	Medium	30 per cent or more, but less than 80 per cent
	High	80 per cent or more

Non-manual union density

As for manual union density substituting NON-MANUAL for MANUAL and Q51 and Q54(a) for Q22 and Q23(c)

Total union density

Numerator	Q23(c) plus Q54(a)
Denominator	number of full-time employees at establishment (Workforce Data Sheet, 1)
Bands	As for manual union density

Other workforce densities

Other workforce densities, such as female density and part-time density, were calculated in a similar way to union densities.

Manual representative structure

Q27 (a) Do the manual unions have stewards or union representatives from the manual unions here, apart from any concerned *exclusively* with Health and Safety? IF YES ASK (b)

      (b) How many? INCLUDE SENIOR STEWARDS OR REPRESENTA-TIVES IN THIS TOTAL

Q28 (a) Are there, at this establishment, any stewards or representatives from the manual unions acting as SENIOR STEWARDS, OR CONVENORS?

Q29 (a) Are there any of these senior stewards or convenors who in practice spend all or nearly all of their working time on trade union affairs concerning this establishment?
IF MANUAL UNION MEMBERS PRESENT BUT NO RECOGNISED MANUAL UNIONS ASK

      (a) Are there manual union representatives who meet management to discuss matters affecting the workforce or sections of it?
IF YES   How many?

Non-manual representative structure
As for manual representative structure but substitute non-manual for manual
and Q58(a)(b), Q59(a), Q60(a) and Q77(a)
for Q27(a)(b), Q28(a), Q29(a) and Q46(a)

Notes
1. The full questionnaires are obtainable from the Policy Studies Institute or the SSRC Data Archive. The Archive also has available a document entitled 'Concordance of Questions' which shows which questions on the various schedules correspond to those on other schedules.
2. See C. Hakim *et al*, *Employers' use of outworkers* (Department of Employment Research Paper, 1983, forthcoming).

Appendix B Technical details of the survey[1]

The sampling frame and the sample

The Department of Employment's *Census of Employment* was chosen as the most suitable sampling frame, the census for 1977 being the latest one available. The files included approximately 135,000 census units, in England, Scotland and Wales, with more than 24 employees. A census unit is essentially a number of employees working at the same address who are paid from the same place. In general there was a sufficient degree of one-for-one correspondence between census units and establishments as required in the survey for the census to serve as a frame from which a sample could be selected by simple random selection procedures. The extent that these procedures had to be modified in minor ways is described in later paragraphs.

Part of the sample (those units with fewer than 1,000 employees) was drawn from the 10 per cent file of the census. This consisted of a randomly selected sub-set of census units. The remaining sample was drawn from the complete census file, since the sampling fractions required were lower than one in ten. Prior to the drawing of the sample, the census files were stratified by four factors: the proportion of the workforce who were full time within the proportion who were male within industry (each of Orders II to XXVII of the Standard Industrial Classification, 1968) within the number of employees (in seven bands, as set out below).

Within the resultant list, samples were selected by marking off at intervals from a randomly selected starting point, using the sampling fractions given in Table B.1, with the object of obtaining a sample of 4,000 units.

The choice of sampling fractions arose from the requirement to provide a minimum achieved sample of, say, 100, in the size band of very large establishments (2,000+ employees), without an unacceptable loss of efficiency in the total sample. A range of sampling fractions that would have produced a more even distribution of units among the size bands would at the same time have substantially reduced the effective sample size. The selected sample of 3,994 units was stratified by Standard Industrial Classification Order within size band and every fourth unit in the list so produced marked off for a reserve pool of about 1,000 units in case the number of ineligible or non-co-operating establishments had been underestimated. In fact during the latter third of

Table B.1 Sampling fractions and numbers of census units drawn

Numbers

	No. of units in census	Sampling fraction (1 in)	Estimated sampled units	Actual sampled units
No. of employees				
25–49	66,959	79	850	849
50–99	33,881	42.5	800	799
100–199	18,340	26	700	700
200–499	10,649	15	700	699
500–999	3,098	6	500	499
1000–1999	1,332[1]	5.5	250	249
2000 or more	571[1]	3	200	199
Total	134,825		4,000	3,994

[1] Estimated subdivision

the fieldwork period further addresses were drawn (systematically from a randomly selected starting point) from the reserve pool, since there seemed to be a possibility of the achieved sample falling significantly below 2,000. These extra addresses were issued to the interviewers in two phases. There were somewhat over 300 extra units selected which meant that the number of addresses in the reserve pool and never used in the survey was 687. The total number of addresses used was therefore 3,307

Among the 3,307 units used there were found to be certain groups of addresses that were, for the reasons indicated below, withdrawn prior to fieldwork and therefore excluded from the sample. One reason for withdrawal was the existence of *multiple census units*. In the early stages of the design it was recognised that some establishments were listed in the *Census of Employment* more than once. Since a census unit consists of employees at the same establishment who are paid from the same place, in some instances a single establishment is represented by more than one census unit. This was confirmed by a comparison, for the manufacturing industries, of the number of establishments in the *Census of Production* with the number of census units in the *Census of Employment:* establishments were appreciably outnumbered by census units of a comparable size The aim was to achieve an equal probability sample of establishments within size bands. Obviously establishments which comprised more than one census unit had received a higher chance of selection than single census units of the same size. The sample of census units was therefore combed for examples of more than one census unit representing one establishment.

Where examples were found, all units bar one for each establishment were randomly deleted. This resulted in the deletion of 61 units from the sample.

Multiple census unit establishments of which only one census unit had been selected in the sample posed a different problem. The solution adopted is described in the paragraphs relating to the weighting of the data.

A second type of withdrawal concerned *aggregate returns*. It became apparent on examination of the sample listing of units that for some establishments (generally schools and colleges) the census return, having been completed at the offices of the local (education) authority, showed not the number of employees at each establishment, but the number of employees for a much larger unit – probably the complete district or county. Since the sampling fractions had been determined by the number of employees at any census unit, these units had therefore been given an incorrect chance of selection. The method devised for coping with the problem was thus. The units were withdrawn from the sample. (There were found to be 48). The local (education) authority to which each of these units belonged was contacted and asked to provide a list of all educational establishments within its area, along with the number of employees. Ideally the number of employees was to have been at 1977 levels. Where this was not available, however, later figures were to be provided. The lists provided were then used as a frame for a series of substitute re-sampling operations. For each of the listed establishments the appropriate inclusion probabilities were worked out and fresh selections made from the list on the basis of these probabilities.

The method could result in any deletion being replaced by 0, 1, 2 . . . and so on substitutes. In the event 25 extra establishments were selected from the 20, out of 48, local authorities who co-operated. The comparatively poor response to this exercise was partly because of the imminence of the school summer holidays when potential respondents would be uncontactable. The overall effect therefore was to decrease the sample base by 23.

Further withdrawals were necessary because some addresses were found to have been printed out incompletely or obscurely. These totalled 36. There were also eight instances of apparent duplicates in the sample.

Finally, among the addresses initially selected were found to be a number of establishments that were known to have been approached during recent Department of Employment surveys, including the pilot work for this survey. These addresses, which totalled 77, were withdrawn. The result of all the withdrawals mentioned above was that the number of addresses actually used was 3,102. At 2,040 of these addresses, successful interviews were obtained with management respondents. The remaining 1,062 are accounted for in a later section.

Questionnaire development and fieldwork

Two separate pilot surveys were conducted during the three months (January to March 1980) available for questionnaire development work. In the first pilot survey interviews at 15 establishments were achieved by four interviewers working in separate areas. Versions of the five main questionnaires were tried out during the survey, but not the contacting procedures. Interviewers made the initial contacts at a sample of establishments picked out from directories. There was no initial contact by the Department of Employment, although letters of authority from the Department of Employment were carried by interviewers. The average length of the management interview, excluding interruptions, was at this pilot 2 hours 25 minutes.

For the second pilot survey, modifications were made to the wording and ordering of the questions and some questions were deleted. The basic questionnaire structure was, however, maintained. For this second pilot the sample consisted of 80 establishments and co-operation was sought by the Department of Employment by letter. Fifty-five addresses were ultimately issued to interviewers. A further 20 replacement addresses (at which there was no time for prior contact by the Department of Employment) were subsequently added to the lists. The addresses were again selected from directories and published lists, greater weight being given in the second pilot to the inclusion of public sector establishments. Interviews were achieved at a total of 42 establishments, in 22 of which interviews with one or more worker representatives were conducted. The total number of interviews achieved with worker representatives was 31. The average duration of the management interview was, at this stage, reduced to 1 hour 54 minutes.

The interviewing for the main survey was carried out by 120 experienced interviewers after an initial approach by letter from the Department of Employment. Six of the interviewers were SCPR employees (from the institute's field staff); 43 had been trained by the institute as senior interviewers/supervisors; the remaining 71 were members of the regular interviewing panel, all members of which have been fully trained by the institute's field staff.

Before fieldwork began a series of six two-day briefings was conducted jointly by staff of SCPR and the Department of Employment's research team. One hundred and one of the interviewers attended one of the briefings in this series. They were responsible for carrying out 90 per cent of the interviews eventually achieved. The remainder attended supplementary briefings held throughout the first month of fieldwork. Fieldwork began immediately after the interviewer briefings and continued until early September 1980.

Approximately 60 per cent of addresses were available for distribution to interviewers at the time of briefing. The remainder were made available throughout the fieldwork period as queries were resolved and permission granted by the head offices or governing bodies of the sampled establishments. The great majority of public sector addresses were not released until early June 1980. Approximately 100 addresses were not, in the event, released until two to three weeks before the end of the fieldwork period. In the great majority of cases interviews with worker representatives took place very close in time to those with management respondents.

Fieldwork quality control was carried out by a postal check on a random sub-sample of establishments after the fieldwork period was over. Replies were received in about four-fifths of cases and about one half of these were without comment. The replies of those who did comment have been summarised in a report to the three sponsoring bodies.

Overall response

The outcome of the sampling, initial approach and fieldwork operations may be judged from the summary statistics in Table B.2.

Ineligible or out of scope addresses fell into three main groups: addresses of establishments which were found to have closed down in the period between 1977 and 1980; addresses of establishments which were found in 1980 to have fewer than 25 employees; and addresses which were found to be vacant or demolished premises or where the establishment had moved leaving no trace of its new whereabouts.

Non-productive addresses fell into two main groups: those for which permission for interview was not granted in response to the original letter sent out by the Department of Employment (404 cases); and addresses at which interviewers failed to obtain a complete interview,

Table B.2 Summary of fieldwork response

Numbers

	Addresses	
Initial sample		3307
Withdrawn at sampling stage	205	
Ineligible or out of scope	376	
Non-productive addresses	686	
Interviews achieved	2040	
		3309

Table B.3 Response rate in relation to size of census unit

| | Number of employees according to census unit | | | | | | |
	25–49	50–99	100–199	200–499	500–999	1000–1999	2000+
Response rate	73	72	75	75	78	80	77

either owing to refusal, non-contact or for other reasons (282 cases). Of the total 686 non-productive addresses, the great majority were straightforward refusals, a little over one half of these being made at the stage of initial contact by letter. The overall rate of response, judged by the completion of at least a satisfactory management interview, was 75 per cent.

The response rate was analysed by region, industry and establishment size. In regional terms the response varied from 67 per cent in Yorkshire and Humberside to 86 per cent in East Anglia (by far the smallest region in terms of the whole sample). The remaining regions lay within the range 71 per cent (Greater London) to 78 per cent (the South East, excluding London). The range of response rates for different industrial sectors was rather greater. Excluding mining, which was mentioned in Chapter I as an almost complete failure to gain access, the response rates varied from 66 per cent in the financial and business services sector to 83 per cent in electrical engineering. The response rate varied less than this according to the size of the census unit as Table b.3 shows.

Response among worker representatives
Within the 2,040 establishments at which interviews were obtained with management respondents, manual negotiating groups were identified in 1,344 cases and non-manual in 1,255. There were a small number of establishments (not included in the figures above) in which negotiating groups were not positively identified, although it was clear that the management at the establishment did recognise the unions' right to negotiate in respect of pay and conditions. The reasons for the lack of positive identification were that negotiation took place outside the establishment and that there were no worker representatives at the establishment. These conditions did not invariably lead to a lack of positive identification of negotiating groups. Those establishments at which they did numbered 31 in respect of manual recognition and 27 in respect of non-manual recognition.

Interviewers were required to seek an interview with the representative of the primary negotiating group for manual employees and, separately, with the representative of the primary negotiating group for non-manual employees, *where such a representative was present at the sampled establishment.*

For each category of negotiating group, a proportion of the establishments at which groups were identified was excluded because no representative could be identified at establishment level. The details of response rates therefore exclude such establishments (192 manual groups, 171 non-manual groups). The response rates for manual and non-manual representatives of primary negotiating groups were 84 per cent and 85 per cent respectively.

At certain establishments there were found to be no formal arrangements between management and employees for negotiating pay and conditions, but there was a joint committee of employees and management to discuss matters of mutual interest. At such establishments, interviewers were required to seek to interview an employee representative on this committee. This added a further 66 interviews with manual worker representatives and 94 with non-manual worker representatives. Of these the majority were not trade union members.

At those establishments at which a second manual negotiating group was identified, interviewers were required to seek an interview with the representative of that group, provided that manual employees formed the majority of employees at the establishment. A similar instruction was given in respect of non-manual employees. There was, therefore, a maximum of one secondary worker representative respondent at any one establishment. Response among secondary worker representatives is shown in Table B.4.

Table B.4   Response among secondary worker representatives

		Numbers
	Manual	Non-manual
Number of establishments identified with two or more negotiating groups	469	319
Less:		
Establishments at which relevant employees were the minority	132	117
Establishments at which relevant employees were in the majority, but no representative present	49	38
Establishments where secondary worker representative interview was required	288	164
Interview obtained with representative	208	115

Table B.5   Number of worker representative interviews

Primary manual interviews	1,040
Primary non-manual interviews	1,016
Secondary manual interviews	216
Secondary non-manual interviews	167
Total	2,439

The response rates for secondary manual and non-manual respondents were therefore 72 per cent and 70 per cent respectively. In a further 60 cases the shorter interview schedules for secondary worker representatives were completed where a longer schedule for primary respondents was unobtainable. The total number of worker representative interviews is shown in Table B.5.

Weighting of the data
All the results presented in the main text of this report, unless otherwise specified, were adjusted by weighting factors to compensate for the inequalities of selection that were introduced by the differential sampling of census units according to their number of employees[2]. The variations in response rates according to region, industry and size described in an earlier section of this appendix were not considered to be so substantial as to justify any additional corrective weighting.

No weighting was introduced to compensate for possible differential response rates among the sample of worker representatives, nor was any introduced to compensate for the absence, from the sampling frame, of establishments that had come into being in the three year gap between the completion of the census forms and the survey fieldwork. Any such 'new' establishments are likely to belong to the smaller size bands.

After the completion of fieldwork the achieved sample was compared with the cómplete *Census of Employment* files in order to identify those census units at which interviews had been carried out that were in fact part of multiple census unit establishments. To do this the census files were combed for any instances of units of the *same employer with the same postcode* as those at which interviews had been achieved. The sample was found to include 76 examples of such multiple census units. Since the true probabilities of inclusion for each of these units was not that of their size band, they were excluded from the size band weighting. Separate weighting factors for each of these units were calculated on the basis of the probabilities of inclusion for each of the units within the establishment. The resulting individual weights

Table B.6 Weighting factors

Number of employees in census unit	Interviews achieved	Weighting factor	Weighted total
25–49	359	2.4857	892
50–99	395	1.3377	528
100–199	374	0.8182	306
200–499	356	0.4721	168
500–999	264	0.1890	50
1000–1999	128	0.1735	22
2000 or more	88	0.0941	8
	1,964		1,974

Table B.7 Comparison by industrial sector of weighted sample and population

Percentages

	Weighted sample (establishments)	Census of Employment units
Food, chemicals (3, 4, 5)[1]	4	4
Metals, mechanical engineering (6, 7, 12)	9	8
Electrical engineering (8, 9)	2	3
Vehicles (10, 11)	1	1
Textiles, clothing (13, 14, 15)	4	5
Miscellaneous manufacturing (16, 17, 18, 19)	7	6
All manufacturing (3 to 19)	27	27
Construction, extraction (20, 2)	7	8[2]
Utilities, transport, communications (21, 22)	8	8
Distribution (23)	13	13
Financial services (24)	5	6
Professional/scientific services (25)	19	16[3]
Miscellaneous services (26)	12	12
Public administration (27)	9	9

[1] Figures in brackets indicate Orders of the Standard Industrial Classification, 1968
[2] 0.8 per cent of census units are in Order 2 (Extraction)
[3] This sector contained the largest number of multiple census unit establishments. See text

Table B.8 Comparison by size band of weighted sample and population

Percentages

Number of employees	Weighted sample	Census of Employment units	
		Sample	Adjusted[1]
25–49	45.0	50.2	45.6
50–99	26.6	25.1	26.9
100–199	15.4	13.2	14.5
200–499	8.7	7.7	8.6
500–999	2.6	2.6	2.9
1000–1999	1.2	0.9	1.0
2000 or more	0.4	0.4	0.5
Total	2,000	13,763	

[1] The data has been re-percentaged to take into account the proportion of census units in each size band that were found to have either closed down or to have become ineligible on grounds of having too few employees in the period between the completion of the census return (1977) and fieldwork (1980)

ranged from 0.056 to 1.251 and the weighted total of these units amounted to 26.

For the remainder of the sample (the single census unit cases) the weighting factors were as given in Table B.6. Tables B.7 and B.8 demonstrate the extent of agreement between the achieved sample after weighting and the 1977 *Census of Employment* (10 per cent sample file) which is the best available measure of the population of establishments.

As was mentioned in Chapter I of this report, the weighting scheme described above was considered satisfactory for the type of analysis that the report contains, most of which centres on patterns of variation in practices between establishments with different characteristics. Methodological work carried out by SCPR in parallel with the preparation of this report has revealed that the average size of establishments in the achieved sample was substantially higher than the average size of establishments in the population, at least as indicated by the size distribution of census units. There are several possible reasons for the difference, only some of which are amenable to empirical testing. Further work is in progress on this matter and the results will be published in due course.

The work carried out so far has suggested that, in order to make grossed-up estimates of the absolute numbers of employees having characteristics identified in the survey, an alternative weighting scheme

Table B.9 Additional weights for grossed-up estimates

Number of employees in establishment	Weights
25–49	88.41
50–99	66.05
100–199	53.26
200–499	51.04
500–999	35.69
1000 or more	34.55

should be employed. This involves the application of additional weighting factors, according to the size of the establishments at the time of the interview (1980), as given in Table B.9. These weights have to be applied in addition to the weights previously specified since it is still essential to adjust for differential sampling. The additional weights would permit grossing up to employees in all establishments with 25 or more workers in 1980, but only by assuming that establishments that grew to 25 or more employees between 1977 and 1980 were no different in relation to the survey variables from the ones that had 25 or more employees at both points in time. This alternative weighting scheme has not been used in the preparation of this report.

Coding and editing of the data

Coding and editing of the data took place over a period of eight months and presented some particular difficulties. In the first place, the novelty of the design in terms of the selection of respondents and the definition of sub-units within the establishment necessitated a number of checks of the structure of each set of questionnaires prior to coding. Secondly, the prospective use of the data for secondary analysis through the SSRC Data Archive made it desirable to code open questions with a comparatively detailed coding frame which could be used flexibly by other researchers. Because of the unevenness with which different segments of the sample were represented in the different months of the fieldwork period, the coding frames had to be kept open for virtually the whole of the coding period, so that the full range of answers was captured. In consequence the proportion of answers simply coded as 'other' is very small.

Throughout the coding and editing of the questionnaires reference was made back to interviews or respondents or both to clarify obscurities in the data collected or to attempt to collect data missing from the original questionnaire. In particular, considerable effort was put into

Table B.10   **Estimated sampling error for a selection of survey variables**[1]

Percentages

	Sampling error
Manual union members present	1.4
Manual unions recognised	1.4
All manual employees in closed shop	1.1
Non-manual union members present	1.4
Non-manual unions recognised	1.4
Some non-manual employees in closed shop	0.4
Formal procedure for disputes over pay and conditions	1.4
Formal procedure for discipline and dismissals	1.1
Formal procedure for individual grievances	1.2
Job evaluation scheme present	1.1
Consultative committee present	1.3
Industrial action by manual employees	0.8
Industrial action by non-manual employees	0.8

[1] Source: management questionnaires

retrieval of any missing *Basic Workforce Data Sheets*. As a result of the follow-up after the fieldwork period, only one per cent of the achieved sample was, in the event, deficient in respect of the *Basic Workforce Data Sheet*. In these cases the minimal amount of data necessary to make the questionnaires usable was imputed by the research team from the establishment's original census information and any relevant figures on the questionnaires. All serious cases of missing data or inconsistencies within the set of questionnaires for an establishment were discussed fully by the research team. Eleven sets of questionnaires had inconsistencies that could not be resolved or had unacceptable omissions and were rejected.

The data, after keying, were transferred to a computer file, where they were subjected to rigorous edit checks, incorporating range, filter and structural checks. Errors detected by the computer edit were resolved after reference back to the individual schedules by the editing team.

Sampling errors
The design of the survey sample, for reasons given earlier, involved both stratification and disproportionate sampling according to size strata with the result that sampling errors were greater than those for a simple random sample of equivalent size. A further complication was introduced by cases for which individual weights were calculated. For estimating sampling error, these were treated as if they were drawn

from the stratum with the nearest weighting factor to their own. Although this introduced imprecision, it was unavoidable, and was unlikely to have a major effect on the estimates.

Table B.10 gives the estimated sampling error[3] for a number of major survey variables. These values have to be doubled to obtain the sampling error for a 95 per cent confidence level. By comparing these and other estimates with equivalent figures for a simple random sample, it was found that for the majority of variables the increase in sampling error was between 20 per cent and 30 per cent. The table of approximate confidence intervals given in Chapter I therefore assumes an increase of 25 per cent (in other words a design factor of 1.25).

Notes

1. The material in this appendix is drawn very largely from an unpublished initial report on the survey by Colin Airey and Andrew Potts of SCPR. Their fuller account is available to prospective analysts of the survey data from the SSRC Data Archive.
2. These weighting factors are also contained in the data records held at the SSRC Data Archive.
3. Ignoring finite population correction factors.

Index

WORKPLACE INDUSTRIAL RELATIONS IN BRITAIN

The DE/PSI/ESRC Survey